The Avila of Saint Teresa

THE AVILA OF SAINT TERESA

Religious Reform in a
Sixteenth-Century City

Jodi Bilinkoff

Cornell University Press

Ithaca and London

First published 1989 by Cornell University Press.

International Standard Book Number 0-8014-2203-5
Library of Congress Catalog Card Number 89-42886
Printed in the United States of America
*Librarians: Library of Congress cataloging information
appears on the last page of the book.*

⊚ The paper used in this publication meets the minimum requirements of the American National Standard for Permanence of Paper for Printed Library Materials Z39.48–1984.

6-6-91

To my parents

Contents

Maps and Illustrations

Preface

Teresa de Ahumada y Cepeda never expected to live a long life. As a young nun in the Spanish city of Avila in the 1530s she suffered a series of illnesses that crippled her limbs and wracked her body with pain. Once she slipped into a coma, and family members, taking her for dead, dropped wax on her eyelids and prepared her for burial.

But this extraordinary woman, the future Saint Teresa of Jesus, witnessed the better part of an extraordinary century. Her lifetime (1515–82) spanned the great movements in European culture now known as Renaissance, Reformation, and Counter-Reformation. Her experience of these movements, and the changes and conflicts they brought, had an enormous impact on her life and work as a mystic, a writer, and a religious reformer.

Teresa spent most of these sixty-seven years in her native city of Avila. Here, in this urban setting, she found many of her models for the religious life, as well as the individuals and institutions that helped to shape her concepts of prayer and monastic reform. These influences have often been overlooked in traditional studies of her life, which emphasize its final seventeen years, when she bustled about Castile founding convents, *la santa andariega* (the wandering saint). Teresa is closely associated with the city of her birth; indeed, she is often referred to as Saint Teresa of Avila, rather than as Teresa of Jesus, her religious name. Despite this, little has been written about the social and religious milieu of sixteenth-century Avila. This book, then, attempts to examine Saint Teresa of Jesus and her reform of the Carmelite order in the context of the religious and social changes that transformed European society in the sixteenth century, as experienced in the city of Avila.

Teresa was born one year before Ferdinand of Aragon died and two years before Martin Luther initiated his revolt. By this time Avila was an important regional center and diocesan seat, and was politically controlled by an entrenched oligarchy. Members of the urban aristocracy dominated religious life, as well. Noblewomen, in particular, played a critical role in founding and endowing monastic institutions in Avila throughout the entire early modern period.

The saint grew up in the age of Charles V, when Spain was emerging as a major European and overseas imperial power and the defender of Catholic orthodoxy in a religiously divided Europe. In the early sixteenth century, Avila underwent rapid demographic and economic growth that was due in large measure to expansion in Castile's wool trade. The challenges and problems posed by these changes affected relations between social groups in the city and, ultimately, the mood and character of the city's religious life as well.

By mid-century, inspired by the late medieval *devotio moderna* and the Spanish exponents of Christian humanism, a group of reformers in Avila were fostering the values of education, poor relief, clerical training, and apostolic service to the urban community as a whole. Supported in part by an influential group of non-noble "rich men"—merchants, financiers, professionals, and minor clerics—these reformers founded institutions that offered alternatives to the traditional dynastic form of religious expression embraced by members of the city's hereditary elite. The books, the figures, and the ideas of Catholic reform then sweeping much of Europe were brought to Teresa of Jesus through this dynamic reform movement in sixteenth-century Avila. In this setting, too, she found the earliest supporters of her efforts to reform the Carmelite order.

By the time of Teresa's death in 1582, the Spain of Philip II was beginning to experience serious economic and demographic problems at home and threats to its hegemony abroad. In the aftermath of the Council of Trent (1545–64), religious authorities actively discouraged the individual and institutional experimentation that had characterized the first half of the century, and instead placed a high premium on conformity, quiescence, and obedience in the religious life.

By the time Teresa of Jesus was canonized in 1622, Avila had suffered several decades of plague and drought, the destruction of its wool trade, and the removal of its elites to the court at Madrid. The city could hardly afford to sponsor celebrations in Teresa's honor—indeed, with much of its population and resources gone, Avila rapidly faded in importance. Later visitors commented on the stagnation and poverty of this provincial backwater, even as they marveled at its many elegant palaces and monasteries. These monuments serve as reminders of the city's golden age in the sixteenth century, when Avila formed part of a mighty empire and nurtured one of the world's most beloved saints.

By far the most pleasant part of completing a project of this size is acknowledging the many individuals who helped to make it possible. My first word of thanks must go to Natalie Zemon Davis, my teacher, adviser, and friend. Her erudition, imagination, and energy never cease to amaze and inspire me. J. H. Elliott generously shared his time and immense knowledge of Spanish history with me; this book greatly benefits from his penetrating remarks and careful reading.

Preface

Others have commented on all or parts of this work at various stages of its development: James Amelang, Miriam Chrisman, W. A. Christian, Jr., Teófanes Egido, Richard Kagan, J. Mary Luti, Francisco Márquez Villanueva, JoAnn McNamara, Sara Nalle, T. K. Rabb, Stanley Stein, Fr. John Sullivan, and Ronald Surtz. I especially thank Serafín de Tapia for sharing his excellent research on the demographic and economic history of sixteenth-century Avila, and for his friendship. My colleagues in the history department at the University of North Carolina at Greensboro have been supportive and enthusiastic from the start. Jeffrey Patton and his class in advanced cartography prepared the maps, which appear with his permission. The staff of the Academic Computer Center and William Link and Paul Mazgaj offered much useful technical advice. My thanks also go to Jackie Wehmueller for her careful copyediting and to my editors at Cornell University Press.

I received financial support for this project from Princeton University's Department of History and Committee on European Studies, a Woodrow Wilson Women's Studies Grant, a Charlotte W. Newcombe Dissertation Fellowship, and a UNCG Excellence Fund Faculty Summer Research Grant. The book owes its current shape and probably its very existence to my wonderful year as a Research Associate and Visiting Lecturer in Women's Studies in Religion at the Harvard Divinity School in 1985–86. I am grateful to Constance Buchanan and my fellow research associates for their companionship and stimulation. My parents and grandparents also provided support over the years, financial and otherwise.

Finally, I'm grateful to Rich Haney. He knows how much I owe to him.

JODI BILINKOFF

Greensboro, North Carolina

Abbreviations

ADA	Archivo Diocesano, Avila
AGS	Archivo General del Estado, Simancas
AHN	Archivo Histórico Nacional, Madrid
AHPA	Archivo Histórico Provincial, Avila
ARC	Archivo de la Real Chancillería, Valladolid
ASA	Archivo del Seminario, Avila
BAH	*Boletín de la Real Academia de Historia*
BN	Biblioteca Nacional, Madrid
CNRS	Centre National de la Recherche Scientifique
CODOIN	Colección de Documentos Inéditos de la Historia de España
CSIC	Consejo Superior de Investigaciones Científicas
FUE	Fundación Universitaria Española
MHSJ	Monumenta Historica Societatis Jesu
RAH	Real Academia de Historia, Madrid
SEVPEN	Service d'Edition et de Vente des Publications de l'Education Nationale

The Avila of Saint Teresa

AVILA

I

The City of
Saint Teresa

The history of Saint Teresa's city begins in the violent struggles of Spain's medieval Reconquest from the Moors. The North African Muslims first invaded the Iberian Peninsula in 711 A.D.; three years later they conquered the previously Roman, then Visigothic, settlement known as Abula. For over three hundred years Christian and Muslim battled for possession of this region high on the central Castilian plateau, with its strategically located mountain passes between the Duero and Tagus valleys. Beyond the sierra lay the Visigothic capital of Toledo, the key to the domination of Castile. The area fell alternately into Moorish and Christian hands, and constant warfare reduced it to a barren no-man's land.[1]

Finally, in 1083, Christian forces under King Alfonso VI of Castile gained definitive control; two years later they oc-

1. For the early history of Avila, see such general works as Juan Martín Carramolino, *Historia de Avila, su provincia y obispado* vol. 2 (Madrid: Librería Española, 1872–73) pp. 5–190; José María Quadrado, *Salamanca, Avila, y Segovia* (Barcelona: D. Cortezo, 1884), pp. 302–303; Enrique Ballesteros, *Estudio histórico de Avila y su territorio* (Avila: Tip. de M. Sarachaga, 1896) pp. 16–21; Luis Ariz, *Historia de las grandezas de la ciudad de Avila* pt. 2 (Alcalá de Henares: L. Martínez Grande, 1607), 11–71.

cupied Toledo. Alfonso charged his son-in-law, the French knight Raymond of Burgundy, with establishing a new city on the site of the old Abula. In what is referred to as Avila's Repopulation, settlers arrived from northern Spain and France to found the frontier city.[2] Many landmarks, such as the Cathedral of San Salvador, the beautiful basilica of San Vicente, several parish churches, and most important, the massive city walls, were constructed during the Repopulation of the late eleventh and early twelfth centuries. Designed by foreign "masters of geometry" and built in part by Moorish prisoners of war, the formidable walls of Avila were meant to last centuries, for enemies still threatened the city on all sides.[3]

In this "society organized for war," military strength and prowess were highly valued.[4] Ennobled warriors quickly came to dominate a city of residents dependent upon them for protection. The legacy of military activity and noble hegemony would continue to influence Avila throughout the Middle Ages and early modern period. The city came to be called Avila de los Caballeros, Avila of the Knights.

Occasionally women penetrated this man's world of warfare. A popular legend of medieval Avila celebrates a certain Jimena Blázquez. According to the story, once, in the early days of the Reconquest when all the men were away at battle, the Moors surrounded the city, confident of its easy capture. But Jimena Blázquez, the valiant wife of the royal governor, organized all of Avila's women and inspired them with courage. Dressed in their husband's hats and armor, the women climbed the battlements and furiously clattered their pots

2. Carramolino 2:191–210. *Crónica de la población de Avila,* ed. Amparo Hernández Segura (Valencia: Textos Medievales, 1966) pp. 17–19. Claudio Sánchez-Albornoz y Menduiña *Despoblación y repoblación del Valle del Duero* (Buenos Aires: Instituto de Historia de España, 1966) especially pp. 344–390.

3. Carramolino 2:203. Ariz pt. 2, 7r, 12v.

4. Elena Lourie, "A Society Organized for War: Medieval Spain," *Past and Present* 35 (1966): 54–76.

and pans. Hearing the dreadful clamor, the Moors feared that there were twice as many warriors as usual and fled without a fight. In some accounts, the grateful city offered Jimena Blázquez and her sisters full status as citizens (*vecinos*) and the right to vote in the *concejo*, or city council, but they refused this privilege.[5]

Whether or not Jimena Blázquez actually existed, her legend illustrates certain values. In this male-centered society, women who demonstrated toughness, initiative, and independence were thought so unusual that they were labeled (by male writers) *varonil*, manlike. Jimena Blázquez, noisy, brave, and arrayed in armor, in some sense *became* male and, by becoming male, achieved honor and greatness.[6] Her refusal to accept political power is consistent with ideas regarding female abnegation and humility, however. One wonders if this part of the legend was formulated at a later date to justify the complete exclusion of women from the political scene. We shall see that, although internalized and spiritualized, the ideal of *la mujer fuerte*, "the strong woman," persisted in Avila well into the seventeenth century.

By the late Middle Ages, the city had acquired another name, Avila del Rey, Avila of the King, which was also the device borne on its coat of arms. Avila established close ties with the Castilian monarchy, sheltering the boy-king Alfonso XI during his minority in the early fourteenth century and receiving many royal privileges in return. The city attained the right to send its representatives to the *cortes*, a parliamentary assembly. In the troubled mid-fifteenth century, influential citizens of Avila, perhaps precisely because of their strong conception of kingship, opposed the vacillat-

5. This legend is recounted in all the general histories of Avila. See, for example, Carramolino 2:263–265; Ballesteros pp. 101–102; Quadrado pp. 307–308.

6. Malveena McKendrick, *Woman and Society in the Spanish Drama of the Golden Age. A Study of the mujer varonil* (London: Cambridge University Press, 1974).

The Avila of Saint Teresa

ing and reputedly impotent king Henry IV in favor of his half-sister, the princess Isabella.[7] Moreover, Isabella was an *abulense*, a native of the province of Avila, born in Madrigal de las Altas Torres in the extreme north and raised in the convent of Santa Ana in the capital. Avila's gamble paid off as Isabella won her bid for power. Thus, by the end of the fifteenth century tight bonds between city and monarchy had once again been forged.

Avila at the Birth of Saint Teresa

When Teresa de Ahumada y Cepeda was born in 1515, Avila could claim between four thousand and six thousand inhabitants. Like other European cities at the time, Teresa's birthplace was just beginning a period of sustained demographic and economic growth. Because this period essentially coincided with Teresa's lifetime, the saint grew up in an atmosphere of dynamic, but sometimes disturbing, urban change.[8]

Sixteenth-century Avila was an amalgam of diverse social groups. Even in the city's earliest frontier days, residents organized themselves in barrios or neighborhoods according to occupation, rank, and ethnic diversity. These criteria formed the basis of the city's social geography.[9]

In 1515 most abulenses worked as artisans, especially in the manufacture of woolen cloth. Simply put, wool produc-

7. William D. Phillips, *Enrique IV and the Crisis of Fifteenth Century Castile, 1425–1480* (Cambridge, Mass.: Mediaeval Academy of America, 1978) especially p. 79.

8. Serafín de Tapia, "Las fuentes demográficas y el potencial humano de Avila en el siglo XVI," *Cuadernos Abulenses* 2 (1984): 61–70, 86–88. Tapia records 1,043 *vecinos* (citizens or heads of households) in 1514, according to a municipal census, and 1,366 in 1517. He argues persuasively for a rather low coefficient of 3.7, which I have rounded off to 4 to account for nobles, clerics, and others not counted because exempt from or unable to pay taxes. For European trends of demographic growth and urbanization in this period, see Harry A. Miskimin, *The Economy of Later Renaissance Europe, 1460–1600* (Cambridge: Cambridge University Press, 1977) pp. 20–46.

9. Ariz pt. 2, 7r–21v. Ballesteros pp. 96–98.

4

tion was the backbone of Avila's, and of Castile's, economy. At the end of the fifteenth century, the Catholic Monarchs, Ferdinand and Isabella, had taken measures to encourage sheepraising in Castile, giving nearly free rein to the *mesta*, the powerful herders' guild. Most of the highly prized Spanish merino wool was exported to foreign manufacturing centers, particularly those in Flanders. Some, however, was kept within Castile, providing the raw material for a native cloth industry.[10]

Avila's location virtually ensured its participation in this vital and lucrative wool trade. One of the three major royally protected systems of sheepwalks, the Segovian, passed through the province. This route of transhumance originated in the northeast corner of Castile, in La Rioja, and linked the cities of Burgos and Segovia, the financial and industrial centers of the wool trade. The massive herds of sheep were pastured in the mountains in the summer, and in winter they migrated west and south through the province of Avila, entering the warm plains of Extremadura through passes in the Val de Corneja. For this reason, many placenames in Avila contain the word *cañada* (sheepwalk).[11]

Much of the wool raised in the province, especially that used for making high-quality cloth, went to the nearby city of Segovia. Dozens of men and women in Avila, however, found employment in the production of the cheap, coarse woolens made mainly for local consumption. About 20 percent of Avila's active population was involved in the production of textiles in the early part of the sixteenth century. By the 1560s and 1570s this figure rose to over 30 percent.[12]

Avila's numerous wool workers—weavers, dyers, card-

10. The basic reference for these developments remains Julius Klein, *The Mesta: A Study in Spanish Economic History, 1273–1836* (Cambridge: Harvard University Press, 1920). I have used the latest Spanish edition: *La Mesta: Estudio de la historia económica española, 1273–1836* (Madrid: Alianza, 1981) pp. 215–234. Also, Ramón Carande Thobar, *Carlos V y sus banqueros* (Madrid: Sociedad de Estudios y Publicaciones, 1965) pp. 71–114.

11. Klein pp. 31–45. Carande pp. 95–97.

12. Serafín de Tapia, "Estructura ocupacional de Avila en el siglo XVI," in *El pasado histórico de Castilla y León* vol. 2, *Edad Moderna*, ed. Jesús

ers, combers, spinners, fullers—as well as artisans involved in leathermaking, metalworking, construction, and other trades, clustered in certain neighborhoods. One of these was las Vacas, located outside the city walls. Enrique Ballesteros, a local historian of the nineteenth century, commented in describing this section of Avila that it had always been inhabited by "people of the most humble condition."[13] When the holy woman Mari Díaz moved to the city in the 1530s, she settled among the artisans and laborers of las Vacas. Her neighbor, the father of the future priest Julián de Avila, worked, according to the cleric's biographer, as a weaver.[14]

The barrio of San Esteban, sloping west of the city's center, lying roughly between the small church of San Esteban and the ancient bridge on the Adaja River, was Avila's "industrial end" par excellence. In his 1609 history, Luis Ariz recounted its settlement by "men who performed the mechanical arts, dyers, tanners, millers, fullers and halberd-makers."[15] In the seventeenth century, Gil González Dávila attested to the operation of seventeen grist mills on the banks of the Adaja, as well as several fulling mills and washing troughs for the production of various grades of woolen cloth.[16] San Esteban also gained a reputation as a bad neighborhood, at least in the eyes of the political and ecclesiastical elites whose opinions have come down to us. Behind the church of San Esteban, for example, stood one of Avila's *casas de la mancebía* (houses of ill repute).[17]

Crespo Redondo (Burgos: Junta de Castilla y León, 1983) pp. 210–223. AGS Expedientes de Hacienda (hereafter Exp. Hac.) 50–3 for 1561 household survey of Avila.

13. Ballesteros p. 254. Even today this is a working-class neighborhood.

14. "Información de la Vida, muerte, y milagros de la Venerable María Díaz," ADA Códice (hereafter Cód.) 3.345. Gerardo de San Juan de la Cruz, *Vida del Maestro Julián de Avila* . . . (Toledo: Impr. de la viuda é hijos de J. Peláez, 1915) pp. 10–11.

15. Ariz pt. 2, 20r–v.

16. Gil González Dávila, *Teatro eclesiástico de las ciudades e iglesias catedrales de España* . . . (Salamanca: A. Ramírez, 1618) p. 194.

17. Quadrado p. 546n. AHPA Actas Consistoriales (hereafter Actas Consist.) legajo (hereafter leg.) 278, 1567–68.

Most of the evidence for the unsavoriness of this area is derived from the debate over the proper location for the relics of Avila's first bishop, San Segundo, discovered in 1519 in the chapel of San Sebastián on the Adaja, across from a large grist mill. González Dávila, some forty years after the relics had been transferred to the cathedral, cited among the reasons for the move that the place was inconvenient, that "the maintenance of the physical plant was very poor," and that "the faithful attended very infrequently because of the great distance of the chapel." Attendance at the shrine was, in fact, regular enough, but not by the class of people who would have to travel through the "bad part of town" to get there.[18] The ecclesiastical notary Antonio de Cianca, a major proponent of the move, pointed to the proximity of the chapel to foul-smelling tanneries, the animals that wandered unchecked into the shrine, and the thieves and "low-life men and women who [went] there to chat and have lascivious relations." And although the patrons of the neighborhood-based confraternity protested that the chapel was in a "comfortable and cheerful location, well above the river, mills and tanneries," in 1594 Avila's bishop and cathredal canons decided that the sacred relics, for security reasons, must be placed "in the middle of the city" (that is, where the upper class lived) and out of this "bad neighborhood of tanneries and mills and other inconveniences caused by the animals."[19]

Perhaps we should not be surprised that city elites eventually succeeded in having the body moved. More remarkable is that the brothers of the San Segundo confraternity managed to keept the saint's relics for some seventy years in a peripheral neighborhood where thieves and prostitutes mingled with artisans and visiting peasants, the incessant sounds of mills grinding grain and fulling cloth filled the air, and the unpleasant smells of tanned leather, dyestuffs, and manure filled the nostrils.

18. González Dávila 1:305.
19. Antonio de Cianca, *Historia de la vida, invención, milagros, y translación de San Segundo* . . . bk. 3 (Madrid: Luis Sánchez, 1595) 5r–6r, 15v–25r.

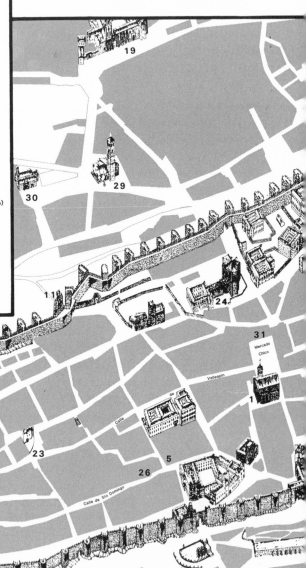

AVILA

Parish Churches

1 San Juan
2 San Pedro
3 San Vicente
4 Santiago
5 Santo Domingo
6 Santo Tomé
7 San Andrés
8 San Nicolás

Monasteries

9 La Antigua
10 Santo Tomás
11 N. S. del Carmen
12 San Francisco
13 San Gil (later San Jerónimo)
14 San Antonio

Convents

15 Santa Ana
16 Santa Catalina
17 Las Gordillas
18 N. S. de Gracia
19 La Encarnación
20 San José

Other Churches and Shrines

21 San Millán
22 San Sebastián (later San Segundo)
23 San Esteban
24 Chapel of Mosén Rubín
25 Cathedral
26 Santa Escolástica
27 La Magdalena
28 N. S. de las Vacas
29 San Martín
30 N. S. de la Cabeza

Other

31 City Hall (Consistorio)
32 Fortress (Alcazar)

AVILA

12

14

15

17

13

20

6

16

25

21

2

9

Mercado Grande

32

27

28

18

4

10

More centrally located were Avila's two marketplaces, the Mercados Grande and Chico. Here commerce and trade flourished in the early sixteenth century as the city played an important role as a regional distribution center. Numerous fairs and markets attracted farmers from the surrounding countryside and brought business to shopkeepers and dealers in agricultural products as well as revenue to the city government. Municipal ordinances promulgated in 1485 mention the market held every Friday in the Mercado Chico, a tradition that continues to this day.[20] Avila's commercial district also provided a place for gossip, communication, and entertainment. The country visitor in town to sell his or her wares might see a morality play staged in the courtyard of the Hospital of la Magdalena, off the Mercado Grande, or witness the equally theatrical execution of a criminal in the Mercado Chico. Religious processions and civic parades wound their way through the district, the true heart of Avila. Taverns, frequently operated by women, accommodated travelers and traders.[21] It was off the Mercado Chico, in a shop on the busy Cal de Andrín, that Saint Teresa's paternal grandfather, Juan Sánchez, grew wealthy dealing in silks and fine woolens. He belonged to Avila's small but dynamic commercial and professional class, a group that would grow in both number and influence during the sixteenth century.

20. The "Ordenanzas de Avila" were published by Manuel de Foronda in BAH 71 (1917): 381–425, 463–520, and 72 (1918): 25–47.

21. For theater in the patio of la Magdalena, see Abelardo Merino Alvarez, *La sociedad abulense durante el siglo XVI: La nobleza* (Madrid: Impr. del Patronato de Huérfanos, 1926) p. 161. RAH MS 9.3594, 263v. The most famous occasion was the presentation of the liturgical drama *San Segundo de Avila* by Lope de Vega, performed there to commemorate the transfer of the relics of Avila's first bishop in 1595. Cianca refers to la Magdalena as the place "donde se representan las comedias" (bk. 3, 68v). Women played significant roles in provisioning trades in early modern Avila, for which see AGS Exp. Hac. 50–3. For this phenomenon throughout Europe, see *Women and Work in Preindustrial Europe*, ed. Barbara A. Hanawalt (Bloomington: Indiana University Press, 1986), especially articles by Bennett, Reyerson, Kowaleski, and Davis.

Despite its considerable manufacturing and mercantile activity, in 1515 Saint Teresa's city still looked decidedly rural. Farming in the Valley of Amblés extended right up to the city gates. Neighborhoods such as that of San Nicolás retained a semirural character until quite recent times. Families had their chickens and pigs, orchards and gardens, as did monasteries and convents. The municipal ordinances of 1485 sternly threatened with fines residents who let their pigs or cows roam the streets and trample vineyards and gardens.[22]

In the northern agricultural district of Ajates, between the adjacent chapels of San Martín and Nuestra Señora de la Cabeza and the parish church of San Andrés, many of Avila's *moriscos* made their home. During the Middle Ages a group of Muslims living under Christian rule, known as *mudéjares*, had settled in Avila. Their descendants, who converted to Catholicism en masse in 1502, were known as *moriscos*.[23] The moriscos composed a relatively small sector of Avila's population, their numbers certainly never exceeding 15 percent of the total. Most supported themselves as farmers, as local placenames such as Huerta del Moro (the Moor's Garden) suggest. Many found employment in metalworking trades, and they practically monopolized the manufacture of pots and pans. As carters and haulers, craftsmen and small shopkeepers, moriscos contributed to Avila's economic development. Some morisco families were even able to amass considerable fortunes.[24]

Substantially more is known about Avila's other ethnic minority, the Jews. Jews made their first appearance in Avila during the Repopulation of the late eleventh century, when a

22. Foronda. Carramolino 3:75–83.
23. Tapia, "Estructura," pp. 209–210, 217–219. For a general introduction to the topic, see Antonio Domínguez Ortíz and Bernard Vincent, *Historia de los moriscos: Vida y tragedia de una minoría* (Madrid: Revista de Occidente, 1978) ch. 1.
24. Tapia, "Estructura," pp. 217–219. Idem, "La opresión fiscal de la minoría morisca en las ciudades castellanas: El caso de la ciudad de Avila," *Studia Historica* 4 (1986): 17–49.

group led by Rabbi David Centén entered the city.[25] A sizable community developed during the Middle Ages, most Jews living in the central commercial district where they gained their livelihoods. Pilar León, in her important study *Judíos de Avila*, stresses that most Jews lived humble, even impoverished, lives as artisans and shopkeepers. Some, however, did make great fortunes in trade, moneylending, tax collecting, and medicine.[26]

Avila's Jews coexisted peacefully with their Christian neighbors throughout the medieval period. They seem to have been spared the violent horror of the pogroms of 1391 which destroyed some of the largest Jewish communities in Castile and Aragon. But in the late fifteenth century the mood of toleration swiftly changed. Laws passed by the cortes of Madrigal (1476) and Toledo (1477), for example, prohibited Jews from wearing ornaments of gold or silver and luxury fabrics, and banned usury.[27] Upon the publication of these laws in Avila, Jewish leaders retaliated by ordering community members simply to stop lending money. The municipality, in desperate need of funds during Castile's war against Portugal, ordered the Jews to make loans. They complied, and later their debtors refused repayment, claiming that the interest rate had been usurious.[28]

The late 1470s and the 1480s witnessed an increasing number of fiscal and legal complaints directed against the Jews of Avila, in large part by financially strapped taxpayers who

25. Ariz pt. 2, 20r. Pilar León Tello, *Judíos de Avila* (Avila: Diputación Provincial de Avila, Institución "Gran Duque de Alba," 1963) p. 5.

26. León pp. 1–32. Yitzhak Baer, *A History of the Jews in Christian Spain* vol. 1 (Philadelphia: Jewish Publication Society of America, 1961) pp. 191–198.

27. Luis Suárez Fernández, *Documentos acerca de la expulsión de los judíos* (Valladolid: CSIC, 1964) pp. 27–28. León pp. 10, 19. For the worsening relations between Christians and Jews in late medieval Castile, see José María Monsalvo Antón, *Teoría y evolución de un conflicto social: El antisemitismo en la Corona de Castilla en la Baja Edad Media* (Madrid: Siglo Veintiuno, 1985).

28. Suárez pp. 27–28, 158–160. Francisco Cantera Burgos, *La usura judía en Castilla* (Salamanca: Establecimiento tipográfico de Calatrava, 1932).

The City of Saint Teresa

vented their frustrations at their Jewish creditors. In addition, in November 1489, the Jewish community lost its time-honored right to have its own organs of government and courts, its members ordered henceforth to appear before the *justicias ordinarias*.[29] Finally, Jews were forced to live within a crowded ghetto, or *judería*, located in and around the streets of Santo Domingo and Santa Escolástica, the site of the city's original Jewish settlement in 1086. Their main synagogue probably stood on the corner of these two streets.[30]

Anti-Jewish feelings in Avila reached a climax in 1491, with the famous trial of the so-called Santo Niño de la Guardia (Holy Child of La Guardia). On this occasion several Jews from Toledo were accused of kidnapping a boy from the Toledan village of la Guardia, crucifying him, and using his heart and a consecrated host in demonic rituals. Captured in Avila, they eventually confessed to these crimes under torture. For reasons that remain unclear, officials of the Inquisition of Toledo decided to try the case in Avila, and sent the unfortunate Jews to the stake in the Mercado Grande. Common people lashed out by stoning individual Jews and attacking the *judería*.[31] Within the year, the Catholic Monarchs, citing as justification the blasphemy and murder committed in the la Guardia case, gave their Jewish subjects the choice of conversion to Christianity or permanent exile from the kingdoms of Castile and Aragon.[32] In Avila, as in other parts of Spain, this decision had profound consequences. While León's estimate of three thousand Jews expelled seems very

29. Suárez pp. 151–160, 194–195, 333–334.
30. Ibid. pp. 31–36. Marvin Lunenfeld, *Keepers of the City: The Corregidores of Isabella I of Castile (1474–1504)* (Cambridge: Cambridge University Press, 1987) pp. 126–127.
31. León p. 27. Fidel Fita, "La verdad sobre el martirio del Santo Niño de la Guardia," BAH 11 (1887): 7–134. For a classic analysis of accusations of ritual murder and desecration, see Joshua Trachtenberg, *The Devil and the Jews: The Medieval Conception of the Jew and Its Relation to Modern Antisemitism* (Philadelphia: Jewish Publication Society of America, 1983) pp. 109–139.
32. Edict of Expulsion, published in León pp. 91–95.

13

large, it is clear that the city lost an important segment of its population and that its productive and financial resources, at least in the short run, were significantly diminished.[33] A great many, probably the majority, of Avila's Jews converted to Catholicism in the years after the expulsion. Far from ending conflict, however, these conversions led to more complications. Instead of a "Jewish problem," Avila now had a "New Christian (converso) problem." "Old Christians" remained profoundly suspicious of these converts and their descendants. After all, Old Christians reasoned, these conversos changed their names but continued to exercise the same professions and live in the same neighborhood, now known as the Judería Vieja, the Old Jewish Quarter.[34] What was to prevent them from secretly observing their ancestral customs and religious practices?

Conversos, for their part, began to struggle to establish impeccable Catholic credentials and to deny that their families had ever been "tainted" with Jewish blood. This part of Avila's legacy—of a Jewish past hidden and in disgrace—had a profound effect on Teresa de Ahumada y Cepeda.

In the beginning of the sixteenth century, then, a variety of social groups, artisans, peasants, merchants, converted Muslims and Jews, all made their homes within and without Avila's massive walls. An entrenched oligarchy dominated all the inhabitants of the city, controlling the organs of political and also religious life. It is to this powerful class, their values and concerns, that we now turn.

33. Ibid. pp. 117–163. Tapia, "Fuentes," p. 62.

34. A 1513 *visita* (inspection of houses owned by the cathedral chapter) records many tenants with names found traditionally among Avila's Jews living in the Judería Vieja and in and around the two marketplaces. Others used placenames, such as de Bonilla and del Barco, a common converso practice. The evidence strongly suggests that these merchants, physicians, artisans, and tax farmers were New Christians. AHN Cód. 466-b. For converso professions and names and a good introduction to this uniquely Iberian problem, see Antonio Domínguez Ortiz, *Los judeoconversos en España y América* (Madrid: Ediciones Istmo, 1978).

2

Aristocratic Dominance
and Monastic Foundation,
1480–1520

In an aristocratic age Avila was, in the words of the great Spanish social historian Antonio Domínguez Ortiz, a "thoroughly aristocratic city" ("una ciudad eminentemente nobilaria"). By the late fifteenth century in Avila, as in other European cities, a small number of elite families dominated the organs of political power, notably the city council.[1] These families asserted a profound influence on religious institutions as well, supplying the cathedral chapter and monastic houses with most of their personnel and financial backing. Just as critically, if less tangibly, the urban aristocracy articulated a set of social values based upon family honor and continuity which permeated many levels of Avila's society. The effort of local elites to found and patronize religious houses between 1480 and 1520 powerfully symbolized the values so deeply cherished by this dominant class.

Avila's oligarchy consisted of between two and three hundred families in the first half of the sixteenth century. It

1. Antonio Domínguez Ortiz, *La sociedad española en el siglo XVII* vol. 1 (Madrid: CSIC, 1963) p. 150. For a general discussion, see articles in *The Rich, the Wellborn, and the Powerful: Elites and Upper Classes in History*, ed. F. C. Jaher (Urbana: University of Illinois Press, 1973).

usually accounted for about 10 percent of the city's total population, although this figure at times climbed as high as 20 percent. Most elite families lived in the central districts of San Juan and San Pedro, at the city's geographical and social summit. These neighborhoods also housed the majority of Avila's domestic servants and tailors.[2]

Upper-class families in early modern Avila, as in other Castilian cities, could be divided roughly into two categories, titled nobility and "gentlemen." The extremely small group of titled nobles derived their wealth and power from the fixed incomes (rentas) of large estates they owned in the territory around Avila. These estates included whole villages, and the nobles frequently maintained seigniorial rights over their inhabitants. A notable example of a nobleman of this type would be Don Pedro Dávila, lord of the landed estates of Villafranca and las Navas founded by his grandfather in 1431. In the sixteenth century, Don Pedro's income was estimated at ten thousand ducats a year. His lands encompassed at least four towns and approximately 1,350 families. In a collection made for a municipal granary in 1528, "El magnífico Señor" pledged the largest individual contribution, fifty fanegas of wheat. By contrast, the merchant and financier Alonso Sánchez de Cepeda, father of the future Saint Teresa, pledged two fanegas. Don Pedro's acceptance of the title of first marquis of las Navas from Charles V in December 1533 climaxed a long and distinguished career that had included military service to both Isabella the Catholic and Charles V, participation in Charles's royal council, and a seat on Avila's city council.[3]

The majority of Avila's elite families belonged to the lower

2. Serafín de Tapia, "Estructura ocupacional de Avila en el siglo XVI," in *El pasado histórico de Castilla y León* vol. 2, *Edad Moderna*, ed. Jesús Crespo Redondo (Burgos: Junta de Castilla y León, 1983) pp. 209, 216; idem, "Las fuentes demográficas y el potencial humano de Avila en el siglo XVI," *Cuadernos Abulenses* 2 (1984): 59–70.

3. Abelardo Merino Alvarez, *La sociedad abulense durante el siglo XVI: La nobleza* (Madrid: Impr. del Patronato de Huérfanos, 1926) pp. 53–55, 146–151. Luis Ariz, *Historia de las grandezas de la ciudad de Avila*, pt. 3

rank of Spanish nobility, the *hidalgos*. They were distinguished from their non-noble neighbors by privileges such as exemption from taxation and the right to affix the polite titles of *Don* or *Doña* before their names.[4] Like the titled nobility, they owned property, but often their holdings were more diversified, including properties within the city of Avila as well as farmland, pastures, orchards, and vineyards throughout the countryside.

An inventory of the property of Don Diego Alvarez de Bracamonte made on December 10, 1562, describes the economic resources of an affluent hidalgo family in sixteenth-century Avila. Apart from movable goods such as cattle, jewelry, furniture, and other household effects, Don Diego possessed land in four rural districts and three enclosed fields in the mountain villages around Avila, including one that produced an annual income of 13,000 *maravedís*. He owned an unspecified number of houses in country villages and collected mortgage payments (*censos*) on an additional three houses and four rural properties. Don Diego also owned several large houses and some smaller ones in the city of Avila, near the Hospital of Santa Escolástica, on the border between the fashionable San Juan district and the Old Jewish Quarter. Tenants paid him censos on four houses in another part of the city, as well. A member of a large and influential family of politicians and clerics, Don Diego sat on the city council during the first two decades of the sixteenth century.[5]

Don Pedro Dávila and Don Diego Alvarez de Bracamonte

(Alcalá de Henares: L. Martínez Grande, 1607) 35r. AHN Cód. 458-b. Jesús Molinero, "La alhóndiga de Avila en 1528 y D. Alonso Sánchez de Cepeda, padre de Santa Teresa," BAH 65 (1914): 258–268, 344–350. For gradations of nobility in Spain, see J. H. Elliott, *Imperial Spain, 1469–1716* (New York: New American Library, 1966) pp. 109–114.

4. Annie Molinié-Bertrand, "Les 'Hidalgos' dans le royaume de Castille à la fin du XVIe siècle: Approche cartographique," *Revue d'Histoire Economique et Sociale* 52 (1974): 51–82.

5. Merino pp. 191–193. For description and analysis of various types of landholding, see David Vassberg, *Land and Society in Golden Age Castile* (Cambridge: Cambridge University Press, 1984) especially pp. 90–119.

shared many of the experiences and goals of other European elites. Both derived their wealth primarily from the ownership of rural property. Both held seats on the city council. And both exhibited considerable concern for perpetuating their families' power, wealth, and prestige in succeeding generations. Don Pedro constructed a magnificent palace in Avila in 1541. Its façade proudly displays his family's coat of arms and proclaims the family's motto, "Where one door closes, another opens."[6] Don Diego attempted to consolidate his varied economic holdings in 1562 by creating a *mayorazgo*, or entailed estate. This way, in theory at least, his male heirs, in perpetuity, would inherit his patrimony intact.[7]

Being a noble in sixteenth-century Avila entailed embracing a whole set of social values based upon the concepts of honor and lineage. Avila of the Knights participated wholeheartedly in the obsession with honor which gripped Spain in the early modern period.[8] This concept of honor had multiple levels of meaning. The most important pertained to the question of lineage (*linaje*). For Avila's elites, claims to honor and prestige hinged upon claims of descent from a family with a long pedigree, preferably with origins in the city's medieval Reconquest and Repopulation. Tracing one's family back to

6. Merino p. 150. Natalie Zemon Davis, "Ghosts, Kin, and Progeny: Some Features of Family Life in Early Modern France," *Daedalus* 106 (1977): 87–114, on concern for family continuity.

7. Merino pp. 194–197. Bartolomé Clavero, *Mayorazgo: Propiedad feudal en Castilla, 1369–1836* (Madrid: Siglo Veintiuno, 1974). Theoretically entailed estates could not be divided or alienated, but in fact sometimes they were. Charles V granted permission to Don Francisco de Avila and his wife, Doña Isabel Mexia, to mortgage goods of their *mayorazgo* on October 28, 1522. He allowed Don Rodrigo de Valderrábano to sell off parts of his estate on May 22, 1542. In both cases the nobles needed cash to pay for their daughters' dowries. Manuel de Foronda y Aguilera, *Estancias y viajes del Emperador Carlos V* (Madrid, 1914) pp. 210, 516.

8. Bartolomé Bennassar, *The Spanish Character: Attitudes and Mentalities from the Sixteenth to the Nineteenth Century* (Berkeley and Los Angeles: University of California Press, 1979) pp. 213–236. Claude Chauchadis, *Honneur, morale, et société dans l'Espagne de Philippe II* (Paris: CNRS, 1984).

the Reconquest served the dual purpose of establishing roots at Avila's inception and identifying, and allowing families to identify with, heroic warrior ancestors. Military valor, after all, was a virtue highly valued by this class.

Thus, interest in genealogy, heraldry, and local history ran high in sixteenth-century Avila, with the emphasis on local history of a decidedly aristocratic flavor.[9] The authors of histories commissioned by individual members of the city council or by the body as a whole celebrated the city's glorious past in language reminiscent of the popular chivalric novels of the day. These histories featured lengthy genealogies (accurate or otherwise) and recitations of the heroic deeds of the purported ancestors of the historians' patrician patrons. Gonzalo de Ayora, commissioned to record Avila's history in 1519, ended his account with these stirring words: "And thus, all this being true, a fine thing it is that the descendants of such ancestors and settlers of the people might strive to emulate their forebears and [even] outdo them in virtue, if such a thing were possible."[10] In 1519 both Don Pedro Dávila and Don Diego Alvarez de Bracamonte sat on the city council.

9. Merino p. 117: "La historia de Avila toma carácter esencialmente nobilario durante el siglo XVI" (the written history of Avila takes on an essentially aristocratic character during the sixteenth century). For noble interest in genealogy, heraldry, and so forth, see pp. 107–128 in Merino. He notes that Don Pedro de Avila avidly collected old stones, inscriptions, and weapons and traced the history of the previous lords of las Navas (p. 119). A similar trend emerged in England in this period. "One of the most striking features of the age was a pride of ancestry which now reached new heights of fantasy and elaboration. . . . Genuine genealogy was cultivated by the older gentry to reassure themselves of their innate superiority over the upstarts; bogus genealogy was cultivated by the new gentry in an effort to clothe their social nakedness. . . . A lengthy pedigree was a useful weapon in the Tudor battle for status." Lawrence Stone, *The Crisis of the Aristocracy, 1558–1641* (Oxford: Oxford University Press, 1967) pp. 16–18.

10. Gonzalo de Ayora, *Epílogo de algunas cosas dignas de memoria pertenecientes a la . . . ciudad de Avila* (Salamanca, 1519). "Y pués todo esto es así verdad, justa cosa es que los descendientes de tales raices y moradores de tal pueblo se les fueren a parecer a sus antepasados y sóbrales en toda virtud si fuere posible." In 1517, the industrious corregidor Bernal de Mata discovered the ancient "Crónica" of Avila, composed around 1256, in the

The desire of Avila's elite families to claim illustrious ancestors in the city's remote, even mythical, past could not disguise the fact that most had arrived much more recently.[11] Luis Ariz, in his 1607 history of Avila, asserted an ancient Reconquest past for many families but was hard-pressed to find a verifiable line of descendants before the mid-fourteenth century. He specifically traced the Bracamonte family (as well as other distinguished families such as the Guiera, Guillamás, Bullón, Rengifo, Henao, and Cimbrón) to knights who "came from France to fight for King Henry." The Trastámara king Henry II (1369–79) depended heavily upon outside support to defeat his half-brother, Peter the Cruel, in a series of bloody dynastic wars. He was noted for liberally rewarding his followers with grants of land and noble status. Other families active in the political, economic, and religious life of sixteenth-century Avila, such as Pacheco, Vera, Manrique de Lara, Ochoa, Aguirre, and Medina, could be dated locally from the fifteenth century. Only a few lineages, such as various branches of the Dávila, the Serrano, and the Vela, may have actually had roots in Avila's earliest resettlement.[12]

The definition of honor in early sixteenth-century Spain also had a uniquely Iberian feature—the concern for "pure" Christian blood. Masses of Jews had converted to Chris-

---

possession of the regidor Nuño González del Aguila. He ordered the manuscript copied and bound and had it kept in the strongbox of the city council so the councilors could read of the "bondades y señalades virtudes de los antiguos pobladores de esta ciudad y su tierra." BN MS 1745.

11. The medieval "Miscelánea de antigüedades de Avila," recopied "por un regidor de Avila" in 1607, credits Hercules with the city's foundation. RAH MS 11–1–6–193.

12. Ariz pt. 4, especially 251–v. Merino pp. 29–47. For the formation of a "new nobility" in fifteenth-century Castile, see Salvador de Moxó, "De la nobleza vieja a la nobleza nueva: La transformación nobilaria castellana en la baja Edad Media," Cuadernos de Historia (Anexos de la revista Hispania) 4 (1969): 1–210. Marie Claude Gerbet, "Les Guerres et l'accès a la noblesse en Espagne de 1465 á 1592," Mélanges de la Casa de Velázquez 8 (1978): 295–325.

tianity following the series of violent pogroms in 1391. During the fifteenth century many of these converso families intermarried with Old Christians, including, in some cases, members of the nobility. As we have seen, Avila possessed a large and dynamic Jewish population in the Middle Ages.[13]

In the late fifteenth century, however, the doctrine of *limpieza de sangre*, purity of blood, gained enormous strength and influence and added a new dimension to the notion of honor. True honor was now defined by ethnicity, by blood, as well as by rank and pedigree. The idea of a strain of Moorish or, more likely in Avila, Jewish blood as a "stain" on one's reputation and standing affected families of relatively remote Jewish heritage as well as those of more recent Christian conversion.[14] Accordingly, families took great pains to conceal any information regarding Jewish ancestors. For many families in Avila, their insistent claims of pure Christian descent may have been as tenuous as their claims to Reconquest origins.

In establishing his *mayorazgo*, Don Diego Alvarez de Bracamonte expressed concern over the purity of his descendants, when he ordered his heirs to keep the family line free of the "taint" of Jewish blood. He specified that "he who succeeds to the said estate, be it a man or a woman, at no time shall be married to or marry a woman or man who belongs to the race of the Jews, but only [a spouse] that be an Old Christian on all sides." Don Diego charged each descendant with "looking to the conservation and purity of his lineages . . . [and] guarding and defending them in all purity against the caste and race of the Jews."[15] For all his protes-

13. Antonio Domínguez Ortiz, *Los judeoconversos en España y América* (Madrid: Ediciones Istmo, 1978) pp. 16–27.

14. Albert A. Sicroff, *Los estatutos de limpieza de sangre: Controversias entre los siglos XV y XVII* (Madrid: Taurus, 1985) especially pp. 336–343. Juan Ignacio Gutiérrez Nieto, "La estructura castizo-estamental de la sociedad castellana del siglo XVI," *Hispania* 125 (1973): 519–563.

15. Bracamonte family documents published by Merino pp. 34, 194–197: "El que sucediere en esta dicha mejora e mayorazgo, ora sea varón o embra,

tations of pristine Old Christian credentials, Don Diego Alvarez de Bracamonte may in fact have descended from conversos. His ancestor Admiral Mosén Rubín de Bracamonte founded the family line when he emigrated from France to fight in the dynastic wars of the late fourteenth century. Several historians, noting the Semitic sound of the Frenchman's name and examining patterns of intermarriage, have surmised the Jewish background of this family.[16] Don Diego's apparent disdain for the tainted "race" of Jews, rather than constituting proof of his family's "pure" lineage, may instead reveal a keen sensitivity on his part regarding the family's origins.

In the late fifteenth century and early sixteenth century many urban aristocrats in Avila found themselves in the process of consolidating positions of power and influence only relatively recently achieved. For this reason they, like other European elites, demonstrated an intense interest in matters of precedence, seniority, and etiquette. Through the articulation of an elaborate set of rituals and the adoption of a chivalric, almost archaic, way of life, Avila's oligarchs enthusiastically participated in the traditions of a medieval past from which few of them derived.

For example, a series of bitter and drawn-out debates over the question of parish antiquity preoccupied Avila's aristocrats during most of the sixteenth century. The members of several churches, all of which dated from the early twelfth

---

en ningún tiempo se aya casado ni case con mujer ni con varón que tenga rraça de judío, sino que sea cristiano viejo por todas partes . . . Están obligados a mirar por la conserbación e limpieça de sus linaxes . . . guardados e defendidos en toda limpieça de casta e rraça de Judíos." Ariz pt. 4, 411r.

16. Ariz pt. 4, 39v. Teófanes Egido, "The Historical Setting of St. Teresa's Life," Carmelite Studies 1 (1980): 153 n. 129. For conversos in Castilian oligarchies see Stephen H. Haliczer, "The Castilian Urban Patriciate and the Jewish Expulsions of 1480–92," American Historical Review 78 (1973): 35–61, and Francisco Márquez Villanueva, "Conversos y cargos concejiles en el siglo XV," Revista de Archivos, Bibliotecas, y Museos 53 (1957): 503–540.

century, stubbornly maintained, above the claims of rivals, that theirs was founded earlier. The noble parishioners of the churches of San Juan and Santiago engaged in numerous legal conflicts over the relative ages of their churches. Finally, in 1598, the city council decided in favor of San Juan, probably due in part to close relations between the church, which was located across from city hall, and the municipal government. When San Vicente and San Pedro maintained a similar rivalry, the case was decided in favor of San Pedro.[17]

The real issue at stake in both these legal battles was a point of honor, precedence in religious and civic processions. To representatives of the city's oldest parish went the privilege of accompanying the Host during the annual Corpus Christi processions, in which each parish carried its distinctive banner (pendón). Despite the decision in favor of San Pedro, in the conflict between San Pedro and San Vicente, a practical compromise had to be reached, perhaps owing to San Vicente's unique ecclesiastical position as a basilica and depository of some of Avila's most revered relics, not to mention the influence of its powerful parishioners, such as the Bracamonte, Estrada, and Esquina families. During several public processions, members of the church of San Pedro marched at the head for the first half of the route, but were then compelled to cede their place near the body of Christ to the parishioners of San Vicente.[18] Rituals such as these helped to underscore the

17. Juan Martín Carramolino, *Historia de Avila, su provincia y obispado* vol. 1 (Madrid: Librería Española, 1872) pp. 497, 478. Copy of 1598 decision in archive of parish church of San Juan. Gabriel María Vergara y Martín, *Estudio histórico de Avila y su territorio* (Madrid: Hernández, 1896) p. 180.
18. Carramolino 1:477–480. Vergara p. 180. Bartolomé Fernández Valencia, *Historia y grandezas del insigne templo ... de ... S. Vicente* vol. 1 (Avila, 1676) AHPA libros 2454–2455 pp. 88–89. Ronald Weissman describes how elites in sixteenth-century Florence also fought for positions close to the Eucharist, that is, for "a place in Christ's bodyguard," in Corpus Christi processions. *Ritual Brotherhood in Renaissance Florence* (New York: Academic Press, 1982) pp. 233–235. See also Edwin Muir, *Civic Ritual in Renaissance Venice* (Princeton: Princeton University Press, 1981). On devotion to the Host in late medieval Europe, see Charles Zika, "Host, Proces-

values of tradition, pedigree, and family continuity shared by members of Avila's oligarchy in the early modern period.

The City Council

A seat on the city council was both a cause and an effect of status in sixteenth-century Avila, as in other Castilian towns. The council served as the city's main administrative body. It consisted of two parts, the fourteen *regidores*, or city councilors, and the *justicia* ("the law"), police officials such as the *alguacil mayor*, or sheriff, who were subordinate to the regidores and responsible for enforcing their demands. The city council functioned simultaneously as a legislative, police, and in some matters, judicial institution.[19]

Every Tuesday and Saturday, with the bells of the nearby parish church of San Juan chiming, "according to usage and custom," the regidores met in the city hall located in the Mercado Chico. There they heard grievances, commissioned members to investigate complaints, and made decisions regarding a multitude of urban problems. They authorized the construction of public works. They negotiated with the cathedral chapter and other ecclesiastical institutions over religious affairs, for example, arrangements for the annual Corpus Christi processions. Avila's councilors particularly occupied themselves with the provision and maintenance of the city, including ensuring the supply of food and water, the disposal of garbage, and the repair of roads and bridges, concerns that became increasingly urgent as the city grew. Trade

sions, and Pilgrimages: Controlling the Sacred in Fifteenth Century Germany," *Past and Present* 118 (1988): 25–64.

19. José Fernández Mayoral, *El municipio de Avila: Estudio histórico* (Avila: Diputación Provincial de Avila, Institución "Alonso de Madrigal," 1958) pp. 4off. Luis G. de Valdeavellano, *Curso de historia de las instituciones españolas* (Madrid: Revista de Occidente, 1968) pp. 541–554. After around 1520, the number of regidores varied between fourteen and twenty-three.

regulations held an important place on the council's agenda, and the city controlled prices and supplies and appointed a battery of *veedores* (inspectors) to check the quality of many crafts, sometimes to the chagrin of the craftsmen. The councilors also decided in matters of *vecindad*, that is, whether an immigrant to the city should receive the status of citizen.[20]

In theory, all these functions of city government fell under the aegis of an agent of the Crown called the *corregidor*. Isabella the Catholic, striving to extend centralized royal authority after a chaotic period of civil wars in the fifteenth century, resumed a practice begun in the thirteenth century of using appointed officials to oversee the governing of the often factious Castilian towns. The corregidor would take on two-year, renewable stints of duty in towns of which he was not a native. He held responsibility for a broad range of administrative and judicial tasks, taking charge of adequately provisioning cities, upholding public order, and preventing local aristocratic and ecclesiastical elites from infringing upon royal prerogatives. The corregidor also heard civil and criminal cases that arose within his jurisdiction, although his judgment could be, and frequently was, appealed to Castile's higher courts, the *chancillerías*, or, eventually, to the Royal Council of Castile. In principle, then, a representative of the crown oversaw all aspects of municipal government.[21]

Day-to-day practice did not always conform to theory, however. In Avila, as in other Castilian cities, the crown-

20. The city hall was constructed in 1509; municipal records date from this time. Before this the regidores met in the parish church of San Juan. AHPA Actas Consist., for public works, e.g., libro 12, April 17, 1562; for Corpus Christi arrangements, e.g., leg. 278, April 8, 1567, libro 15, April 14, 1571, libro 12, April 17, 1563; for provisioning, e.g., libro 4, July 1, 1522 (water), libro 9, October 1537 (coal), libro 11, April, October 1558 (bread); for economic controls, e.g., libro 4, February 1522 (adjustment of price of bread). Inspectors were usually appointed at the beginning of each year. For criterion of *vecindad* see Valdeavellano p. 543.

21. Elliott pp. 91–96. Robert S. Chamberlain, "The Corregidor in Castile in the Sixteenth Century and the Residencia as Applied to the Corregidor," *Hispanic American Historical Review* 23 (1943): 222–257.

appointed corregidores performed their duties with varying degrees of enthusiasm. While some vigorously carried out public works projects, others, barely mentioned in municipal records, seem to have involved themselves very little in civic affairs. A more serious problem was posed by aristocratic city councilors, who often opposed individual corregidores and successfully resisted royal efforts to diminish their own political power.[22] Thus, in fact, the powerful local oligarchy determined the tenor of political life in early modern Avila.

The composition of the city council remained amazingly stable, and essentially aristocratic, throughout the period. Analysis reveals continuity of family names to be a striking feature of this fundamental governing body. Castilian monarchs appointed regidores to lifetime posts. After a councilor's death or resignation, in theory the position reverted back to Crown control. By the sixteenth century, however, regidores in Avila, as in many other towns, passed their offices from father to son, holding them, in effect, as hereditary possessions.

Typically, a councilor would nominate his son for office, receiving essentially automatic approval from the Crown.[23] If he had no sons, he might turn to other kin members. When the regidor Don Alvaro Serrano died young, his brother Don

22. For conflicts between corregidores and "entrenched urban oligarchs," see Marvin Lunenfeld, "Governing the Cities of Isabella the Catholic: The *Corregidores*, Governors, and Assistants of Castile (1476–1504)," *Journal of Urban History* 9 (1982): 31–55. In March 1500, Avila's regidores complained to the Crown that corregidor Alonso Martínez de Avila refused to visit outlying areas of the district. Idem, *Keepers of the City: The Corregidores of Isabella I of Castile (1474–1504)* (Cambridge: Cambridge University Press, 1987) p. 157. In April 1523, when corregidor Don Francisco Hurtado de Mendoza fell ill, the councilors petitioned Charles V to appoint as his replacement acting deputy Don Francisco de Mendoza rather than the royal candidate, deputy Sancho de Guevara. They reported that Guevara was in Almería and they claimed that it was Mendoza who actually kept the city in "mucha paz y sosiego." AGS Cámara de Castilla (hereafter Cám. Castilla) leg. 159–22.

23. Ariz. pt. 4, 36v.

Juan succeeded "in his place and rule."[24] Both Don Sancho Cimbrón and his brother-in-law Don Antonio de Barrientos held office in the years 1589–1600. Men often entered the council at a very young age and remained their entire adult lives. The councilor Don Francisco Dávila de Ulloa, who gave his age as 48 in the 1620 beatification proceedings for the holy woman Mari Díaz, had entered the city council in 1594, when he was 22 years old. Juan de Henao retained his position for some twenty-nine years, licentiate Martín Pacheco de Espinosa, twenty-seven, and Antonio de Muñohierro, thirty-one. The recordholder was undoubtedly Pedro del Peso, a regidor from 1519 until 1562, at which time the documents refer to him as "el Viejo," the "old man."[25]

Pedro del Peso's family offers a good example of a multigenerational conciliar family, one of many within Avila's oligarchy. The first notice of a Peso in the city council is in a royal privilege of John II in 1431, confirming Blasco Núñez Vela as lifetime regidor at the retirement of his father, Juan Blázquez Núñez. Among the councilors mentioned in this document was a Diego Gómez del Peso.[26] After a seventy-year gap in the city council records, Peso family members appear in a nearly unbroken series. Pedro del Paso, who allied himself through marriage to the Sánchez de Cepeda family of wealthy converso merchants, held office from 1504 to 1523. A Cristóbal del Peso, probably a relative of his, served during some of the same years, from 1516 to 1523. By 1519, the Pedro del Peso who became known as el Viejo was sitting with his aging father in council. At the "old man's" death in 1562, his son Antonio del Peso took over, serving until at least 1573 as both regidor and *procurador* (representative) of Avila to the cortes, a position that offered even more opportunities for wealth and influence. His son Don Pedro

24. Ibid. 17r.
25. This information comes from an analysis of AHPA Actas Consist. and genealogical material provided in Ariz and other sources.
26. Ariz pt. 4, 36v.

del Peso de Vera was active politically from 1589 to 1598, inheriting the offices of councilor and representative to the cortes from his father—and his first name from his grandfather, a common contemporary naming practice. His grandson Don Pedro del Peso y Vera served as councilor from 1598 to 1600. Francisco del Peso y Quiñones, perhaps a descendant of Cristóbal del Peso's, served as councilor from 1589 to 1609.[27] Thus, for at least five generations, a Peso helped to direct Avila's political fortunes. Similar narrations of the fortunes of the Cimbrón, Núñez Vela, Henao, and Guillamás families, and various branches of the Aguila and Dávila families, would also reveal this pattern of political power and dynastic continuity in early modern Avila.

The Cathedral Chapter

By the late fifteenth century, certain elite families also administered the important and lucrative bishopric of Avila. In theory, the major responsibility for this lay with bishops, men nominated by kings and appointed by popes. As with the corregidor and the city council, however, the real situation was often quite different. First, bishops were frequently absent from their sees: they were preoccupied with business at court (most bishops of Avila used the designation "of the Royal Council" after their name), were in Rome, were attending church councils, or were away on diplomatic missions. When residing in the diocese, many preferred to handle affairs from the episcopal estate at Bonilla de la Sierra, in an idyllic mountain setting removed from the center of activity.[28]

27. AHPA Actas Consist. See case of the licentiate Pacheco, regidor and *procurador* to the cortes, whose service to Charles V gained him financial advantages and posts as chaplain and member of the Royal Guard for his two sons. *Corpus documental de Carlos V*, ed. Manuel Fernández Alvarez, vol. 4 (Salamanca: CSIC, 1973) p. 383.

28. Angel Barrios García, *La catedral de Avila en la edad media: Estructura socio-jurídica y económica* (Avila: Caja Central de Ahorros y Prés-

The bishops who did attempt to assume a more active role in the bishopric sometimes found themselves embroiled in conflicts with members of the influential cathedral chapter. From 1463 to 1466, Bishop Alonso de Vilches (bishop 1456–69) grappled with the chapter over economic matters and sticky questions of procedure regarding the discipline of beneficed clergy. These disputes were settled only by papal intervention. Vilches's successor, Alonso de Fonseca (bishop 1469–85), did not hesitate to appoint his own relatives to diocesan positions. As a result, he encountered strong opposition from chapter members who were determined to control patronage themselves. These tensions were undoubtedly exacerbated by the fact that, like corregidores, bishops were "outsiders," men who almost always came from other parts of Spain.[29]

With the bishops so frequently absent, removed by early death or transfer, or deadlocked in debilitating power struggles, the members of the cathedral chapter emerged as the actual administrators of the diocese. It was they who oversaw the exercise of the cult in the cathedral and the parish churches of the diocese, supervised the diocese's numerous clergy, and managed vast landholdings in the city of Avila and its surrounding territory.

---

tamos, 1973) p. 35. Episcopal absenteeism was widespread in Catholic Europe in the first half of the sixteenth century. Representatives to the Council of Trent later took steps to discourage it. *The Canons and Decrees of the Council of Trent*, trans. H. J. Schroeder (Rockford, Ill.: Tan Books, 1978) pp. 55–56.

29. AHN Clero leg. 367. Juan Ramón López Arévalo, *Un cabildo catedral de la Vieja Castilla: Avila, su estructura jurídica s. XIII–XX* (Madrid: CSIC, 1966) pp. 150–155. Vergara p. 140. There were a few exceptions to this pattern. For example, the popular bishop Alonso Tostado de Madrigal (bishop 1454–55), a saintly and scholarly man, was also a "local" from nearby Madrigal de las Altas Torres. Alonso Carrillo de Albornoz (bishop 1496–1514) was a vigorous reformer of monastic houses, and the Franciscan Francisco Ruiz (1514–28) founded several religious and charitable institutions and oversaw the distribution of important relics. Tomás Sobrino Chomón, "Avila," in *Diccionario de la Historia Eclesiástica de España*, ed. Quintín Aldea Vaquero et al., vol. 1 (Madrid: CSIC, 1972) pp. 160–161.

Thus, the dean became the leader of the cathedral clergy, the "chief of the chapter" who celebrated high mass, maintained ecclesiastical discipline, and guarded the official seal of the chapter. In the sixteenth century, parish visitations and arrangements with the city council were almost always handled by the dean, or by officials appointed by him, as were negotiations with donors over the terms of endowments to and burials within the cathedral.[30] All this distinguished the dean of the chapter as one of the city's wealthiest and most powerful men. He was often a member of a prominent family.

The cathedral chapter was a formidable institution that included some 140 clerics and lay employees in a hierarchy ranging from aristocratic canons to bellringers, wax suppliers, and the *perrero*, whose function it was to eject stray dogs from the cathedral.[31] The chapter proper consisted of various ranks of clergymen, of which the most important were the dignitaries (*dignidades*), canons, and prebendaries, appointed through papal authority but maintaining the same principles of family solidarity and continuity evident in the succession of city councilors over generations. The dignitaries—the dean of the chapter, the cantor, the treasurer, the master of theology, and the four archdeacons—possessed the most prestigious and highly paid positions in the cathedral hierarchy. The archdeacons of Avila, Arévalo, Olmedo, and Oropesa supervised each of these geographical districts within

30. Ibid. pp. 81–84, where he calls the dean "el jefe del cabildo." The racionero Juan Sánchez de los Moros made an inspection and inventory of the church of San Millán in December 1545. ASA leg. 7, num. 32. Dean Cristóbal de Medina and three canons argued on the side of the chapter for possession of the San Segundo relics at their discovery in 1519. Antonio de Cianca, *Historia de la vida, invención, milagros, y translación de San Segundo* . . . bk. 2 (Madrid: Luis Sánchez, 1595) 101v–106r. Dean Diego de Bracamonte and the chapter handled almost all the long (1602–48) and laborious negotiations with the Marquis of la Velada over construction of a family chapel within the cathedral. Only once was a bishop, Otaduy, present at the negotiations. AHN Cód. 477-b.
31. López Arévalo pp. 75–81.

the diocese of Avila, presenting candidates for ordination, nominating parish clergy, hearing certain cases of ecclesiastical abuse, and inspecting the parishes in their areas.[32] The other dignidades centered their activities on the cathedral itself. They saw to the correct exercise of the divine office in the choir, to the continuous progression of masses, responses, lessons, and processions, and to the provision of books, vestments, wax, sacred vessels, and all the other things necessary to maintain the cult and clergy of a large and complex religious organization.

These positions, as well as canonries and prebends, offered opportunities for wealth and high position in Avila's society. Prestige, pomp, and income derived from fees for participating in individual religious services such as attending an anniversary mass, and from the benefits of property endowments to the chapter, attracted the sons of the city's elites, especially younger sons who under a system of primogeniture could not inherit the family patrimony.[33] Sometimes cathedral clergy succeeded in working their way up the ladder within the chapter, an institution that, like the city council, valued seniority. Cristóbal de Medina, for example, became dean around 1551, after having served several years as archdeacon of Arévalo. Gonzalo del Barco Guiral, a canon in 1607, was archdeacon of Avila by 1619.[34] In the sixteenth century, Avila's canons and prebendaries usually numbered around twenty. The rest of the chapter consisted of lower clergy such as chaplains and sacristans, and an impressive array of lay servants, musicians, and purveyors.[35]

32. Ibid. pp. 85–90. There had also been short-lived archdeaconries of Bonilla (1475–ca. 1489) and Madrigal (ca. 1523–1534). The archdeaconry of Oropesa was founded in 1481 by Bishop Alonso de Fonseca, who promptly appointed his cousin Juan de Fonseca to the position. For salaries see ibid. pp. 215–225.

33. Barrios García pp. 42–43.

34. Cathedral documents usually listed personnel by seniority: first dignitaries, then canons, then prebendaries.

35. López Arévalo pp. 115–145.

An examination of the composition of Avila's cathedral chapter (that is, of the dignitaries, canons, and prebendaries) in the sixteenth century reveals a continuity of certain family names over many generations, in some cases the same names that appear in city council records. In the case of (presumably) celibate clerics, this was not a matter of sons inheriting the offices of fathers, but rather of brothers providing for brothers, cousins for cousins, and (most often) uncles for nephews, in the classic nepotism of the Catholic church. In Avila, through careful planning and patronage, certain families came to dominate the cathedral chapter, the bishopric's largest and most wealthy religious institution.

The Cabero offer a good example of a capitular family. In October of 1513, the racionero Don Antonio Cabero inspected houses belonging to the cathedral chapter, in one of which lived another prebendary, Luis Cabero, probably his cousin. Antonio, who died in 1557, used a substantial fortune gained through the ownership of land and houses in the city to found a generous endowment (*obra pía*) to provide orphaned girls with dowries and other charitable causes. Present as witnesses to this transaction were Luis Cabero "viejo y mozo" ("the elder and the younger"), Antonio's old cousin and a nephew who held a prebend until at least 1572. Also present was a student named Antonio Cabero, probably a younger nephew, who may have possessed a benefice while he pursued a university education.[36] This Antonio served as prebendary from 1575 to 1611, and also as the administrator (*patrón perpétuo*) of an endowment founded by the canon Escudero in 1590. By December 1612 his brother Felipe had replaced him as both prebendary and *patrón* of the Escudero endowment, posts Felipe Cabero retained until 1620.[37]

36. AHN Cód. 465-b, 466-b. Cathedral clergy were granted permission to absent themselves from the chapter for the purpose of study. *Libro de las constituciones synodales del obispado de Avila* . . . (Salamanca: Andreas Portonaris, 1557), which also lists the statutes of the 1481 synod.

37. AHN Cód. 474-b. For capitular families in the cathedral chapter of Seville, see Ruth Pike, *Aristocrats and Traders: Sevillian Society in the Sixteenth Century* (Ithaca: Cornell University Press, 1972) pp. 55–57.

Members of the Cabero family, frequently named Antonio or Luis, held prebends in Avila's cathedral for four generations, maintaining their position in the religious and economic structures of the city for more than one hundred years. Cabero family members may not have sat on the city council, but the family did establish ties of friendship and patronage with the city's political elites. For example, when in October 1572 the prebendary Luis Cabero purchased a mill on the Adaja, the regidor and future representative to the cortes, Luis Núñez Vela signed as a guarantor of the transaction. These two men had entered the exclusive Confraternity of San Antón on the same day in 1559.[38]

Don Pedro López de Calatayud belonged to a family that had long associations with the cathedral chapter as well as connections on the city council. A Juan López de Calatayud held a prebend in 1503.[39] In 1509, Don Pedro, now dean of the chapter, founded the Hospital of Santa Escolástica in the Old Jewish Quarter. He appointed his nephew, also named Pedro de Calatayud, as patrón.[40] When prebendary Juan López de Calatayud (named for his great-uncle?) made his will in December 1550, he designated his niece Jerónima de Calatayud and her husband, Francisco de Quiñones, administrators of the Hospital of Santa Escolástica, now in the third generation of Calatayud control. Francisco de Quiñones served at this time as regidor, and later he served as a representative to the cortes; he was related through marriage to the conciliar Peso family partially traced above.[41] The mother of Jerónima de Calatayud and sister of the prebendary Juan López de Calatayud was Isabel de San Juan, undoubtedly related to the canon and treasurer Don Cristóbal de San Juan. In his will of

---

38. AHN Cód. 472-b. Accounts of the Confraternity of San Antón in the archive of the parish church of San Juan.

39. Ibid.

40. "Constituciones del Hospital de Santa Escolástica, 1509," AHN Cód. 47-b. RAH MS 9.3594 261r–263v. AHN Cód. 74-b. He provided his niece Doña Francisca de Calatayud with a dowry to enter la Encarnación on February 5, 1511. AHN Clero leg. 278.

41. AHN Clero leg. 342. AHPA Actas Consist.

December 1559 Cristóbal named as principal heir his brother Don Hernando de San Juan, who after his death held the position of canon and treasurer. Between 1577 and 1597 a Francisco Suárez de San Juan (their nephew?) held a canonry in the cathedral of Avila.[42]

The fascinating if complex bonds of inheritance, patronage, and intermarriage by which aristocratic families solidified their positions in Avila's most important political and religious institutions are also evident in the Mújica family. In May of 1615, Don Francisco de Mújica, an inquisitor of the Holy Office in Toledo, dictated his last will and testament. As canon and archdeacon, he had served the cathedral chapter of his native Avila for many years, as had his uncle Don Diego de Bracamonte, dean from 1577 to 1607. Don Francisco divided his considerable estate among his three siblings. The principal heir, his brother, Don Nuño de Mújica, sat on Avila's city council from 1608 until at least 1621, and boasted the prestigious title of knight of the Order of Santiago. His sister Doña Mariana de Mújica had married a nobleman of the city of Zamora, a knight of Alcántara. The final share of his inheritance went to the Franciscan convent of las Gordillas in Avila, where his sister Doña Francisca de Bracamonte resided as a professed nun.[43]

The Mújica-Bracamonte parents of these children had planned well. Themselves products of a marriage between two of Avila's most powerful families, they bestowed the patrimony upon their oldest son, who attained the corresponding political post of regidor. Probably with the help of their Bracamonte relative, the dean of the cathedral, the parents secured for their second son a lucrative position in the chapter, launching him into a successful career in the ec-

42. AHN Clero leg. 348, 448-2; Cód. 477-b, 474-b. Another nephew, the canon Gonzalo de San Juan, held a chaplaincy in the parish church of San Juan between 1564 and 1566. AHN Clero leg. 388.

43. AHN Clero libro 803. "Información de la Vida, muerte, y milagros de la venerable María Díaz," ADA Cód. 3.345 pp. 130–133. For Mújica and Bracamonte nuns in las Gordillas, AHN Clero leg. 452.

clesiastical hierarchy. Clearly the church and the city council both offered avenues to power and prestige, and Avila's elites took full advantage of these effective methods of perpetuating their families' fortunes over succeeding generations.

Monastic Foundation, Lineage, and Liturgy

The desire of certain elite families in Avila to enhance their power and influence was reflected in their foundation and patronage of religious institutions, especially monastic houses. By this time, lay endowment of religious houses was a long-established tradition in Western Christianity. The style of spirituality expressed within these institutions frequently took on the aristocratic character of the patrons who sponsored them. This was certainly the case in Avila of the Knights, a circumstance that would have profound implications for Saint Teresa's personal and spiritual development, and would lead in part to her eventual rejection of the traditional dynastic form of religion in her own foundations.

Throughout the Middle Ages, lay patrons endowed monastic institutions and the religious showed their gratitude to benefactors by offering intercessory prayers on their behalf. Typically, a patron would make a donation to a monastery or church in exchange for burial at a certain altar or chapel, prayers for his soul in perpetuity, and other conditions he might specify. This arrangement existed in some form all over Europe and holds an important place in the history of both ecclesiastical organization and liturgy.[44] However, in

44. Of the abundant literature on this topic, see, for example, Barbara Rosenwein and Lester Little, "Social Meaning in the Monastic and Mendicant Spiritualities," *Past and Present* 63 (1974) especially pp. 7–8; Alan Kreider, *English Chantries: The Road to Dissolution* (Cambridge: Harvard University Press, 1979); Samuel K. Cohn, *Death and Property in Siena, 1205–1800: Strategies for the Afterlife* (Baltimore: The Johns Hopkins University Press, 1988) esp. pp. 102–113.

the late fifteenth century in Avila, as in many parts of Europe, elites became very active in founding new monastic houses and churches and reconstructing or reforming already existing ones. Before 1450 the city housed only four monasteries and one female Cistercian community divided among three small convents. Between 1450 and 1510 five new religious houses were established (four of them female), three of the older houses were rebuilt or reorganized, and many of Avila's shrines, hospitals, hospices, and chapels were founded. What caused this sudden burst of foundational activity?

A large part of the explanation lies in the movement for reform and renewal of the Church which characterized much of Western Christendom in the later Middle Ages. In the late fourteenth century and in the fifteenth century, concerned Catholics considered ways of countering the spiritual decay and institutional corruption they perceived in the Roman church. They advocated not only the correction of many clerical "abuses," a regrettable but longstanding feature of medieval Catholicism, but also the establishment of a purer form of Christian spirituality. In northern Europe this took the form of the interiorized *devotio moderna*, while in Spain and Italy greater emphasis was laid on reform of the clery and reform of monastic orders.[45]

Frustrated by the ineffectiveness of popes in resolving the serious problems of the Church, some secular leaders attempted to take religious reform into their own hands. Of these, none were more active than the "Catholic Monarchs," Ferdinand of Aragon and Isabella of Castile, who were not unaware of the political advantages of a program of ecclesiastical reform initiated and directed by the state. The upsurge in religious foundation and restoration in Avila mostly

---

45. On the "pre-reformation" of the fifteenth century, see, for example, H. O. Evennett, *The Spirit of the Counter-Reformation* (Notre Dame, Ind.: University of Notre Dame Press, 1975) pp. 23–42; Francis Oakley, "Religious and Ecclesiastical Life on the Eve of the Reformation," in *Reformation Europe: A Guide to Research*, ed. Steven Ozment (St. Louis: Center for Reformation Research, 1982) pp. 5–32.

coincided with the period of state-fostered ecclesiastical reform in Spain.[46] Queen Isabella began formulating plans for the reorganization of monastic houses in Castile early in her reign. A report to the pope carried by her ambassadors in 1478 reflected the spiritual climate of her time, but also the practical concerns of the administrator of an expanding state. Isabella sought papal approval for her projects, claiming

> In our kingdoms there are many religious houses, both male and female, very dissolute and disorderly in their way of life and in the administration of their temporal and spiritual goods, which gives birth to many scandals and embarrassments . . . so that Our Lord is very badly served, . . . and if these houses were reformed and made as respectable as they should be [*puestos en la honestidad que deben*], it would be a great service to God Our Lord and very beneficial and edifying for the life and morals of the towns in which they are located.[47]

Reform, for Isabella, contained two key features. The first was a question of behavior or lifestyle. She perceived that many "dissolute and disorderly" monks and nuns lived apart from their communities, had relations with members of the opposite sex, refused to obey their superiors, and generally immersed themselves in the vanity and corruption of the world. To her this was a serious problem because she believed that clerics guilty of such abuses rendered poor service to God and offered a bad example to the rest of society. For the greater glory of God, as well as the formation of well-behaved subjects who respected religion and authority, the queen must see to the decorous and devout comportment of the clergy.[48]

46. Marcel Bataillon, *Erasmo y España* (Mexico: Fondo de Cultura Económica, 1950) pp. 1–10.
47. Quoted in José García Oro, *Cisneros y la reforma del clero español en tiempo de los Reyes Católicos* (Madrid: CSIC, 1971) pp. 40–41.
48. Ibid. pp. 36–38.

Second, inept financial management and neglect had led to the impoverishment and physical decay of many religious houses. In 1493, Pope Alexander VI appointed the influential prelate Alfonso Carrillo de Albornoz inspector of the religious houses of Spain. Four years later, as bishop of Avila, Carrillo de Albornoz visited the three Cistercian convents of Santa Ana, Santa Escolástica, and San Millán in his episcopal seat. The reformer made the following observations concerning Santa Escolástica and San Millán, houses greatly reduced in size and vitality since their foundation in the fourteenth century: "[They] have no dormitory, nor refectory nor choir. . . . The nuns are poor and have little income and cannot sustain themselves in a reasonable manner." In a particularly revealing passage, the bishop noted, "Very few nuns reside there . . . and there does not remain a sufficient number for the choir."[49]

To Bishop Carrillo de Albornoz, as well as to Isabella, reform essentially meant establishing religious houses that were well built and well organized and sufficiently endowed, so that monks and nuns might live comfortably and free from financial worry. This way they could attend full time to their traditional work, the "opus dei," the continual vocal recitation of prayer in choir. Carillo's reform of Avila's Cistercian convents in 1502 consisted of closing San Millán and Santa Escolástica and combining the nuns of the two houses with those of the larger and richer Santa Ana. By pooling the personnel and income of three houses he hoped to create a single convent with sufficient economic resources to attract nuns of good families and provide for their material needs so that they could maintain the exercise of the cult.[50]

Avila's elites eagerly responded to the call for reform, for building and rebuilding and maintaining religious houses.

49. Quoted in the historical introduction by Olegario González Hernández to María Vela y Cueto, *Autobiografía y Libro de las Mercedes*, ed. Olegario González Hernández (Barcelona: Juan Flors, 1961) pp. 50–52.
50. Ibid. p. 52.

This period of spiritual renewal coincided with their own efforts to consolidate their positions within the city's political and ecclesiastical structures and to ensure the perpetuation of their families' power and prestige. The single most active builder of religious institutions in fifteenth-century Avila was the captain Juan Núñez Dávila (d. 1469). This military man sponsored the reconstruction of the old Benedictine and Carmelite monasteries of la Antigua and Nuestra Señora del Carmen, founded the shrine of Nuestra Señora de las Vacas, and repaired the small churches of San Silvestre, Cristo de la Luz, and San Millán, affixing to their walls his heraldic coats of arms.[51]

Núñez Dávila's vigorous "campaign" substantially altered the physical and spiritual architecture of his native city, but it was a group of women, the widows and daughters of knights and landowners, who established most of Avila's new religious houses. The foundational efforts of Catalina Guiera, María Dávila, Elvira González de Medina, Mencía López, and María de Herrera reflect the pervasive concern for family and lineage, and suggest that religious patronage served as a means for women to express economic and spiritual independence.

Houses of *beatas*, or *beaterios*, became extremely popular in the charged spiritual climate of fifteenth-century Castile. "Holy women" lived alone or in groups, engaging in prayer and penitence and performing acts of charity. Many of them made private vows of chastity, wore distinctive habits, and observed a religious rule of some kind, but without formally entering a monastic order.[52] In February of 1463, Doña Cata-

51. Carramolino discusses the "valeroso capitán" several times in 1:504–572. For religious patronage as part of a revived chivalric ideal in late fifteenth-century Castile, see Miguel Angel Ladero Quesada, *España en 1492* (Madrid: Hernando, 1978) pp. 35–36, 39.

52. For a working definition of *beata*, see William A. Christian, Jr., *Local Religion in Sixteenth Century Spain* (Princeton: Princeton University Press, 1981) p. 16, and Jodi Bilinkoff, "The Holy Woman and the Urban Community in Sixteenth Century Avila," in *Women and the Structure of Society:*

lina Guiera dictated her last will and testament. The daughter of the knight Pierre Guiera, who had come from France to fight in the Trastámara Wars, Catalina Guiera married Hernando de Belmonte, but the couple had produced no children. Doña Catalina stipulated that a large share of the legacy of farm, pasture, and woodlands and houses in the city which she inherited from father and husband go toward institutionalizing an arrangement by which she had lived for several years. She specified that "the houses in which [she] live[d], with their corrals and possessions, be endowed as a house for devout and honorable women" ("beatas e personas de buena vida"). In 1478 this rather informal foundation became the Dominican convent of Santa Catalina.[53]

Little is known about Doña Catalina Guiera, but probably after the death of her husband she dedicated herself to a life of prayer in the company of several like-minded women. She never specified how many beatas she lived with, but the number was probably small. The evolution of this foundation suggests that the women lived as tertiaries of the Dominican order, which offered a powerful role model for female spirituality in the person of Saint Catherine of Siena, the house's patron and possibly its founder's namesake.[54] Doña Catalina established herself as the community's first abbess, providing for her "daughters" in her will.

Selected Research from the Fifth Berkshire Conference on the History of Women, ed. Barbara J. Harris and JoAnn K. McNamara (Durham, N.C.: Duke University Press, 1984) pp. 74–80. For similar trends among women in late medieval Europe, see Ernest McDonnell, The Beguines and Beghards in Medieval Culture (New Brunswick, N.J.: Rutgers University Press, 1954); Brenda Bolton, "Mulieres Sanctae," Studies in Church History 10 (1973): 77–95; idem, "Vitae Matrum: A Further Aspect of the Frauenfrage," in Medieval Women, ed. Derek Baker (Oxford: Basil Blackwell, 1978) pp. 253–273.

53. The will of Doña Catalina Guiera, dated February 18, 1463, is in AHN Clero leg. 449.

54. The biography of Catherine of Siena by Raymond of Capua and her letters and prayers were translated and published in Spain, at the instigation of Cardinal Cisneros, in 1511 and 1512. Pedro Saínz Rodríguez, La siembra mística del Cardenal Cisneros y las reformas en la Iglesia (Madrid: FUE, 1979) pp. 104–105.

The pattern that Doña Catalina Guiera established was continued by other women in Avila, widows who endowed religious foundations that began informally in their homes. Doña María Dávila, married to two extremely wealthy and powerful men and twice widowed without children, "gave birth" to several religious institutions in the late fifteenth century. She founded the important Dominican monastery of Santo Tomás in 1482, following the wishes of her first husband, Hernando Núñez Arnalte, royal treasurer to the Catholic Monarchs. She also rebuilt the Marian shrine of Nuestra Señora de Sonsoles, located several leagues outside Avila. In 1494, after the death of her second husband, the viceroy of Sicily, Fernando de Acuña, Doña María went to live in a beaterio of twelve pious women connected to the Franciscan convent of la Consolación, in the town of Calabazanos, near Palencia. In June of 1502, she wrote a detailed will by which was established a new convent of Poor Clares, based on the model of the Calabazanos foundation, on her family's estate in a place called las Gordillas, twenty kilometers from Avila. The nuns moved to the city of Avila in 1552, but to this day the convent is known as las Gordillas rather than by its official name, Santa María de Jesús. Doña María Dávila made this foundation the sole heir of the enormous estate that as an only child she had inherited from her father, as well as the inheritances she had received from two highly paid and aristocratic husbands, providing for up to fifty-five nuns. She became its first abbess, serving in this capacity until her death in 1511.[55]

Somewhat different circumstances surrounded the founder of the Carmelite convent of la Encarnación, Doña Elvira González de Medina. While she never actually married, she may be considered in the company of these noble widows, for

55. Manuel de Castro, *Fundación de "las Gordillas"* (*convento de clarisas de Santa María de Jesús de Avila*) (Avila: Caja Central de Ahorros y Préstamos, 1976). This lovely and useful book consists mainly of a facsimile of Doña María Dávila's will, with facing transcription. There is also a seventeenth-century copy of the will in ADA.

Doña Elvira maintained a relationship for many years with the cathedral canon and archdeacon Don Nuño González del Aguila, a scion of a powerful family of clerics and city councilors and lord of the extensive estate of Villaviciosa. Doña Elvira bore Nuño González del Aguila four children. According to the convent's historian, Nicolás González, clerical concubinage was a common occurrence in late medieval Avila, as it was in Europe as a whole.[56] Before his death in 1467, the canon sought to provide for his companion by selling her all or part of his property, a transaction later disputed by their son Diego del Aguila. Lawsuits, which lasted until 1478, finally restored most of Doña Elvira's wealth. By 1479, no doubt exhausted and disillusioned by legal procedures, family conflicts, and the loss of her "husband," and perhaps, as González suggests, looking for a way to compensate for the "sins" of her past, Doña Elvira established a beaterio in her house, in the company of two devout female companions. The reformed "concubine" was to serve as "madre, patrona y administradora" of a house of fourteen women living by the Carmelite rule. In 1495, the Catholic Monarchs gave the community the site of the Jewish cemetery of Avila for the construction of a new convent, which officially opened in 1515. During the next twenty years la Encarnación experienced enormous expansion, housing over one hundred nuns by 1535, when the future Saint Teresa of Jesus entered it.[57]

The female foundation about which we know the least is the Augustinian convent of Nuestra Señora de Gracia. Its

56. Nicolás González y González, *El monasterio de la Encarnación de Avila* vol. 1 (Avila: Caja Central de Ahorros y Préstamos, 1976) pp. 31–32: "En aquella época los amancebamientos eran notorios en todas las clases sociales." For some other cases in late fifteenth-century Avila, see Lunenfeld, *Keepers*, pp. 118–119. For concubinage among the canons of Seville, see Pike pp. 57ff. For the practice in Europe as a whole, see Steven Ozment, *The Age of Reform, 1250–1550: An Intellectual and Religious History of Late Medieval and Reformation Europe* (New Haven: Yale University Press, 1980) pp. 211–212.
57. González 1:27–65.

founder, Doña Mencía López, married to the wealthy silversmith Jorge de Nájera, may have descended from a distinguished family, as her possession of the title *doña* at an early date suggests. Her husband died in 1504, and by 1507 she, two daughters, and a female friend had agreed to live in her home, observing the rule of Saint Augustine. The cathedral chapter of Avila granted Doña Mencía permission to purchase a shrine dedicated to Saints Justo and Pastor, commonly thought to have been a mosque, and convert it to a convent. Doña Mencía López, like the other founders under discussion, served as the house's first abbess, adopting the name in religion Mencía de San Agustín.[58]

To complete this brief survey of female foundations in Avila's early period of urban growth, we must mention the important chapel of Nuestra Señora de la Anunciación, known as the chapel of Mosén Rubín. The chapel was founded by Doña María de Herrera, heir to landed estates in Velada and Colilla, widow of the regidor Andrés Vázquez, and, judging by the tone of her will of 1512, a woman of forceful character. The huge endowment she specified included funds for a magnificent chapel, a residence for six chaplains, and a hospital to care for up to twenty poor and elderly but respectable citizens of Avila. The poor were to maintain a semi-monastic existence, separated by sex, clothed in a distinctive "habit," and required to attend the many religious services offered by the chaplains. Doña María apparently had no surviving children, and she left all her personal property to the chapel.[59]

The founders of these five houses possessed several common features. They all were widows of means. The three of

58. AHN Clero leg. 230. Efrén Montalva (de la Madre de Dios) and Otger Steggink, *Santa Teresa y su tiempo* vol. 1 (Salamanca: Universidad Pontificia, 1982) pp. 149–154.

59. Manuel de Foronda, "Mosén Rubín—su capilla en Avila y su escritura de fundación," BAH 63 (1913): 332–350. The document belongs to a private collection.

the five who had no children, unlike most women in premodern Europe, maintained complete control of considerable economic resources. Joining a convent, and thereby nullifying the possibility of remarriage, allowed all of them to preserve their status as widows of means.[60] But these particular widows did more than merely enter religious houses. They established themselves as abbesses, as the heads of the houses to whom the other members owed absolute obedience. Like their male relations on the city council and cathedral chapter, they held this office for life. In the world daughters and wives of important men, supervisors of large households and owners of estates, women such as Doña Catalina Guiera and Doña María Dávila in religion retained their impulses to direct and command. In fact, as founders of institutions they had particularly good opportunities to exercise their administrative instincts, detailing in their wills exactly how their foundations were to be established and function, from the box in which official papers were to be kept at las Gordillas, to the ration of wine allowed the poor at Mosén Rubín. These founder/abbesses succeeded in embracing the religious life while reserving for themselves an impressive degree of power. They could be tough-minded and resolute, like the Jimena Blázquez of medieval legend.

The founders of these religious houses showed a keen

60. The literature on widows and widowhood in medieval and early modern Europe is extensive. One example that treats aristocratic widows as patrons of religious institutions or movements is Suzanne F. Wemple, *Women in Frankish Society: Marriage and the Cloister, 500 to 900* (Philadelphia: University of Pennsylvania Press, 1981). "Noble [Merovingian] widows also often transformed their dead husbands' property into a monastic community, gaining not only security for their old age but also the opportunity to provide patronage for their own kin, build a cemetery for relatives, and establish a family cult center" (pp. 61–62). Another example is Nancy L. Roelker, "The Appeal of Calvinism to French Noblewomen in the Sixteenth Century," *Journal of Interdisciplinary History* 2 (1972): 391–418. An observer at the court of Catherine de Medici commented that many French noblewomen deliberately remained widows "in order to keep their grandeur, dignity, possessions, titles and good treatment" (p. 397).

awareness of family and lineage. Perhaps it was precisely women without children who recognized most clearly the need to strengthen ties of kinship and family identity over generations. Doña María Dávila, for example, named as lay patron of her convent the lord of the House of Villafranca and las Navas, "from whose line [she] succeed[ed]." She charged him with enforcing the terms of her will, a task he would surely undertake as an "affair of his lineage" ("cosa de su linage").

She also appointed her personal confessor, Alvaro de Castro, a relative, to the important position of the house's chaplain, maintaining in the religious life an established bond of patronage and clientage.[61] Doña Elvira González de Medina, who no doubt was particularly sensitive to the issues of family and inheritance, reserved the right to appoint the house's patron as well as her successor as abbess. Her son Pedro del Aguila and a grandson served as the first two patrons, and her daughter Catalina del Aguila followed her as abbess, in what González astutely characterizes as the "Aguila empire" of la Encarnación's first seventy years.[62] Perhaps also, by associating her children with this important religious foundation, Doña Elvira hoped somehow to "legitimate" the offspring of her irregular liaison.[63]

The most explicit statement linking lay patronage of religious foundations and lineage comes from the will of the forthright Doña María de Herrera. Doña María named as "Patron, Governor and principal administrator" of her chapel her closest relation, Diego de Bracamonte, the husband of her dead husband's sister, "and after his days, Mosén Rubín de Bracamonte, his legitimate son . . . and after him, his legitimate male descendants, one after the other, that are to suc-

61. Castro pp. 38–39, 76. She also made provisions in case female relations would enter as nuns (p. 74).
62. González 1:45. Eventually the community of Carmelites elected abbesses for three-year terms. The woman who succeeded Doña María Dávila as abbess of las Gordillas came from the family of her second husband. AHN Clero leg. 369.
63. This suggestion came from Natalie Zemon Davis.

ceed to the entailed estate of Fuente el Sol."[64] In this case, the dynastic identification developed to the point that the foundation, located directly across from the Bracamonte palace, became known as the chapel of Mosén Rubín. Thus, families entrenched in Avila's political and clerical hierarchy extended their influence further by gaining control of wealthy religious endowments.

In their wills and charters the affluent founders took care to involve their present and future kin members, establishing the offices of lay patron and abbess as lifetime and hereditary positions, and reserving to the family the right to name the institutions' chaplains, a common way of providing for relatives and retainers. They took great pains to include deceased kin in their foundations by charging the religious order with reciting prayers for their souls. This powerful expression of the pervasive concern for salvation also served to strengthen the links between generations and commemorate family unity even after the demise of family members. It was the cornerstone of the system of religious foundation in early modern Avila.

Doña Catalina Guiera, in her small and informal foundation of beatas, specified only that the women "live well and beg God for the soul[s]" of her and her lord (Hernando de Belmonte). She had previously donated anniversary masses to the monastery of San Francisco and the parish church of San Juan, where her husband and parents lay buried.[65] In the later and more elaborate foundations of las Gordillas and Mosén Rubín, however, aristocratic patrons explicitly established houses that doubled as family chapels. Doña María Dávila set down her wishes in considerable detail. She ordered that the

> convent of Santa María de Jesús and its abbess and nuns be obligated to have said in the church of the said convent . . .

64. Foronda p. 346. Mosén Rubín, today a Dominican convent, still falls under the patronage of the House of Fuente el Sol.
65. AHN Clero leg. 449.

every day in perpetuity for ever and ever four masses, one for the souls of Gil Dávila and Doña Inés de Zabarcos, my lords and parents. . . . And the other for the soul of the treasurer Hernando Núñez Arnalte, my lord. . . . And the other for . . . Hernando de Acuña, my lord. . . . And the other for my soul, with a collect pro defunctis for each one of the souls of those who inherited before me the said goods which I leave to the said convent.[66]

In addition to mandating specific prayers for specific people, Doña María guaranteed the identification of the convent with herself and her family by the use of iconography. Most important to her, as to other European aristocrats, were the popular dynastic coats of arms. Doña María had the shield of the Dávila family plus the shields of her two husbands carved over the convent's main entrance and placed in other conspicuous spots. She also commissioned a magnificent alabaster sepulcher for herself, complete with full-sized tomb sculpture and, again, the three sets of *escudos*. Visitors to the chapel at las Gordillas would have no trouble making the connection between the convent and its founder and the lineage from which she descended.[67]

At Mosén Rubín, too, heraldry and tomb sculpture figured prominently. Doña María de Herrera went so far as to procure papal permission to move the remains of several of her relatives from their original graves to her chapel. She had her grandfather, great-aunt, parents, aunt, and sister reburied there, and commemorated each with an alabaster bust. She reserved the area in front of the main altar for two large sepulchers for herself and her husband, Andrés Vázquez. His coats of arms were to be placed "in all parts of the said hospital and its chapel."[68] Doña María specified elements of the chapel's liturgical program as resolutely as the founder of

66. Castro p. 74.
67. For some of the many references to *escudos*, *armas*, and *blasones*, see ibid. pp. 35 and 78 and photographs.
68. Foronda pp. 339–342.

Sepulcher of Doña María Dávila with dynastic coats of arms, ca. 1527, in convent of Santa María de Jesús (las Gordillas), Avila. Photograph courtesy of Eduardo Ruiz Ayúcar.

las Gordillas, requiring that the resident poor at Mosén Rubín attend the three daily masses celebrated by the foundation's chaplains, and that "each one of them very piously recite the Paternoster with the Ave Maria . . . for the souls of the said Andrés Vázquez [her] lord and [herself] and for the souls of [their] ancestors [nuestros difuntos]."[69]

By endowing religious foundations, elite women fulfilled their own spiritual needs while expressing the concern for the continuity of lineage which was characteristic of their class. Doña María Dávila gave up her life of pomp and elegance in the viceregal court in Sicily to become a beata, albeit

69. Ibid. p. 342.

one with a great deal of administrative and financial influence. Yet, in leaving her estate to a convent, she also kept her wealth intact and provided for family members past, present, and future. These aristocratic founder/abbesses contributed immeasurably to the effort to consolidate and perpetuate dynasties in early modern Avila.

Donors could reap the spiritual and familial rewards of religious endowments without establishing new religious houses by founding *capellanías*, or chaplaincies, in monasteries, convents, parish churches, or the cathedral. After the foundational and reconstruction campaigns of the late fifteenth century, the choice of sites for religious endowments was much wider than before. The sixteenth century was the golden age of capellanías in Avila.

Patrons usually left an annual income to a religious house or church in exchange for burial in a particular chapel. They mandated prayers for their souls and those of their heirs in perpetuity; they often included their parents, even if, as in the case of Doña María de Herrera, this entailed moving remains from one location to another. By 1623, Don Diego de Guzmán, in his foundation at the new Jesuit college of San Ignacio, had gained the right to bury members of his family and to disinter bodies already there.[70]

In Avila, as elsewhere, most religious benefactors belonged to the elite, and their endowments reflected the concerns of their class. Landowners, city councilors, and prominent clerics ordered prayers for their kin and clients, appointed the foundations' chaplains, and placed their families' escudos on the chapel walls. Don Diego de Vera, a dignitary of the Cathedral of Salamanca and son of regidor Pedro del Peso, provided for members of his lineage in his 1598 endowment to the cathedral of Avila. He left money for a dowry for a female relative with the surname Peso, Vera, or Venera, named as patrons his nephew the regidor Don Pedro del Peso y Vera

70. AHN Jesuitas leg. 489–1.

and his heirs to his estate, and stated his preference for chaplains by the name of Henao.[71] The documents concerning the capellanía of the Villalba-Aguila family at the Carmelite monastery of Nuestra Señora del Carmen refer to the sponsors as *señores de la capilla* (lords of the chapel), just as the *comendador* Diego de Villalba was *señor* of his extensive landholdings. His capellanía helped to guarantee that people in future generations would recognize his family's position and wealth as clearly as did his tenants in the present one.[72]

The regular and secular clergy of Avila's religious institutions, especially its monastic houses, practiced a style of spirituality appropriate to the dynamic concerns of their benefactors. The concept of reform then current favored respectable and sufficiently endowed institutions in which the religious, unburdened with material needs, would be free to fulfill their traditional task, the continual vocal recitation of prayer. Anniversary masses and other commemorative and intercessory prayers chanted for the souls of patrons and their kin and clients made up a significant portion of the liturgical program.[73]

The endowment of Bernardo Robles at la Encarnación illustrates the implications of vocal commemorative prayer for family honor and patronage in early modern Avila. This example is particularly well documented but is not unique. In his 1513 will, the licentiate Bernardo Robles left the Carmelite convent the impressive sum of 800,000 maravedís for the construction of its main chapel and for payment of other expenses, rescuing the house from a severe financial crisis. In exchange for this endowment Robles specified in minute detail how and where he was to be buried, and required that one nun continually kneel before the Blessed Sacrament,

71. AHN Clero leg. 344. I have seen dozens of documents referring to sixteenth-century capellanías in Avila, and only a few mention capellanías founded by artisans or *labradores*, usually in parish churches.

72. Ibid. 283, 288.

73. See, for example, the busy calendar of anniversary masses in the cathedral's "Libro de pitanzas, sepelios y aniversarios," AHN Cód. 914-b.

holding a candle in her hand, and pray for his soul. He placed his heirs in charge of the money, ordering them to withhold payments if the nuns should fail to carry out his requirements.[74] Bernardo Robles's extreme concern for his salvation, and his desire that his name be associated with "his" chapel, meant that nuns had to succeed each other in one-hour shifts throughout the day and night. They went through with the burdensome ritual for only a few months before appealing to the pope to commute the obligation on the grounds that it violated the Carmelite rule, which called for nocturnal silence. By 1533 the community had dispensed with the vigils. The heirs of Bernardo Robles found out about this turn of events and immediately threatened to stop the payments. The sisters had no choice but to resume the required vigils. Negotiations between convent and benefactors began in the 1540s and dragged on for some thirty years. The matter finally ended with a victory for the nuns in 1574, during the priorship of Mother Teresa de Ahumada.[75]

Because the prayers specified by patrons of foundations and capellanías were *vocal* prayers, benefactors or their descendants could ascertain during mass whether the religious fulfilled the terms of their endowments. It was extremely important that they determine this, because anniversary masses

74. This kind of check by patrons apparently was not unusual. In his endowment of two chaplaincies in the cathedral in 1559, the canon Cristóbal de San Juan, who was no doubt well aware of the realities of capitular life, instituted a fine of one *real* for each day the chaplains failed to say mass. AHN Clero leg. 345. Doña María de Herrera also included a system of fines in her foundation of Mosén Rubín. Foronda p. 343.

75. González 1:177–195. In another instance the canon Don Diego López Beato set aside four hundred ducats for a charitable endowment at Avila's public jail. After his death his heir, the licentiate Juan Núñez de Ortega, fought to ensure that the money would be used for this express purpose, even bringing the case before the Royal Chancillery in Valladolid. On December 23, 1516, Avila's city council appointed two trustworthy vecinos to oversee this capellanía. One of them was Alonso Sánchez de Cepeda, the father of Teresa of Jesus. Fidel Fita, "D. Alonso Sánchez de Cepeda, padre de Santa Teresa: Nuevos datos biográficos," BAH 65 (1914): 138–150.

and other commemorative prayers helped the soul of the deceased toward salvation and proclaimed the power and continuity of his dynasty as surely as the family escudos carved upon the chapel walls. Eventually a nun who had begged on her knees for the soul of Bernardo Robles would develop a new vision of the religious life based upon voluntary poverty and interior, *mental*, prayer. Saint Teresa's reform represented a daring alternative to the fundamentally aristocratic style of sprituality articulated in Avila during the first decades of the sixteenth century.

3

Public Works, Private Goals,

1520–1540

In the first half of the sixteenth century Avila, like many other European cities, experienced intense growth and development. Opportunities for work and leisure, commerce and mendicancy, attracted immigrants of all social classes. Public and private building and increased economic activity accompanied the demographic surge. Urban growth brought problems, too. The press of humanity alone began to stretch the city's resources to the limit, but the pressures of rapid expansion also strained relations between social groups, underscoring, in particular, the aspirations of an increasingly influential group of non-noble merchants, financiers, and professionals. Teresa de Ahumada y Cepeda grew up in this dynamic if sometimes tense atmosphere of demographic and social change in Avila, in which "new men" began to challenge the exclusive control of the city's hereditary oligarchy. Eventually she would seek the support of these "new men" in her efforts to reform the Carmelite order.

At first Avila's population grew somewhat sporadically. An epidemic known as the pestilence of Valladolid raged for six months in 1518–19, provoking emergency measures on the part of the city council and penitential processions by the Dominican friars of Santo Tomás. An even more severe plague of 1523–24 followed a year of disastrous harvests. Crop failures and epidemics would continue to cause occasional fluctuations in the city's demographic patterns throughout the early sixteenth century.[1] Overall, however, Avila's population expanded steadily. In 1530 the city had about 7,000 inhabitants; by 1550, over 10,000 people lived in Avila. Population growth reached a peak in 1572, when between 12,000 and 13,000 residents were recorded. Put simply, during Teresa's lifetime, the population of Avila doubled.[2]

Adhering to the general European demographic pattern, Avila grew mainly through in-migration. Nobles, lured by the availability of social contacts and luxury goods, increasingly left their county estates to settle in Avila, where the sixteenth century proved to be the great age of urban palace building. These aristocrats in turn attracted men and women of humble station to work as domestic servants, and a steady stream of peasants from the surrounding countryside moved to the city.[3] Hoping to find work in textile production, construction, or domestic service, many instead found them-

1. On March 20, 1519, Bishop Francisco Ruiz reported to Charles V's secretary that he was unable to visit the diocese of Avila as he was stricken with "la indispusición y pestilencia de Valladolid." AGS Cám. Castilla, leg. 148–26. Serafín de Tapia, "Las fuentes demográficas y el potencial humano de Avila en el siglo XVI," Cuadernos Abulenses 2 (1984): 63–65.
2. Tapia pp. 63–70, 86–88. Felipe Ruiz Martín, "La población española al comienzo de los tiempos modernos," Cuadernos de Historia 1 (1967): 189–202.
3. Luis Ariz, Historia de las grandezas de la ciudad de Avila pt. 1 (Alcalá de Henares: L. Martínez Grande, 1607) 53r–54r. Abelardo Merino Alvarez, La sociedad abulense durante el siglo XVI: La nobleza (Madrid: Impr. del Patronato de Huérfanos, 1926) pp. 146–151. AGS Exp. Hac. leg. 50–3. For other cases of migration from countryside to city in sixteenth-century Castile, see Alberto Marcos Martín, Auge y declive de un núcleo mercantil y financiero de Castilla la Vieja: Evolución demográfica de Medina del Campo durante los siglos XVI y XVII (Valladolid: Universidad de Valladolid, 1978) pp. 271–272; Antonio Collantes de Terán Sánchez, Sevilla en la Baja Edad Media: La ciudad y sus hombres (Seville: Sección de Publicaciones del Excmo. Ayuntamiento, 1977) pp. 144–146; Bartolomé Bennassar, "Medina del Campo: Un exemple des structures urbaines de l'Espagne au XVIe siè-

selves reduced to begging. In times of drought or famine the stream became a torrent, as desperate people pursued the grain supplies, charitable institutions, and alms they thought an urban center had to offer. These rural newcomers often settled in Avila's outlying semiagricultural districts such as las Vacas and San Nicolás.[4] By 1557, rural migration was such a well-known and widespread phenomenon that ecclesiastics attending an episcopal synod debated whether a person owed his tithes at the village in which he was born or at the urban parish in which he was presently residing.[5]

As the population grew, Avila embarked upon what one local historian has described as a period of "feverish urban activity."[6] Municipal authorities made particular efforts to repair the city's roads, which were narrow, muddy, and full of potholes. Paving dirt roads with cobblestones proved necessary as heavy, horse-drawn carts entered the city loaded with agricultural products, building materials, firewood, and the raw wool and pelts vital to the expanding production of textiles and leather goods. New bridges also helped to link the city with the surrounding province and foster trade with nearby towns such as Escalona and Talavera de la Reina.[7]

cle," *Revue d'Histoire Economique et Sociale* 4 (1961): 474, where he mentions the "afflux constant de gens de campagnes voisines." Domestic servants constituted between 5.7 and 9.7 percent of the active population of Avila during the sixteenth century. Serafín de Tapia, "Estructura ocupacional de Avila en el siglo XVI," in *El pasado histórico de Castilla y León* vol. 2, *Edad Moderna*, ed. Jesús Crespo Redondo (Burgos: Junta de Castilla y León, 1983) pp. 207, 216, 222–223.

4. Tapia, "Fuentes," pp. 65–68; idem, "Estructura," pp. 208–209.

5. *Libro de las constituciones synodales del obispado de Avila* . . . (Salamanca: Andreas Portonaris, 1557).

6. José Fernández Mayoral, *El municipio de Avila: Estudio histórico* (Avila: Diputación Provincial de Avila, Institución "Alonso de Madrigal," 1958) pp. 80–90. Interestingly, Bennassar uses almost the same phrase, "fièvres de constructions," to describe urban growth in sixteenth-century Medina del Campo (p. 474).

7. AHPA Actas Consist. libro 12, 1562–1563. AGS Cám. Castilla leg. 146–110, 162–50. Tapia, "Estructura," pp. 62–63. Jesús Molinero, "Actas municipales de Avila sobre la fundación del monasterio de San José por Santa Teresa," BAH 66 (1915): 172. For studies of urbanism in early modern

Private building flourished, too. The era of noble palace building coincided with the expansion of artisanal neighborhoods such as San Nicolás. This "construction boom" provided employment for nearly 10 percent of Avila's working population in the early sixteenth century. The city council soon began to control the prices and supply of building materials such as timber and clay.[8] Construction of religious institutions continued apace in this period. Monastic houses figured prominently among the parties requesting wood and other building supplies from the city. Convents such as Santa Catalina and la Encarnación, established as small foundations in the late fifteenth century, greatly expanded in size and moved to larger and more elaborate quarters. The Franciscan convent of las Gordillas moved from Doña María Dávila's country villa to a house in the capital in 1552. In addition, the fifteenth-century effort to repair and embellish churches and the cathedral continued into the sixteenth century. One indication of the amount of activity is the levying of fines by the clerics attending the 1557 synod for the exaction of unfair prices and other abuses they believed were perpetrated by workmen repairing churches.[9]

In this period of growth and expansion, urban problems proliferated. Space became a valuable resource, overcrowding a serious concern. Documents such as the transactions of Avila's city council record the multiplication of conflicts

Europe, see *The Early Modern Town*, ed. Peter Clark (New York: Longman, 1976).

8. AHPA Actas Consist. libro 4, 1519–1523; libro 9, 1536–1540. Manuel de Foronda, "Las ordenanzas de Avila de 1485," BAH 71 (1917): 484–485. For workers in construction trades see Tapia, "Estructura," pp. 207, 222–223.

9. AHPA Actas Consist. libro 9, 1536–1540; libro 11, 1558–1562. The friars of San Francisco made frequent requests for building materials after the monastery burned down in 1522. AGS Cám. Castilla leg. 168–101. Nicolás González y González, *El monasterio de la Encarnación de Avila* vol. 1 (Avila: Caja Central de Ahorros y Préstamos, 1976) pp. 91–112. Manuel de Castro, *Fundación de "las Gordillas"* (convento de clarisas de Santa María de Jesús de Avila) (Avila: Caja Central de Ahorros y Préstamos, 1976) pp. 34–36. *Libro de las constituciones synodales.*

over the recognition of boundaries, the use of common lands, and the definition of public and private property. For example, neighborhood residents and the Premonstratensian canons of Sancti Spiritus clashed over rights of passage through fields next to the monastery. Another conflict resulted when the nuns of Nuestra Señora de Gracia attempted to annex a narrow street or alley alongside their convent. These represent only two of the many cases involving borders between adjacent properties, as abulenses became increasingly sensitive to the limitations of space.[10]

Individuals and institutions continually petitioned the regidores to be granted use of the city's common lands, pastures, wastelands, and forests. Lawsuits over access to common grazing lands in Avila began as early as 1506.[11] By the mid-sixteenth century, overcrowding and housing shortages had become acute. In 1558 the regidores noted that people had taken up residence under the arched colonnade of the Mercado Grande (perhaps in shacks of some sort?). The authorities did not object to these squatters, but they did object to the fact that citizens living in the plaza rented the squatters space in front of their homes. The city councilors pointed out that the plaza belonged "to the city of Avila and [was] common and for the service of [all] its citizens," and that "no one can rent that which is not his." Prohibiting, on pain of fine, the rental of this property, they nevertheless apparently accepted the condition of people living, in effect, on the street. Four years later the councilors banned construction within the Mercado Chico, which they claimed was already so crowded, "gentlemen cannot turn their horses."[12]

10. AHPA Actas Consist. libro 11, 1558–1562; leg. 278, 1567–1568. José María Quadrado, *Salamanca, Avila, y Segovia* (Barcelona: D. Cortezo, 1884) p. 429. See AHN Clero leg. 384 for dispute between cathedral and monastery of Santo Tomás over certain pastures, settled by the corregidor.
11. AHPA Actas Consist. libro 4, 1519–1523; libro 12, 1562–1563; leg. 278, 1567–1568. AGS Pueblos leg. 2, núm. 230.
12. AHPA Actas Consist. libro 11, 1558–1562; libro 12, 1562–1563. The "Ordenanzas" of 1485 ordered the churches of San Juan and la Magdalena to keep the Mercado Chico and Mercado Grande, respectively, free of objects

In dry, rocky Castile, water presented an especially difficult problem, one that still troubles the residents of Avila. Sheer lack of rainfall was compounded by the inability to retain and store water. City councilors frequently confronted the bewildering situation in which residents who lived on the top of the hill petitioned desperately for more water, while those who lived at the bottom complained of flooding. Municipal authorities worked urgently to develop technical solutions to this dilemma, which was intensified by population pressure. Beginning in the 1520s they constructed new fountains, pipes, and wells. In 1536 a special investigator inspected the location and working condition of each of the city's fountains and pointed out the need for repairs. Occasionally the regidores called in outside "experts" in an effort to find new sources of water and ways of storing it in the future. When technical attempts failed (as they usually did), abulenses turned to their spiritual "expert," the beloved Marian image of Nuestra Señora de Sonsoles, which they carried into the city in penitential processions. As Nicolás González notes, Teresa of Jesus, who developed the metaphor of "the Four Waters" to illustrate her method of prayer, grew up in a city that experienced a perpetual shortage of water.[13]

In the cities of sixteenth-century Europe the hardships of dearth, overcrowding, and disease affected all residents, but especially the poor. Urban elites became increasingly aware of the miserable condition and the growing number of poor people and beggars flocking to their cities. Municipal govern-

---

during public use of these spaces, such as bullfights and jousts. BAH 72 (1918) pp. 313–316.

13. AHPA Actas Consist. libro 4, 1519–1523; libro 9, 1536–1540; libro 11, 1558–1562; etc. AGS Cám. Castilla leg. 162–50. For Nuestra Señora de Sonsoles, see Ariz pt. 1, 42r–v. Richard C. Trexler analyzes a Marian image as "the rain image of the city" in "Florentine Religious Experience: The Sacred Image," *Studies in the Renaissance* 19 (1972): 7–41. See González 1:113–123 for a fascinating chapter on the "batalla del agua" fought over certain fountains between the convent of la Encarnación and private individuals, a battle that lasted into the nineteenth century.

ments, churches, and private individuals all attempted to establish permanent institutions of poor relief. Their efforts undoubtedly indicate a sense of Christian charity and civic responsibility as well as the need to reduce tensions in a society in which a large gap existed between rich and poor.[14] Avila presented no exception to this trend. The institution founded in 1509 at the former Cistercian convent of Santa Escolástica by Don Pedro de Calatayud, dean of the cathedral chapter, was the city's first hospital for the poor. Don Pedro donated generous portions of his many benefices in the province of Avila and enlisted the alms of others in order to provide a home for the sick, the wounded, and, especially, abandoned children (niños expósitos). These children were to be brought up as servants so that "they should not beg." Don Pedro also cautioned the hospital's staff, which included a general administrator, doctor, barber-surgeon, apothecary, male and female nurse, and cook, to raise the children "soberly," in case the parents were later found.[15]

14. Tapia points out that during the epidemic of 1524, population in the San Nicolás district, one of Avila's poorest, dropped by 13.4 percent; other neighborhoods, by contrast, suffered very little loss ("Fuentes" p. 65). See also his "Estructura," pp. 214–215. There is a large literature on charity and poor relief in late medieval and early modern Europe. See, for example, Natalie Z. Davis, "Poor Relief, Humanism, and Heresy: The Case of Lyon," in her *Society and Culture in Early Modern France* (Stanford: Stanford University Press, 1975) pp. 17–64; R. M. Kingdon, "Social Welfare in Calvin's Geneva," *American Historical Review* 76 (1971): 50–69; Brian Pullan, *Rich and Poor in Renaissance Venice: The Social Institutions of a Catholic State, to 1620* (Cambridge: Harvard University Press, 1971). Most relevant for this study are Linda Martz, *Poverty and Welfare in Habsburg Spain: The Example of Toledo* (Cambridge: Cambridge University Press, 1983), and Maureen Flynn, "Charitable Ritual in Late Medieval and Early Modern Spain," *Sixteenth Century Journal* 16 (1985): 335–348.

15. "Constituciones del Hospital de Santa Escolástica," AHN Cód. 47-b. In 1558 the cathedral chapter of Avila spent 192,548 *maravedís* on *niños expósitos* left at its door. Juan Ramón López Arévalo, *Un cabildo catedral de la Vieja Castilla: Avila, su estructura jurídica s. XIII–XX* (Madrid: CSIC, 1966) pp. 196–197. On the care of foundlings in Toledo, see Martz pp. 224–236; in Salamanca and Valladolid, Flynn p. 343 n. 22. Doña María Dávila, the founder of las Gordillas, also established a hospice for poor pilgrims visiting

The Hospital of Santa Escolástica did not accept patients with contagious, incurable, or venereal diseases. This gap was partially filled by the Hospital of San Lázaro, founded under Bishop Francisco Ruiz around 1520, which specialized in the treatment of leprosy. The Hospital of la Magdalena, established around 1511, housed the Confraternity of the Souls in Purgatory, whose members visited prisoners in jail and attended burials. Other foundations followed, and by mid-century, Avila possessed at least twelve hospitals for the poor.[16]

These measures may have relieved somewhat the plight of the most destitute among Avila's poor, but crop failures and distribution problems led to food shortages that affected a large portion of the city's less privileged classes. When the royal official Antonio Pérez arrived in Avila in 1502, he discovered that someone had taken more than ten thousand fanegas of grain from the city's stockpiles and brought them to Medina del Campo and Valladolid in preparation for an official visit of the royal princes. This rash act had caused the price of grain to soar. Poor people now lived in such misery that one or two had already died of starvation. Pérez organized emergency relief measures, obtaining alms from the Church and private individuals and forbidding the removal of any more grain. Even then, he lamented, "one third of the people walk[ed] around begging for the love of God."[17]

---

the shrine of Nuestra Señora de Sonsoles around 1480, and left money for the annual distribution of food to the poor at the shrine of Nuestra Señora de las Nieves in her 1503 will. Castro pp. 30–32. Gabriel María Vergara y Martín, *Estudio histórico de Avila y su territorio* (Madrid: Hernández, 1896) p. 142.

16. Ariz bk. 1, 42r–v. Juan Martín Carramolino, *Historia de Avila, su provincia y obispado* vol. 1 (Madrid: Librería Española, 1872) pp. 536, 562–573; vol. 3 (1873) pp. 36, 98–99, 122–123, 290. Vergara pp. 142, 159, 163. AHN Cód. 1091-b, 465-b. Enrique Ballesteros, *Estudio histórico de Avila y su territorio* (Avila: Tip. de M. Sarachaga, 1896) p. 300. Gil González Dávila, *Teatro eclesiástico de las ciudades e iglesias catedrals de España . . .* (Salamanca: A. Ramírez, 1618) p. 295.

17. "Copia de carta o memorial del licenciado Antonio Pérez," April 24, 1502, CODOIN 36:447–454.

City councilors made attempts to regulate the price and available quantities of the city's grain, wine, and meat. In 1513 the municipality purchased houses belonging to a certain Fernando Guillamás "so that there might be a slaughterhouse of meat . . . for the provision" of the city. Officials placed ceilings on the cost of bread in 1522, after widespread famine catapulted the price of wheat from 102 to 170 maravedís per fanega. They kept a sharp watch over firewood and coal, as well, commodities also in high demand and short supply. Hunger and hardship, however, were often close at hand.[18]

In 1528 the price of wheat doubled, to 340 maravedís per fanega. The emergency that ensued finally compelled municipal authorities to put into action plans for a public granary which they had begun discussing in 1521 and which Antonio Pérez had recommended in 1502.[19] The project began in November, when the Dominican preacher Juan de Victoria reported to the assembled regidores on the "great necessity and hunger" suffered by the poor people in Avila. After several years of bad harvest ("algunos años esteriles de pan"), many poor people could not "even buy the bread necessary for their subsistence," he noted.[20]

Before this date authorities had relieved food shortages on an ad hoc basis, collecting alms and distributing bread at

18. AGS Pueblos leg. 2, núm. 250. AHPA Actas Consist. libro 4, 1519–1523; libro 9, 1536–1540; libro 11, 1558–1562; leg. 278, 1567–1568; etc. Examples of other studies of the problem of provisioning cities in early modern Spain are Cristóbal Espejo, "La carestía de la vida en el siglo XVI y medios de abaratarla," *Revista de Bibliotecas, Archivos, y Museos* 41 (1920): 36–54, 169–224, 329–354; 42 (1921): 1–18, 199–225; Manuel Fernández Alvarez, "El Madrid de 1586," in his *Economía, sociedad, y corona (Ensayos históricos sobre el siglo XVI)* (Madrid: Ediciones Cultura Hispánica, 1963) pp. 281–303; Marcos Martín pp. 213–216.

19. AHN Clero leg. 445–2 gives prices at which the cathedral chapter sold wheat and barley between 1520 and 1558.

20. "Papeles pertenecientes al patronato de la Alhóndiga," AHN Cód. 458-b. Jesús Molinero, "La alhóndiga de Avila en 1528 y D. Alonso Sánchez de Cepeda, padre de Santa Teresa," BAH 65 (1914): 258–268, 343–350.

subsidized prices in the city's main plaza and marketplaces. Now the regidores began to follow the European practice of institutionalizing and centralizing food distribution; they concentrated operations in a public granary, or *alhóndiga*, located in the Mercado Grande and administered by a committee of city councilors, cathedral clergy, and other local notables. The committee solicited donations from Avila's more affluent residents, lay and clerical, and received pledges for a certain amount of grain which was to be baked into bread and sold below the market price.[21] The foundation of a public granary resolved the subsistence crisis of 1528, but famine, drought, and disease continued to create serious problems for the burgeoning city throughout the sixteenth century.

"Personas Ricas": Avila's "New Men"

Fray Juan de Victoria directed his plea for help in relieving the plight of Avila's poor in 1528 toward "the gentlemen and rich people of this city" ("los cavalleros e personas ricas de esta dicha cibdad").[22] In so doing, the Dominican recognized an important new social reality: the existence of a group of wealthy but non-noble citizens who played an increasingly crucial role in the city's economic life. Their wealth did not automatically bring them high social status or political power, however, in a society that valued "honor" based upon birth, ethnic purity, and the leisured possession of land. The

21. AHN Cód. 458-b. Bread was to be sold at one *real* (thirty-four maravedís) below market price. Similar institutions were founded in other parts of Europe. For the *aumône générale* of Lyon, founded in 1529, one year after the *alhóndiga* of Avila, see Davis, "Poor Relief." For the grain office of Venice and the *abbondanza* of Florence, Fernand Braudel, *The Mediterranean and the Mediterranean World in the Age of Philip II* vol. 1 (New York: Harper and Row, 1972) p. 329. For the grain *pósito* of Toledo, Martz pp. 137–139, 145–146.

22. Molinero, "Alhóndiga," p. 258.

strong aspirations to the prestige and privileges of the city's traditional elite on the part of these "new men," and the determination by members of the oligarchy to maintain control of Avila's political and religious institutions, created serious social tensions in the early decades of the sixteenth century.

Documents such as the list of people who contributed to the public granary indicate the formation of a tightknit circle of "new men" who were active in Avila's expanding economy, particularly in the lucrative wool trade, in finance and moneylending, in tax farming, and in the liberal professions. Certain family names predominate: Gallego, del Barco, de las Navas, Salcedo. The del Barco family was undoubtedly one of the most influential. The successful cloth merchant Francisco del Barco frequently lent money, his clients including "el Señor Alonso Navarro," a city councilor who borrowed fifteen thousand maravedís at high interest on August 8, 1536. Francisco del Barco contributed to the *alhóndiga*, as did Cristóbal del Barco and Juan de Avila del Barco. Furthermore, when Charles V made an official tour of Avila in June of 1534, he visited the house of the financier Gregorio del Barco.[23]

Blood, marriage, business, and trust bound members of these families to each other and to members of other families. For example, the brothers Silvestre Gallego and Lope Fernández Gallego both traded woolen cloth. Diego Salcedo and his nephew Gregorio served as witnesses to one of Francisco del Barco's lending transactions. Gregorio's brother Isidro exercised the liberal profession of public scribe.[24] Ethnic identity may have forged another link between these mer-

23. AHPA Protocolos (hereafter Prot.) 6.393, August 8, 1536. These records report other transactions concerning the del Barco family, as well. Molinero, "Alhóndiga," pp. 260–266. Manuel de Foronda y Aguilera, *Estancias y viajes del Emperador Carlos V* (Madrid, 1914) p. 389.

24. AHPA Prot. 6.393, June 3, 1526. ARC Sala de Hijosdalgo leg. 115, exp. 6; leg. 96, exp. 15. Isidro and Cristóbal de Salcedo also made large contributions to the *alhóndiga*.

cantile families. Their names and professions strongly suggest Jewish ancestry. Most came from neighborhoods traditionally inhabited by conversos, such as the Mercados Grande and Chico, the Cal de Andrín, the Cal Toledana, and the barrio Santo Domingo, the Old Jewish Quarter.[25] As they consolidated their wealth and cemented their personal and professional associations, Avila's "new men" developed strategies for achieving that which they still lacked: social prestige and political power. No member of the families named above held a seat on the city council during the sixteenth century, a position that would have ensured direct participation in the city's political life. They were forced, therefore, to seek alternative means of achieving influence and status.[26]

One method was to buy, in effect, one's way into the ranks of the lower nobility by using a legal procedure known as the *pleito de hidalguía.* Many conversos in early modern Spain utilized the courts to establish their status as "gentlemen" and to claim certain privileges, notably exemption from taxation.[27] The 1519 suit involving members of the Sánchez de Cepeda family, father and uncles of Teresa of Jesus, is an exceptionally well documented but not unusual case. It demonstrates how a wealthy converso family could use cash payments, the institution of marriage, and legal maneuvers to "prove" its gentility.

In 1519 the four Cepeda brothers, Alonso, Pedro, Ruy, and

25. Molinero, "Alhóndiga," pp. 260–266. Fita pp. 344–350. AHN Cód. 466-b. AGS Cám. Castilla leg. 144–89. AGS Patronato Real leg. 5. Antonio de Cianca, *Historia de la vida, invención, milagros, y translación de S. Segundo . . .* bk. 2 (Madrid: Luis Sánchez, 1595) 101v–106r. AHPA libro 2.902.

26. A Vicente de Salcedo held the relatively modest post of racionero in the early decades of the sixteenth century. Otherwise, these family names are absent from the cathedral chapter records as well.

27. For this practice, see introduction to Teófanes Egido, *El linaje judeo-converso de Santa Teresa (Pleito de hidalguía de los Cepeda)* (Madrid: Editorial de Espiritualidad, 1986) pp. 9–31. Albert A. Sicroff, *Los estatutos de limpieza de sangre: Controversias entre los siglos XV y XVII* (Madrid: Taurus, 1985) pp. 336–343.

Francisco, refused to pay taxes in the village of Hortigosa in the jurisdiction of Avila. In response to the town's demands for revenues the brothers instigated a pleito de hidalguía at the Royal Chancellery of Valladolid in August of that year.[28] All four men, affluent merchants and tax farmers, were, in fact, citizens of Avila; only one of them, Pedro, owned land in Hortigosa, in the hamlet of Majálbalago, where he resided occasionally. Why, then, did they bring suit against Hortigosa and not Avila? The chancellery official (fiscal) in charge of defending the king's interests and investigating claims to noble status, a Dr. Villaroel, asked the same question. He alleged that the four plaintiffs had "made a common front and reached an agreement with the town council of Hortigosa . . . that [the council] arrest them but not pursue legal action."[29] Apparently the wily brothers, rather than directly confront the city council of Avila, provoked litigation and then bought off a few small-town elders. This left prosecution of the case in the hands of the municipal official in charge of the towns and lands under the city's jurisdiction, known as the procurador general de los pueblos y tierras. In 1519 this office was held by the powerful regidor Francisco de Pajares. A hostile witness at the 1519 pleito claimed, perhaps with some exaggeration, that Francisco de Pajares "ruled absolutely in the city of Avila" ("a mandado asolutamente la dicha cibdad de Avila").[30]

Pajares maintained extremely close ties with the Sánchez de Cepeda family and was certainly their most important ally on Avila's city council. He lived in the posh San Juan parish, as did at least two Cepeda brothers, Alonso and Ruy. In 1506 or 1508 Pedro Sánchez de Cepeda married Doña

28. For what follows, see Egido pp. 9–31 and accompanying documents.
29. Ibid. pp. 14–15, 93–95. "E que hagora los dichos partes contrarias . . . hizieron frente e se conzertaron con el concejo e hombres buenos del lugar de Ortigosa . . . que los prendasen e no syguiesen el pleito, ni hiziesen probanza alguna."
30. Ibid. pp. 166–168.

Catalina del Aguila, whose sister Doña Ana del Aguila was Pajares's wife. Thus, these two men were brothers-in-law. At the birth of his daughter Teresa in 1515, Alonso Sánchez de Cepeda asked Pajares's daughter Doña María del Aguila to serve as the child's godmother. Alonso's second wife, Doña Beatriz de Ahumada, named her husband and Pajares as coexecutors of her estate in her 1528 will.[31]

During the 1519 hearings, four residents of Avila slated to testify against the Cepeda family abruptly changed their minds and agreed to testify instead in the brothers' favor. Under questioning they admitted that Pajares had brought them together and given them the means of traveling to Valladolid, "and that Francisco de Pajares gave the money to pay the witnesses and that which was necessary which came to three hundred maravedis for each witness."[32] Many commentators in early modern Spain bemoaned the widespread bribery, fraud, and coercion in these pleitos de hidalguía. Perhaps this level of corruption was not too surprising given the society's crippling obsession with honor.[33]

Finally, a total of twelve witnesses testified that the Cepedas lived in the style of gentlemen. In his statement of November 16, 1519, for example, Cristóbal de Salcedo de-

31. Ibid. pp. 15–17. Homero Serís, "Nueva genealogía de Santa Teresa," *Nueva Revista de Filología Hispánica* 10 (1956): 365–384. Efrén de la Madre de Dios (Montalva) and Otger Steggink, *Santa Teresa y su tiempo* vol. 1 (Salamanca: Universidad Pontificia, 1982) pp. 53, 75, 77, 131.

32. Egido pp. 15–17, 112–116. "Dixo que por mandado de Francisco de Pajares, procurador de la Tierra de Avila; e que vino a traer quatro testigos para presentar en el pleito de las hidalguías de los Cepedas de Avila. E que el dicho Francisco de Pajares le dio los dichos testigos para que les traxiese a esta avdiencia. E que el dicho Francisco de Pajares le dio los dineros para pagar los testigos e para lo que más fuese menester, que fueron trecientos maravedís para cada testigo." Dr. Villaroel would not allow their testimony.

33. See cases cited by Claude Chauchadis, *Honneur, morale, et société dans l'Espagne de Philippe II* (Paris: CNRS, 1984) pp. 134, 156–157. Henry Kamen, *Inquisition and Society in Spain in the Sixteenth and Seventeenth Centuries* (Bloomington: Indiana University Press, 1985) pp. 121–122. "The fraud, perjury, extortion and blackmail that came into existence because of the need to prove limpieza was widely recognized as a moral evil. . . . Genealogy became a social weapon."

clared that he had always regarded the members of the Cepeda family as hidalgos. A business partner who had joined the four brothers in a lucrative tax-farming venture, Salcedo reported that they were married to "distinguished women, daughters of gentlemen" ("mugeres principales, fijas de cavalleros"), retained servants and wet nurses, served the king with horses and arms, and "had not paid any taxes whatsoever."[34] His testimony, along with the influence of Cepeda money and connections, helped the brothers to win their case in August 1522. In 1536 the abulenses Sebastián de Salcedo and his uncle Isidro also gained noble status after hard-fought and much-appealed pleitos.[35]

The lawsuit of the Cepedas reveals another method utilized by Avila's "new men" to gain social status: marrying daughters of the city's elites. We have seen that through marriage the Cepedas established strong alliances with the regidor Francisco de Pajares. They had links to another city councilor, as well, Pedro del Peso, for Alonso de Cepeda married his daughter Doña Catalina del Peso y Henao in 1504 (she died in 1507). A witness against the Cepeda brothers in the pleito de hidalguía claimed that only the timely intervention of Pedro del Peso had saved Alonso from paying taxes in the city of Avila some five years earlier.[36]

Marriage united members of the litigious families, as well. In the mid-sixteenth century Alonso's daughter, the nun Teresa de Ahumada, developed a close friendship with the pious Francisco de Salcedo, who was at that time married to Doña Mencía del Aguila, the daughter of Teresa's uncle Ruy Sánchez de Cepeda. One wonders whether Francisco de Salcedo, assiduously referred to by Teresa as "the holy gentleman" ("el caballero santo"), was, like his father-in-law and others with the name Salcedo, a "gentleman" by legal

34. Egido pp. 82–86. Narciso Alonso Cortés, "Pleitos de los Cepedas," *Boletín de la Real Academia Española* 25 (1946): 85–110.
35. ARC Sala de Hijosdalgo leg. 115, exp. 6; leg. 96, exp. 15.
36. Egido pp. 20–23, 105, 156–157. Serís pp. 371–373.

decree only (*hidalgo de ejecutoria*). Neither Luis Ariz, the seventeenth-century chronicler, nor Abelardo Merino, the twentieth-century historian of Avila's aristocracy, listed the Salcedos among the city's traditional noble families.[37] The emotionally charged dispute over the proper location for the sacred relics of San Segundo is another incident demonstrating the frustrations and the resolve of some of Avila's *personas ricas*.[38] In 1519, the same year the Cepeda family began its legal battle for social status, workmen repairing the small church of San Sebastián on the Adaja River discovered relics widely believed to be those of San Segundo, the city's first bishop. The members of the aristocratic cathedral chapter immediately laid claims to the remains of the saint, the reputed companion of the Apostle James and evangelizer of Avila in the first century A.D. The canon Cristóbal de Medina (later dean) and three other clerics went to the site and formally demanded that the relics be moved to the cathedral.[39]

The brothers of the Confraternity of San Sebastián (its name quickly changed to San Segundo) vigorously opposed this plan and insisted upon keeping the relics in this commercial and artisanal district. The confraternity was represented at this time by its *patrones*, Lope Fernández Gallego and his brother Silvestre, Cristóbal del Barco, Pedro de las Navas, and Cristóbal Alvarez, all of them well-known middle-class citizens belonging to affluent mercantile families who were involved, mainly, in the manufacture and trade of woolen cloth.[40] Lope and Silvestre Gallego and Pedro de las Navas

---

37. For Francisco de Salcedo, see Montalva and Steggink 1:346 and notes.

38. For relics and their potential for causing conflict, see Peter Brown, *The Cult of the Saints: Its Rise and Function in Latin Christianity* (Chicago: University of Chicago Press, 1981); Patrick Geary, *Furta Sacra: Thefts of Relics in the Central Middle Ages* (Princeton: Princeton University Press, 1978); William A. Christian, Jr., *Local Religion in Sixteenth Century Spain* (Princeton: Princeton University Press, 1981) pp. 126–141.

39. Cianca bk. 1, 96r; bk. 2, 102r.

40. Molinero, "Alhóndiga," pp. 258–268. Fita pp. 344–50. AGS Cám. Castilla leg. 144–189. Joseph Pérez, *La Révolution des "Comunidades" de Castille (1520–1521)* (Bordeaux: Institut d'études ibériques et ibero-

had also served as representatives of the city's non-noble taxpayers (*la comunidad e homes buenos pecheros*).[41] The patrones were prepared to begin legal proceedings against the cathedral chapter if necessary.

Avila's city councilors, anxious to avoid a confrontation and costly court expenses, hastened to negotiate between chapter and confraternity. Perhaps they were also reluctant to antagonize these "new men" who were their present or potential business partners and creditors. The parties finally agreed upon a compromise: the saint's body would remain in the neighborhood church, while the ring and chalice found with it would receive a special place in the cathedral.[42] Thus, in 1519 the merchants and manufacturers representing the San Segundo confraternity used their influence to win, temporarily, the battle with members of Avila's oligarchy for the city's most sacred religious treasure. The little church on the Adaja now became an important shrine, attracting attention, pilgrims, and donations. The brothers resolved to guard their prize carefully, and managed to resist several other attempts by the cathedral chapter to effect the transfer of the relics over the next several decades.[43]

In the early sixteenth century, then, Avila's "new men" began to gain indirect political influence through their manipulation of economic resources, the legal system, and personal contacts. The lack of direct political power, however, still rankled. As early as 1502, Antonio Pérez, in his report to

américaines de l'Université de Bordeaux, 1970) pp. 488–493. Manuel Danvila y Collado, *Historia crítica y documentada de las Comunidades de Castilla*, in *Memorial histórico español* vol. 35 (Madrid: Est. tip. de la viuda e hijos de M. Tello, 1897) pp. 454–456. AHN Cód. 466-b.

41. Egido pp. 122–132, 155, 168. Perhaps Lope Fernández Gallego also used his money and influence to establish noble status through legal means. In his testimony at the Cepeda trial he identified himself as a hidalgo (p. 155), but in another place in the record he is listed as a representative of the tax-paying comunidad (p. 128). Nowhere is he accorded the honorific title *Don*.

42. Cianca bk. 2, 102r–106r. Ariz bk. 1, 51v–53v.

43. Cianca bk. 3, 101r, 119v, 125v–129r. AHN Clero leg. 345.

the Crown, had noted the resentments that arose from the unequal distribution of power in the city. He observed that in most Spanish towns the representatives chosen by the body of taxpaying citizens attended meetings of the city council. In Avila, he alleged, "There is only one [representative] and he is hand-picked by the regidores." As the non-noble citizens do not feel truly represented, he stated, they "harbor many suspicions" and "complain of the injustices which they say are done to them in the assessment of taxes and other things done by the city." The royal agent recommended that abulenses assemble each year and elect two representatives, one for the hidalgos and one for the taxpayers (*pecheros*), a policy that he believed would avoid "muchas discordias."[44]

Within a generation Pérez's worst fears of "discord" were realized. In 1520, one year after the Cepeda family began their pleito and confraternity members began fighting to retain the relics of San Segundo, many of Avila's "new men" became involved in an uprising that directly and dramatically raised the issue of broader political participation for tax-paying citizens. The city took part in the Revolt of the Comuneros, a nationwide rebellion against the fiscal and administrative policies of the young king Charles V. This complex affair pitted virtually all the cities of Castile against the monarchy, or at least the "bad government" of Charles and his Flemish advisors. In this the rebels from Avila cooperated closely with their counterparts in nearby towns such as Segovia, Medina del Campo, and Toledo.[45] Although Avila never ex-

44. CODOIN 36:448–449. "En todas las cibdades de vuestros reinos hay seismeros, é procuradores é personas puestos por la comunidad que asisten en los consistorios; en esta cibdad solamente hay un procurador nombrado por mano de los regidores, como la comunidad no tenga por su parte puesta persona alguna tienen consigo muchas sospechas, é hánse quejado á V.A. de algunos agravios que dicen que se les han fecho en los repartimientos y en otras cosas que se hacen por cibdad. . . . Quitarán á esta cibdad de muchas discordias é andarán las cosas del regimiento con algund mas concierto que hasta aquí."

45. There is a large literature on the comunero revolt. See, for example, Pérez, *La Révolution*; José Antonio Maravall, *Las Comunidades de Cas-*

perienced the level of violence reached in these other cities, it still witnessed two years of upheaval and the resentments of non-nobles which emerged as soon as the normal structures of municipal life had broken down. Charles V touched off the revolt when he convoked the cortes in the spring of 1520. The purpose of this meeting was clear: the collection of tax subsidies from Castilian towns in order to meet his enormous expenses as Holy Roman Emperor. Avila, still suffering from the effects of the plague, also felt keenly the pinch of an economic recession in the wool trade. The price of bread had risen sharply, and mob violence had already broken out in neighboring Segovia.[46] In this tense situation, Avila's city councilors chose representatives from among their number, but charged them with wresting certain concessions from the king before approving the poorly afforded *servicio*. When the sparsely attended and Crown-manipulated cortes convened at la Coruña at the end of May accepted the tax without gaining any of these demands, a large number of Castilian city dwellers rose in rebellion.[47]

The initial impetus for revolt in Avila came from within the ranks of the city council itself. The regidores, cautious at first, swore loyalty to the monarchy at the beginning of June. But within a few weeks they found themselves divided. At a stormy session of the council held on June 19, 1520, Diego

---

tilla: Una primera revolución moderna (Madrid: Revista de Occidente, 1963); Juan Ignacio Gutiérrez Nieto, Las Comunidades como movimiento antiseñorial: La formación del bando realista en la guerra civil castellana de 1520–1521 (Barcelona: Planeta, 1973); Henry Latimer Seaver, The Great Revolt in Castile: A Study of the Comunero Movement of 1520–1521 (New York: Octagon Books, 1966); Stephen Haliczer, The Comuneros of Castile: The Forging of a Revolution, 1475–1521 (Madison: University of Wisconsin Press, 1981).

46. J. H. Elliott, Imperial Spain (New York: New American Library, 1966) pp. 147–148. Emilio González López, "Los factores económicos en el alzamiento de las Comunidades de Castilla: La industria textil lanera castellana," Revista Hispánica Moderna 31 (1965): 185–191.

47. AHPA Actas Consist. libro 4, 1519–1523. Elliott p. 148.

Alvarez de Bracamonte accused his colleagues present at the cortes of la Coruña of having misrepresented the city's views and having betrayed their charge by voting for the *servicio.* He angrily demanded an investigation of their conduct. He was joined in this swing toward the *comunero* position by the influential Francisco de Pajares, Cristóbal del Peso, and Gil Suárez, and later by Sancho Sánchez Cimbrón, Fernán Gómez Dávila and Suero del Aguila. They elected to repudiate the city's vote in the cortes, refuse to pay the subsidy, and begin negotiations with Toledo for a meeting of Castilian cities. The other regidores either remained loyal to the royal government during the revolt or swore allegiance to the comunidad, but they prudently kept their distance from the mainstream of events.[48]

Several leaders of the city's ecclesiastical hierarchy became involved in the widening revolt, as well. The dean of Avila's cathedral chapter, Alonso de Pliego, and several canons joined the comunero movement, offering the recently constructed chapel of San Bernabé as a meeting place for the junta of Castilian cities. Pliego was a native of Segovia, one of the cities most fervently committed to the comunero cause. He maintained close personal relations with Suero del Aguila, with whom he had established a chaplaincy the previous year. The radical dean was probably at least partly responsible for bringing Aguila over to the rebel side.[49]

In addition, a significant group of merchants, manufacturers, notaries, and physicians joined the comunero revolt in Avila. Three of the five patrones of the San Segundo confraternity, Lope Fernández Gallego, Pedro de las Navas, and Cristóbal Alvarez, participated in the rebellion. These "new men" formed a fragile alliance with dissident city councilors and cathedral clergy during the early stages of the revolt.[50]

48. Danvila 35:392–395. Pérez pp. 436–437. Seaver p. 103.
49. Danvila 35:408–410. Carramolino 3:135–136. AHN Clero leg. 345. Seaver p. 103.
50. Danvila 35:454–456, 36:147ff. Juan Ignacio Gutiérrez Nieto, "Los conversos y el movimiento comunero," *Hispania* 94 (1964): 237–261.

However, the meeting of the "Santa Junta" of Castilian cities in Avila's cathedral on July 29, 1520, revealed a different, and to many elites, disturbing aspect of the rebellion: participation of "the common people" (*la gente común*). Most of these rebels worked as artisans, especially in textile trades, and were the people most severely affected by the economic recession and the rise in taxes. Many contemporaries commented upon the prominent position in the junta given a man named Pinillos. In a complete inversion of the normal order, Pinillos, a cloth shearer from the humble San Esteban district, presided over the council and would let no one speak, "neither gentleman, nor representative, nor ecclesiastic," until he had signalled them with his staff. "In this way," sneered Charles V's chronicler Fray Prudencio de Sandoval, "those who presumed to remedy the problems of the kingdom were commanded by a lowly shearer." Or rather, a "lowly shearer" seized the opportunity to make his voice heard.[51]

At this point a movement that had begun primarily as a revolt of urban elites against royal authority turned more popular, more democratic, and more violent in nature. Even Avila, which, in the words of the nineteenth-century historian Antonio Ferrer del Rio, rose up only "moderately," saw incidents of violence and social protest.[52] Here, as in cities such as Valladolid and Soria, the rebellious comunidad of non-noble taxpayers vented its wrath particularly against the city council, a symbol of fiscal privilege and restricted municipal power.[53] In July crowds sacked and destroyed the

---

51. Fray Prudencio de Sandoval, *Historia de la vida y hechos del Emperador Carlos V...* (Madrid: Ediciones Atlas, 1955) p. 251: "De manera que los que presumían de remediar el reino eran mandados de un tundidor bajo." For artisans in the revolt, see Danvila 35:441–458; Pérez pp. 488–493; Maravall pp. 219–245; AGS Pueblos leg. 2, núm. 265.

52. Antonio Ferrer del Rio, *Decadencia de España: Historia del Levantamiento de las Comunidades de Castilla, 1520–1521* (Madrid: Mellado, 1850) p. 63: "Ninguna población se alzó mas moderamente que Avila."

53. Haliczer p. 167 for violence against city council members in Valladolid; Gutiérrez Nieto, "Comunidades," pp. 336–337 for Soria.

houses of the regidores Diego Fernández Quiñones and Juan de Henao, who had voted for the hated *servicio* at la Coruña. The councilors, warned in advance, fled the city, thereby escaping the fate of the Segovian regidor Tordesillas, who had been lynched a short time earlier by a mob of angry cloth workers. The councilors Antonio Ponce and Pedro de Avila saw their houses attacked and looted when they refused to swear allegiance to the revolutionary comunidad. Others were forced to flee the city during this brief period of popular revolt.[54]

While forming a revolutionary junta to replace the traditional city council, the comuneros made demands that would have significantly broadened the base of political power in Avila. The rebels insisted that parish representatives elect city delegates to the cortes, as opposed to the old method of choosing them from the ranks of the city council. They called for the selection of two cortes delegates, one to represent the interests of the nobles and one for the commoners. Their most radical proposal struck straight at the heart of aristocratic privilege, mandating that nobles "pay taxes and contribute to the fiscal burden and municipal responsibilities like all other citizens."[55]

Events soon tore asunder the uneasy coalition of social groups which characterized the early days of the revolt. After a bloody popular uprising in nearby Medina del Campo in September 1520 in which several regidores were murdered, Avila's elite rebels began to abandon the comunero cause. Undoubtedly they recognized that social revolt from below threatened their privileges and authority more than royal repression from above. Members of the cathedral chapter denied the Castilian junta further use of the chapel of San Bernabé. After the humiliating defeat of the rebel forces at Tordesillas in December 1520, the leaders of Avila's militia,

54. Danvila 35:409, 38:123–126. AGS Cám. Castilla leg. 144–89, 142–126. Merino p. 25 n. 191.
55. Merino p. 96: "Los señores pecharan y contribuyeran en los repartimientos y en las cargas vecinales como otros cualesquiera vecinos."

Suero del Aguila and Fernán Gómez Dávila, who had both been captured during this battle, emerged as moderates. They now offered to serve as intermediaries between the Crown and the rebels and in this capacity were allowed to return to Avila. By the end of February 1521, the city's active participation in the comunero revolt had come to an end.[56]

A document issued in May 1521, following the definitive defeat of the comuneros at Villalar, illustrates the efforts of elite rebels to dissociate themselves from the movement. It contents that "Suero del Aguila and [Fernán] Gómez Dávila and Francisco de Pajares and the dean at first were comuneros, but they quickly found themselves returned to His Majesty's service.... Sancho [Sánchez] Cimbrón was a representative of the city ... and in this capacity went to the king with proposals [but] after he came back he never wanted to return to the comunidad again." And when war broke out with the French in Navarre in June 1521, former comuneros of noble rank rivaled one another in offering military service and professing abject loyalty to the Crown.[57]

The end of the Revolt of the Comuneros dashed the hopes of Avila's merchants and artisans for greater political representation. Peace returned but tensions remained. A royal ban on firearms within the city stayed in effect. In the widespread repression following the uprising many individuals suffered punishment for their disobedience to the monarchy. Some twenty former rebels from Avila were explicitly excluded from Charles V's general pardons of 1521 and 1522. These

56. Danvila 35:531–534. Pérez pp. 436–437. In the words of Merino: "Los caballeros se fueron retirando, al comprender que era mayor la amenaza de la plebe que la de la Corona" (the nobles began withdrawing, recognizing that the threat of the common people was greater than that of the crown) (p. 95).

57. Danvila 36:146–150: "Suero dell aguila e gomez davila e francisco de pajares y el dean al prencipio fueron comuneros pero que brevemente los vido tornados al servicio de su mt.... Sancho de ynbro [sic] fue procurador de la cibdad ... e asy fue con los capitulos al Rey [pero] despues que vino nunca quiso mas bolver a la Comunidad." Elliott pp. 55–56. Pérez pp. 488–493. Abulenses who participated in the war in Navarre included Sancho Sánchez Cimbrón and, reportedly, Alonso Sánchez de Cepeda.

men, for the most part members of the city's middle or artisan classes, faced huge fines or the confiscation of their property. Despite requests for clemency issued by Avila's city council over the next several years, the Crown stood firm. Some ex-comuneros were still paying off their fines as late as 1528, and probably into the 1530s.[58] These abulenses were fortunate compared to the eleven artisans executed in October 1521. These lower-class rebels included the cooper Juan de Osma, labeled "a very great rebel," the spinner Tomé Fernández (or Hernández), "a great rabble-rouser," and the shearer Cohote (or Cogote), "who grabbed the staff of office from the corregidor and his assistants." Death was their punishment for directly threatening the social order.[59]

Having failed in their gamble for power, the taxpayers of the city of Avila and of the towns and villages in its jurisdiction found themselves with an even heavier fiscal burden than before. They were forced to pay for the damages caused by some of their neighbors during the revolt. It took Avila nearly twenty years to complete these onerous indemnity payments.[60] The city's restored oligarchy, shaken by the experience of popular uprising, took steps to avoid the recurrence of violence. As noted earlier, discussions concerning the foundation of a public granary began in December 1521, only six months after the end of the revolt. In 1523 the city created the two new positions of "letrado y procurador para los pobres." These officials would "assist [the poor] in their lawsuits and affairs in the city," functioning, in effect, as public defenders.[61] These measures may have helped to im-

58. Ballesteros p. 156. Danvila 36:146–150; 38:283–284. Pérez pp. 479–497. Serafín de Tapia, "Avila después de Villalar," El Diario de Avila (May 8, 1984) p. 2.
59. AGS Cám. Castilla leg. 143–75, 143–157.
60. Tapia, "Villalar," p. 3. Pérez pp. 668–669. AGS Cám. Castilla leg. 144–89.
61. AHPA Actas Consist. libro 4, 1519–1523. The ubiquitous Francisco de Pajares was instrumental in establishing these offices.

prove the situation of Avila's most needy residents, but they did little to satisfy the political and social aspirations of its ambitious "new men."

Demographic expansion and urban development brought dramatic changes to Avila in the first decades of the sixteenth century. Economic opportunities in textile and construction trades, for example, attracted large numbers of rural immigrants. The city's poor were particularly vulnerable to the shortages of food and water, overcrowding, and unhealthy conditions that affected all abulenses.

The growth of the city and stimulation of trade enhanced the economic position of a group of "new men" in this period. Merchants, manufacturers, financiers, and professionals, many of converso descent, attempted to achieve a degree of political influence and social mobility by using the courts to establish noble status, by forging strategic marriage and business alliances with members of the city's oligarchy, and by asserting local control over key religious institutions and symbols. They also took part in a political uprising that presented a serious if ultimately unsuccessful challenge to the exclusive rule of a hereditary aristocracy.

With the failure of the comunero revolt, Avila's non-noble citizens abandoned their efforts at violent political confrontation: the city experienced no more popular revolts in the early modern period. But its "new men" continued to push for social acceptance and prestige. They may have found some compensation for their lack of direct political power in personal and financial involvement in new religious foundations. In the decades that followed many channeled their energies into supporting religious movements and institutions that reflected the changing conditions of urban life in sixteenth-century Avila, including the monastic reform of Teresa of Jesus.

4

Toward a New Definition
of Reform, 1540–1570

As Avila's population expanded during the sixteenth century, the spiritual climate within the city underwent
changes as well. Religious reform movements, originating
from without as well as from within, addressed the personal
and social problems that were being brought into focus by
accelerated urban growth. Traditional piety, and in particular monastic piety, to a large extent had involved the provision of sufficient endowments for a decorous and numerous
clergy who prayed vocally and continuously for the souls of
departed benefactors and their clients. This system satisfied
the spiritual, economic, and dynastic needs of the hereditary
aristocracy to which, in fact, most monks, nuns, and cathedral clergy belonged. It tended to accentuate the differences
between social groups.

By mid-century new religious reform movements articulated an alternative definition of piety, one that emphasized
the importance of a personal experience of conversion and
penitence and reflected the concern among many to relieve
the condition of the poor and to mediate conflicts among
social groups within the city. It featured a clergy committed
to the active apostolate of a large community of believers, as

well as the development of methods of internalized, mental, prayer which afforded the individual a more immediate and direct experience of the divine. In Avila, the ideals of service to the community and of the spiritual formation of the individual were furthered by a group of concerned clerics and laymen, many of whom ranked among or had links with the city's "new men," and who patronized the Children of Christian Doctrine, the Jesuit College of San Gil, the Seminary of San Millán, the holy woman Mari Díaz, and, eventually, Teresa of Jesus and her reform of the Carmelite order. Teresa, in turn, took many of her ideas concerning religious practice, practical administration, and prayer from the religious movements and institutions that emerged in Avila in the mid-sixteenth century. They fostered an atmosphere in which her own ideas could develop.

The Sacerdotal School of Juan de Avila

In the late fifteenth century, as Spain ended its long crusade against the Moors and several generations of dynastic conflict, it began to feel the effects of intellectual and religious change emanating from Italy, the Netherlands, the Rhineland, and elsewhere. Spaniards enthusiastically embraced the works of Italian humanists and northern European devotional writers, made available through a vigorous publishing campaign fostered by the reformist cardinal Cisneros.[1]

Most influential in promoting the ideals of the *devotio moderna* and the methods of Christian humanism in Spain was the great Dutch thinker Erasmus of Rotterdam. His works, with their emphases on humanist education in the classics, the analysis of scriptural texts, the pursuit of an interior religious life, and the rejection of mechanically per-

1. Pedro Saínz Rodríguez, *La siembra mística del Cardenal Cisneros y las reformas en la Iglesia* (Madrid: FUE, 1979).

formed ceremonies, enjoyed wide circulation. In the early sixteenth century, many Spanish intellectuals and clerics worked to adapt Erasmian models to fit indigenous needs and traditions. The result was an outpouring of ideas concerning education, charity, prayer, the proper role of the clergy, and the nature of the Christian community.[2] This dynamic reform movement would profoundly affect Spanish society, including the city of Avila.

One of the best known of Erasmus's many followers was the famous preacher, writer, and clerical reformer Juan de Avila (1499?–1569), who exercised wide influence in Spain, and later in Italy and France as well.[3] Despite his name he was not from the city of Avila, but rather from La Mancha, and he spent most of his life in southern Spain, where he gained fame as the Apostle of Andalusia. Although he never set foot in Avila, his writings and programs inspired a group of followers there. Maestro Avila, as he was known, corresponded with many of the city's religious reformers, including the nun Teresa de Ahumada.[4] A brief analysis of the life of Juan de Avila and his advocacy of an active, committed clergy, his social ideas regarding poor relief and the rejection

2. Still unsurpassed for these developments is Marcel Bataillon, *Erasmo y España* (Mexico: Fondo de Cultura Económica, 1950), first published in French in 1937. See especially chs. 1 and 2.

3. Juan de Avila, long neglected by historians and theologians, finally began receiving scholarly attention in the 1940s and, especially, in the years surrounding his canonization in 1970. The best study of his life and work is the six-volume *Obras completas del santo maestro Juan de Avila,* edited by Luis Sala Balust and, after Sala's death, by Francisco Martín Hernández (Madrid: Editorial Católica, 1970–71). For his Erasmianism, see Florencio Sánchez Bella, *La reforma del clero en San Juan de Avila* (Madrid: Rialp, 1981) pp. 47–59; Bataillon pp. xv–xvi. Bataillon suggests that it was Juan de Avila, not his disciple Fray Luis de Granada, as previously thought, who prepared a new translation of Thomas à Kempis's *Imitation of Christ* in 1536, "obra que ... era muy leída por los erasmistas españoles" (p. 594 n. 27).

4. For his correspondence with Gaspar Daza, Francisco de Guzmán, Mari Díaz, and Teresa of Jesus, see José Vicente Rodríguez, "Cinco cartas inéditas de San Juan de Avila," *Revista de Espiritualidad* 34 (1975): 366–371. *Obras* 5:573–576, 655–656, 660–661.

of worldly honor, and his contributions to the field of education is essential to an understanding of religious movements in Avila and the environment in which Teresa of Jesus created her reform programs. Juan de Avila encountered the writings of Erasmus as a university student in the early 1520s. He attended the University of Alcalá de Henares, founded some ten years earlier by Cardinal Cisneros, an institution that quickly gained fame as the center of Erasmian thought and humanistic studies in Spain.[5] Maestro Avila began his career as a priest in the late 1520s, charged with the apostolic fervor of the day. He traveled through Andalusia, preaching, hearing confessions, organizing aid for the numerous poor, and educating children and unlearned adults in the fundamentals of Christian doctrine. He believed strongly that the responsibility for remedying the problems of the Church lay in the hands of its clergy. He would eventually write, "It is ordained by God that the harm or benefit of the people depends upon the diligence and care of the ecclesiastical estate as the land depends upon the influences of the heavens."[6]

Armed with this lofty conception of the priestly vocation, Maestro Avila and a group of followers began to redefine the character and function of the clergy, especially on the parish level. He proposed restricting ordination to a small but select group of men who felt a genuine calling, rather than including anyone who wanted to enjoy the material comforts of a benefice and the juridical privileges of clergymen. Potential priests, he claimed, must receive theological and moral training from the earliest age (de mas atrás). By the time he died in 1569, Juan de Avila had established fifteen schools (col-

5. Sánchez Bella pp. 51–56. Bataillon pp. 10–22. For biographical information, see *Obras* 1:3–389.
   6. "Memorial segundo al Concilio de Trento, 1561," *Obras* 6:86: "Ordenanza es de Dios que el pueblo este colgado, en lo que toca a su daño o provecho, de la diligencia y cuidado del estado eclesiástico, como está la tierra de las influencias del cielo."

egios) for young men in addition to several schools intended specifically for the education of priests.[7]

Maestro Avila espoused, and exercised, an active apostolate. He urged priests to imitate Christ in their pastoral work, preaching, hearing confessions, engaging in works of charity and education, and living simple, virtuous lives as an example to *la gente común*. Juan de Avila himself had remarkable success as a popular preacher and spiritual director throughout southern Spain. The Maestro exhorted priests to maintain a commitment to preaching the Word to a large audience, regardless of social standing, and relieving, wherever possible, the wretched condition of the poor. In his writings he criticized the system of capellanías, which bound ecclesiastical organization and religious practice to the needs of a privileged elite, and an ingrained system of patronage and clientage. He bitterly condemned the process by which young men could become priests merely "by virtue of the chaplaincies of their lineages"; there was often no commitment of faith, then, to keep them from neglecting their parishioners.[8]

Early in Juan de Avila's career his outspoken statements against the tendency of donors to concentrate their money in capellanías and exert pressure on clerics to chant vocal prayers for their souls helped bring about his arrest by the Inquisition of Seville. In 1531 informants denounced the young priest from La Mancha for preaching certain dangerous doctrines, among them that "heaven had been made for the poor and those who worked the land and . . . it was impossible for the rich to find salvation," and that "it was better to give alms than to found chaplaincies." Maestro Avila success-

7. "Memorial primero al Concilio de Trento, 1551," *Obras* 6:33–68, 1:162–163. Marcel Bataillon, "Jean d'Avila retrouvé," *Bulletin Hispanique* 57 (1955): 5–44. Sánchez Bella pp. 143–172. Similar concerns over an improved clergy in Italy and elsewhere in the late fifteenth and early sixteenth centuries are discussed in H. O. Evennett, "The New Orders," in *The New Cambridge Modern History* vol. 2, ed. G. R. Elton (Cambridge: Cambridge University Press, 1958) pp. 275–300.

8. For example, *Obras* 6:40, 55, 222–225.

fully defended himself and was aquitted in 1533. Yet even while denying the charges brought against him, he maintained, cautiously, a spiritual program consistent with his social ideals. He explained that not all rich people lost their chance for salvation, only those who neglected their moral responsibility to remedy the plight of the needy. He defended his stand on capellanías by citing the grim social reality of Andalusia, where "in many places there is a sufficient number of masses and extreme misery among the poor."[9]

Many years later Maestro Avila would continue to state his conviction that priests must pray and intercede for all mankind, not merely for those who could afford donations. In a passage from his most famous work, the commentary on Psalm 44, *Audi, filia,* he criticized a social order tied to birth and privilege, here given in the English translation of 1620: "O Vanity, which deserves to be despised, in them that presume upon their descent; whereas all the souls of men are created immediately by God and we have not them by inheritance."[10] His theology, predicated upon the need for charity, the typically Erasmian notion of the Mystical Body of Christ (with its corresponding devotion to the Blessed Sacrament), composed of all believers, and the exercise of interior, mental, prayer, emphasized faith over liturgy, formation over heredity. These ideas attracted many priests who, like Juan de Avila, descended from non-noble converso families. The concentration of New Christians in the sacerdotal school of Juan de Avila frequently aroused the suspicions of ecclesiastical authorities.[11]

9. For a detailed analysis of the inquisitorial trial, see ibid. 1:31–63.

10. "Tratado sobre el sacerdocio," ibid. 3:491–535. *The Audi, Filia, or a Rich Cabinet Full of Spirituall Jewels* (St. Omer?, 1620). As far as I know this is the only English translation of this important work. The Spanish version is in *Obras* vol. 1, and also was edited by Luis Sala Balust and published separately (Barcelona: Juan Flors, 1963).

11. See *Audi, filia,* in *Obras* vol. 1, especially p. 490 ("los prójimos son pedazos del Cuerpo de Cristo"). Sánchez Bella pp. 27–46, 56–57. Eusebio Rey, "San Ignacio de Loyola y el problema de los 'Cristianos Nuevos,'" *Razón y Fe* 153 (1956): 173–204.

Juan de Avila's major contribution to reform in sixteenth-century Spain, including in Avila, was in the area of religious education, especially for the poor. Like other reformers active at the time, he worked to take educational theories promoted by humanists such as Erasmus and popularize them for a mass audience. The Maestro spent years composing catechisms, establishing a system of schools for both children and adults, and developing methods of pedagogy later utilized and expanded by the Society of Jesus and the teaching orders of the seventeenth century. The basis of Juan de Avila's educational program was his catechism "la Doctrina Cristiana." A question-and-answer format based upon the Credo ("That which one must believe") and the Ten Commandments ("That which one must do") was framed in rhyming couplets so that children could sing their doctrine as they walked in the streets. The attractive and adaptable "Doctrina Cristiana" of Maestro Avila enjoyed considerable success in Spain, and also in Italy, where it was published at the suggestion of Ignatius Loyola.[12]

The active apostolate concept advocated by Juan de Avila provided a model for a group of clerics and devout laymen living in Avila in the late 1540s and the 1550s. This coterie centered around Gaspar Daza, a major exponent of the ideas and methods of Juan de Avila. Daza and his "sacerdotal team" became involved in virtually every religious reform movement in mid-sixteenth century Avila.[13]

12. Carlos María Nannei, La "Doctrina Cristiana" de San Juan de Avila (Pamplona: Universidad de Navarra, 1977), includes a transcription of the catechism. For catechisms in Spain generally, see Sánchez Bella pp. 125–142; Jean-Pierre Dedieu, " 'Christianisation' en Nouvelle Castille: Catechisme, communion, messe, et confirmation dans l'Archevêché de Tolède, 1540–1650," Mélanges de la Casa de Velázquez 15 (1979): 261–293; José-Ramón Guerrero, Catecismos españoles del siglo XVI (Madrid: Instituto Superior de Pastoral, 1969).

13. Rodríguez refers to an "equipo sacerdotal" on p. 369. For Daza, see Efrén de la Madre de Dios (Montalva) and Otger Steggink, Santa Teresa y su tiempo vol. 1 (Salamanca: Universidad Pontificia, 1982) pp. 347–348; Silverio de Santa Teresa, Historia del Carmen Descalzo en España, Portugal, y

Toward a New Definition of Reform

Little is known of Daza's life. A seventeenth-century historian mentioned his noble descent, but other sources are silent on this point. In fact, before 1492 many Jews in Avila had the surname *Daça*. Very possibly Gaspar Daza, like Maestro Avila, had converso roots. Daza held the minor position of prebendary in Avila's cathedral chapter. Successive bishops, impressed by his administrative abilities, tried to promote him to a higher position within the cathedral hierarchy, but without success. Reportedly, on at least one occasion he refused a canonry from bishop Alvaro de Mendoza. An impressive record of *obras pías* and donations indicates that he possessed the resources to offer economic as well as spiritual and administrative support to various religious institutions.[14]

Daza gained fame in Avila as a learned and effective preacher. In the 1530s and 1540s, Daza, like Juan de Avila, preached to audiences both in the city and in rural villages. The cathedral chapter of Avila commissioned him several times to deliver the cycle of Lenten sermons. In addition, Daza heard confessions, lodged students in his home, and personally cared for the poor and the sick. One observer wrote, "He consoled them, he made their beds, swept their rooms and washed their cups, with great devotion and humility."[15]

Gradually, also like Maestro Avila, Gaspar Daza "collect-

América vol. 1 (Burgos: El Monte Carmelo, 1935) pp. 368–375; Victoriano Larrañaga, *La espiritualidad de San Ignacio de Loyola: Estudio comparativo con la de Santa Teresa de Jesús* (Madrid: Casa de San Pablo, 1944) pp. 56–62. Baldomero Jiménez Duque, *La escuela sacerdotal de Avila del siglo XVI* (Madrid: FUE, 1981), is useful as a catalogue of names and for its bibliography, but it offers little analysis.

14. Bartolomé Fernández Valencia, *Historia y grandezas del insigne templo... de... San Vicente* vol. 1 (Avila, 1676) pp. 311–321. Pilar León Tello, *Judíos de Avila* (Avila: Diputación Provincial de Avila, Institución "Gran Duque de Alba," 1963). A 1513 survey of houses owned by the cathedral chapter lists Dazas in neighborhoods of heavy converso concentration and mentions a tenant living in a house formerly owned by "Mosé Daza, judío." AHN Cód. 466-b.

15. Fernández Valencia 1:311–321. Silverio de Santa Teresa 1:372–374.

ed and gathered around him" a group of disciples, natives of Avila who formed the core of a "reform party."[16] Many belonged to the network of interrelated non-noble or recently ennobled families which played such a crucial role in the city's economic life. Daza's disciples included Francisco Salcedo, who figured prominently (with Daza) in the spiritual direction of Teresa de Ahumada; Gonzalo de Aranda, another early supporter of Carmelite reform; Francisco de Guzmán of the influential Bracamonte family; and Pedro de las Cuevas, a priest related to Saint Teresa's mother. Daza particularly influenced Julián de Avila, a young priest born to humble parents in Avila's las Vacas district who would eventually serve as the chaplain and biographer of Teresa of Jesus. In the late 1540s Julián spent several years in Seville and Granada, where he almost certainly came into contact with the work of Juan de Avila. He then returned to Avila and joined Daza in apostolic missions to the countryside in which he heard confessions while Daza preached, a method expressly recommended by Maestro Avila.[17]

In 1547 the devout Hernando Alvarez del Aguila, related through marriage to several of the "new men" in Daza's circle, endowed a new educational and charitable institution called "los Niños de la Doctrina Cristiana," the Children of Christian Doctrine, which resembled in both name and character the schools established by Maestro Avila in Andalusia. Poor boys would be given food and lodging at the church of San Millán, formerly a Cistercian convent, and instruction in the basics of Christian dogma. The house would accommodate children from the entire bishopric of Avila, perhaps

16. *Obras escogidas del V. P. Luis de la Puente,* ed. Camilo María Abad (Madrid: Ediciones Atlas, 1958), p. 57: "Había entonces en aquella ciudad un buen número de clérigos virtuosos, que habían recogido y allegando a si el Maestro Daza, varón de ejemplar virtud, para que ayudasen a remediar almas y necesidades de pobres."
17. Miguel González Vaquero, *La muger fuerte: Por otro título, la vida de Doña María Vela . . .* (Barcelona: Geronymo Margarit, 1627) 136v–138r. Gerardo de San Juan de la Cruz, *Vida del Maestro Julián de Avila . . .* (Toledo: Impr. de la viuda e hijos de J. Peláez, 1915) pp. 26–43.

reflecting both a recognition of the problems faced by rural immigrants and current efforts to coordinate poor relief measures within diocesan structures.[18]

Alvarez del Aguila and his associates envisioned a foundation that would form character, not merely distribute alms like many traditional relief institutions. Their hope was that the house would produce candidates for the priesthood, young men without funds or status but imbued with a sense of Christian purpose and morality who would go on to serve the community. The foundation graduated some of the city's earliest Jesuits, and boys from the Children of Christian Doctrine went on to become students at the Seminary of San Millán, Avila's first Tridentine seminary. By the end of the century los Niños de la Doctrina had gained considerable popularity in Avila, and abulenses frequently bequeathed donations to the poor boys in their wills. Residents watched as the boys marched, singing their doctrine at funerals and religious processions, a testimony to a new definition of reform based upon education and moral formation for which Juan de Avila was the most eloquent spokesman.

The Society of Jesus

The goals and methods of Juan de Avila and his sacerdotal school were adopted and expanded by the Society of Jesus,

18. Ferreol Hernández Hernández, "El convento cisterciense de Santa Ana en Avila," *Cistercium* 11 (1959): 136–144. Juan Martín Carramolino, *Historia de Avila, su provincia y obispado* vol. 1 (Madrid: Librería Española, 1872) p. 553. ASA leg. 2, núm. 10. AHN Clero leg. 245, 529. Similar institutions were founded in many other Castilian cities during the sixteenth century. For "Niños de la Doctrina" in Cuenca, see Sara T. Nalle, "The Castilian Catholic Reformation" (Paper delivered at the Sixteenth-Century Studies Conference, Arizona State University, Tempe, Ariz., October 29–31, 1987), especially pp. 6–7. In Toledo, see Linda Martz, *Poverty and Welfare in Habsburg Spain: The Example of Toledo* (Cambridge: Cambridge University Press, 1983) pp. 140–141, 223. In Valladolid, Bartolomé Bennassar, *Valladolid en el Siglo de Oro: Una ciudad de Castilla y su entorno agrario en el siglo XVI* (Valladolid: Ayuntamiento, 1983) pp. 410–411.

the most important of the orders of priests founded in six-teenth-century Europe. Ignatius Loyola, who greatly admired and often corresponded with the Maestro, developed a similar, but much more tightly organized, program of clerical reform centered around the formation of active priests engaged in public preaching, missionary work, education, and poor relief. In Avila as elsewhere, the Jesuits also responded to some of the problems of urban life. In their elaboration of confessional techniques, they addressed the needs of individual laymen. Their organizational structure, which featured a hierarchy bound by a sense of commitment and obedience, offered an alternative to a larger, societal, hierarchy based upon birth and privilege. The Society institutionalized periods of mental prayer and examination of conscience, virtually abolished choral intercessory prayer, and emphasized service to the individual and to a community of believers rather than to particular families.[19] Ignatian spirituality and institutional organization would make a deep impression upon Teresa of Jesus, who counted Jesuits among her most trusted confessors.

Many aspects of Jesuit organization illustrated Loyola's ideal of a society composed of a small number of trained, tested, and highly committed priests. The qualifications listed in the *Constitutions* for entrance in the Society of Jesus included the possession of strong moral virtues, sufficient education, and a willingness to obey superiors and the pope to the point of departing at a moment's notice for service in any part of the world. "The extrinsic gifts of nobility, wealth, reputation and the like," Loyola noted, "are not necessary when the others are present, just as they do not suffice if those others are lacking."[20] At a time when monastic houses

19. Joseph de Guibert, *The Jesuits: Their Spiritual Doctrine and Practice* (St. Louis: Institute of Jesuit Sources, 1964) pp. 544–565. *The Constitutions of the Society of Jesus*, trans. George E. Ganss (St. Louis: Institute of Jesuit Sources, 1970) pp. 261–263.

20. *Constitutions* pp. 107–108, 130.

frequently required noble status and considerable dowries or entrance fees, the early Jesuits represented a very selective, but not socially elitist, organization. Many of Loyola's colleagues, as well as the first Jesuits at the College of San Gil, Avila, descended from bourgeois or even more humble backgrounds. Loyola's extreme reluctance to adopt statutes of purity of blood, and his conflict with Archbishop Silíceo of Toledo over the admission of conversos in the Society, are well known. The many wellborn early Jesuits were chosen on the basis of their commitment to the Society's goals, not their money or family connections.[21]

Jesuits normally lived in one of two types of residences: houses, from which priests would exercise an active apostolate, and colleges, for the training of young men for membership in the Society. Houses were to receive no fixed incomes whatsoever. Jesuit colleges such as San Gil received endowments so students could engage full time in academic pursuits, without having to solicit alms. However, Loyola recognized the problems associated with accepting individual or dynastic patronage and made provisions to preserve the Society's autonomy. He mollified potential donors by mandating that the clergy within a college periodically offer a special mass for the founders and all patrons living or dead; masses for individual donors at times and for people they had specified (a part of most capellanías), however, were prohibited. On the day of this special mass, the members of the college would present the founder or his closest relatives with a

21. See, for example, James Broderick, *St. Ignatius Loyola: The Pilgrim Years, 1491–1538* (New York: Farrar, Straus and Cudahy, 1956) pp. 288–289, for Loyola's companion Bobadilla, a *labrador*. See also Rey pp. 173–204. Albert A. Sicroff, *Los estatutos de limpieza de sangre: Controversias entre los siglos XV y XVII* (Madrid: Taurus, 1985) pp. 315–336. In 1616 the regidores of Avila praised the Jesuits of San Gil for "la enseñanza que hacen a los hijos de los vecinos de esta república sin estipendio ninguno." AHPA Actas Consist. libro 32, October 25, 1616. Of course, as the Society changed over time, Jesuits came to specialize in the education of children of the elite, but their more egalitarian origins should be kept in mind.

candle decorated with his coat of arms or emblem of his devotions, and then place it on the altar during the Sacrament of the Eucharist—an extremely moving spiritual gesture but a far cry from carving a founder's *blasón* on the chapel's walls or venerating his tomb. Loyola stated his intentions clearly: "'This candle signifies the gratitude due to the founders and not any rights of patronage or any claim belonging to them or their successors against the college or its temporal goods. Nothing of this kind will exist.'"[22]

At the College of San Gil in Avila, founded in 1553, one of the most generous of a consortium of backers was Juan Vázquez de Medina, dean of the cathedral chapter and uncle of one of the college's founders, the Jesuit Luis de Medina. Don Juan, in his 1566 will, left money for the "rector, fathers, and brothers of San Gil," and a substantial donation for the upkeep of deserving students (*muy buenos latinos*). He made no mention, however, of anniversary masses, chaplains, tombs, coats of arms or any of the other stipulations usually contained in capellanías. San Gil was a different kind of foundation, and its supporters shared the humanist ideals of education and moral formation as well as the concern for an educated and committed clergy then being articulated at the Council of Trent.[23]

In Avila, as in other places, the Jesuits specialized in public preaching, and they attained great popularity and prestige for their sermons. In addition, Jesuits served as mediators between social groups, an important function in a highly stratified society such as that of Avila. In fact, the first direct encounter between citizens of Avila and the Society of Jesus, in 1550, involved the mediation of social conflict. The Jesuit Miguel de Torres, while traveling through the city, was called

22. George E. Ganss, *Saint Ignatius' Idea of a Jesuit University* (Milwaukee: Marquette University Press, 1954) pp. 18–43. See also Loyola's letter to Antonio Araoz, Provincial of Castile, in *Monumenta Paedogogica Societatis Iesu* vol. 1 (Rome, 1965) pp. 414–419. *Constitutions* pp. 94, 174–176, 281.
23. AHN Jesuitas leg. 491, núm. 3.

upon to settle a dispute that had arisen in a convent housing more than 120 nuns. Although not specified in the sketchy accounts of the incident, this was almost certainly the Carmelite convent of la Encarnación, which, like Avila itself, suffered from the effects of rapid demographic growth. Overcrowded conditions and competition for limited material resources exacerbated the tensions between nuns of wealthy and more modest families which had long plagued the convent. At this time Teresa de Ahumada, aged 35, had spent fifteen years at la Encarnación. Torres, according to the Jesuit chronicler Polanco, spoke only once with the factious nuns, and moved them to such shame and repentance that they fell on their knees asking God for forgiveness. Then, under the Jesuit's guidance, they reconciled their differences. Torres's spiritual authority and ability to negotiate a swift and effective resolution of the nuns' quarrel greatly impressed many people in Avila.[24]

Jesuits demonstrated their aptitude for recognizing the needs and problems of individuals in their roles as spiritual directors. The ability to guide people in reforming their lives through confession and penance became one of the hallmarks of the Society's apostolic program. Here, too, they insisted that one's purpose on earth, namely, to serve God and to work toward one's salvation, precluded undue attachments to things of this world, including one's family. A new set of allegiances, formed between confessor and penitent, competed with and sometimes even replaced the bonds of kinship and patronage fostered by traditional social relations and religious practices.[25]

24. This story, repeated by many Jesuit historians, is taken from the "Historia Societatis Jesu," MHSJ 2:128–129. See also Alberto Risco, "Una opinión sobre los tres primeros confesores Jesuitas de Santa Teresa de Jesús," BAH 80 (1922): 462–469; 81 (1922): 41–52. Nicolás González y González, *El monasterio de la Encarnación de Avila* vol. 1 (Avila: Caja Central de Ahorros y Préstamos, 1976) pp. 143–176.

25. *Constitutions* pp. 92–93: Loyola urged the virtue of "divesting oneself of disordered love of relatives" and claimed that "by closing the gate of

The Jesuit Luis de la Puente's biography of his colleague Baltasar Alvarez, who spent nine years (1558–67) in Avila, provides fascinating insights into the theory and practice of Ignatian confessional technique. Alvarez, according to de la Puente, offered spiritual advice and direction to people of all social backgrounds. He never disdained the humble nor "let his heart cleave to the great" ("dejar pegar su corazon a los grandes"). He bitterly criticized the tendency of confessors to "make a name for themselves through their penitents, applying themselves exclusively to the treatment of high-born people, and no one else."[26] Alvarez's avoidance of "particular and entangling" friendships, and his refusal to bow to special interests, faithfully reflected the central Jesuit tenet of retaining one's spiritual liberty (*santa libertad*), a concept later adopted by Teresa of Jesus.[27]

Jesuits such as Baltasar Alvarez maintained high spiritual standards (some penitents fled Alvarez's presence rather than hear their faults delineated and criticized) while remaining flexible enough to counsel each person according to his or her needs, capabilities, and position in society, a principle clearly set out by Loyola in the *Spiritual Exercises*. Jesuits also distinguished themselves by their readiness to direct women. In Avila, Baltasar Alvarez's female penitents included some truly extraordinary individuals, such as Doña Guiomar de Ulloa, the holy women Mari Díaz and Ana Reyes, and the nun Teresa de Ahumada.[28]

recourse to parents and relatives and of the profitless memory of them [Jesuits] may persevere in their vocation with proportionally greater firmness and stability." He reminded members of the Society that the Gospel "does not say 'give to your relatives,' but 'to the poor.'"

26. Luis de la Puente, *Vida del Padre Baltasar Alvarez* (Madrid: Ediciones Atlas, 1958) pp. 54–55.

27. Ibid. p. 55: "Porque no amaba a los penitentes con amor imperfecto . . . no buscaba dellos interese temporal, ni quería recibir las cosas que le ofrecían . . . por no menoscabar esta santa libertad; no trataba amistad tan particular y pegajosa . . . conservándose libre para mudarse a otra parte."

28. Ibid. pp. 56–60 for Alvarez's treatment of "señoras y mujeres ejemplares."

Confessors urged their penitents to reform their lives through mortification, both external and internal. By external mortification they meant acts of corporal penitence, such as fasts and vigils, although, as always, carefully moderated according to the individual's state of physical health and spiritual development. Jesuits themselves, although encouraged by Loyola to live and dress in a manner "characteristic of the poor," did not generally indulge in feats of heroic asceticism like the holy people Peter of Alcántara and Mari Díaz, who represented a different spiritual tradition. For one thing, members of the Society needed to retain their strength for missionary activity.

Thus, the Jesuits placed greater emphasis on internal mortification, or what de la Puente called "the purification of the heart." This entailed, first, reaching a consciousness of the Crucified Christ through the systematic use of the senses, the religious imagination, and the knowledge of self brilliantly worked out by Loyola in the *Spiritual Exercises.* Next, the penitent had to transform himself or herself by controlling carnal and selfish desires. De la Puente described the holy woman Ana Reyes as having attained *señorío de sus pasiones* (dominion or lordship over her passions), the ultimate spiritual goal for all.[29] Finally, the new person was to live a new life, imitating Christ by doing good works— which, in the Jesuit scheme (as in that of Maestro Avila), essentially meant working to relieve the condition of society's poor. This method of spiritual direction, which emphasized the formation and transformation of the individual and heightened his or her awareness of social needs, touched the lives of many abulenses. Figures cited by the Jesuit historian Astraín, though undoubtedly exaggerated, indicate the degree of popularity reached by the Society of Jesus in Avila within the first decade of its installment there. Confessions heard by Jesuits in Avila numbered 4,388 in the last four

29. Ibid. p. 60. The application of the term *señorío* to a poor woman is striking.

months of 1563 alone, and 5,265 in the first four months of 1564.[30]

The ideas and program of the Society of Jesus found an enthusiastic reception among members of the reforming party associated with Gaspar Daza. Hernando Alvarez del Aguila, founder of the Children of Christian Doctrine, became a Jesuit shortly after 1550, when Miguel Torres preached in the city and resolved the conflict at la Encarnación. After several years of negotiations, Alvarez obtained papal permission to apply his benefices toward the establishment of a Jesuit college in Avila. In 1553 Bishop Diego de Alava y Esquivel, a participant at the Council of Trent and generous supporter of the Jesuits, offered them the old parish church of San Gil, centrally located at the city's summit, as a college for young men.[31]

Alvarez del Aguila, scion of a wealthy and powerful abulense family, possessed extensive ties of friendship and kinship with other elites in Daza's circle, as well as with members of families of probable converso extraction. He was a cousin of Catalina del Aguila, the wife of Pedro Sánchez de Cepeda, Saint Teresa's uncle. His sister, Mencía del Aguila, was married to Francisco Salcedo. Recall that both the Sánchez de Cepeda and Salcedo families had been involved in lengthy pleitos de hidalguía in the early sixteenth century.

---

30. Antonio Astraín, *Historia de la Compañía de Jesús en la asistencia de España* vol. 2 (Madrid: Razón y Fe, 1909) p. 505. Francisco de Guzmán, a scion of the powerful Bracamonte family, was converted by Baltasar Alvarez from a spendthrift and worldly life. When a canonry in Avila's cathedral chapter fell open to him upon the death of his brother, Guzmán used his ecclesiastical incomes "en remediar las necesidades de monasterios, hospitales y pobres vergonzantes" (Puente p. 58).

31. For the origins of the Jesuit college in Avila, see MHSJ 2:108–109, 132, 141; 3:311, 366; 4:584–587; 5:442–444; 6:617–621. See also Astraín 1:419–422; Risco pp. 41–52; Larrañaga pp. 62–68; AHN Jesuitas leg. 491, núm. 30. Bishop Diego de Alava y Esquivel was, like Ignatius Loyola, a Basque. Constancio Gutiérrez, *Españoles en Trento* (Valladolid: CSIC, 1951) pp. 226–232.

Catalina del Aguila's sister Ana married Francisco de Pajares, the regidor, former comunero, and friend of Alonso Sánchez de Cepeda. Their daughter, María del Aguila, had served as godmother to Teresa, an indication of the close relationship shared by these families.[32] A network of related and acquainted individuals patronized the Society of Jesus and other educational and clerical institutions founded in mid-century Avila. Francisco Salcedo made administrative arrangements for the establishment of San Gil and personally donated the value of fifty fanegas of grain to his brother-in-law's foundation every year. His nephew Melchor de la Serna entered San Gil in 1565. Julián de Avila supported the Jesuit college, as did Pedro de las Cuevas, who later became rector of los Niños de la Doctrina. At the time that the cathedral chapter of Avila approved the foundation of San Gil and even offered financial support to the college, Francisco Salcedo's brother Vicente, two relatives of the co-founder Luis de Medina, and the indispensable Gaspar Daza all held positions in the chapter.[33] The reform party constituted a system within the wider system of patronage and communication among Avila's elites. The difference was that this sub-system included middle-rank conversos such as the Sánchez de Cepeda family, and clergymen of humble origin such as Julián de Avila and Pedro de las Cuevas. This group emphasized the horizontal kin and collegial connections between its members rather than dynastic links of family over generations, and it fostered religious institutions such as the Jesuit college of San Gil, which in its organization and liturgical program stressed formation over heredity and service to the individual and to a community of believers over intercession for particular families.

32. Montalva and Steggink 1:75–76, 346–347. Larrañaga pp. 62–68. Homero Serís, "Nueva genealogía de Santa Teresa," *Nueva Revista de Filología Hispánica* 10 (1956): 365–384.

33. AHN Jesuitas leg. 491, núm. 2, 3; leg. 490–2, núm. 17; leg. 489–1, núm. 51; leg. 67–2, núm. 74.

Mari Díaz: The Holy Woman and the Seminary Idea

The reforms initiated by the sacerdotal school of Juan de
Avila and the Society of Jesus constituted an effort to pre-
pare trained, virtuous, and committed priests who would
serve a community of believers through education, poor relief, preaching, and spiritual direction. A contemporaneous
movement was the articulation of a different form of spirituality, one that featured the practice of extreme asceticism
and the reception of a direct experience of God on the part of
extraordinary and largely autonomous individuals. Unlike
the clerical reform movement sketched above, this form of
spirituality was open to both women and men, though it was
perhaps embraced more intensely by women. The affective,
often mystical, women's spiritual movement that pervaded
much of Europe during the twelfth, thirteenth, and fourteenth centuries only fully emerged in Castile in the late
fifteenth century.[34] The sixteenth and seventeenth centuries
witnessed an explosion of female religious activity and writing, a consideration that is critical for understanding the
context of Saint Teresa's life and work.[35]

34. For asceticism in the Christian tradition and its meaning for women,
see Elizabeth A. Clark, *Ascetic Piety and Women's Faith: Essays in Late
Ancient Christianity* (Lewiston, N.Y.: Edwin Mellen, 1986). Of the large
literature relating to the late medieval women's spiritual movement, see
R. W. Southern, *Western Society and the Church in the Middle Ages* (Harmondsworth: Penguin, 1970) pp. 318–331, and, most recently, Caroline
Walker Bynum, *Holy Feast and Holy Fast: The Religious Significance of
Food to Medieval Women* (Berkeley and Los Angeles: University of Califor-
nia Press, 1987) ch. 1.

35. Manuel Serrano y Sanz, *Apuntes para una biblioteca de escritoras
españolas desde el año 1401 al 1833*, 2 vols. (Madrid: Ediciones Atlas, 1975).
A significant portion of the writers catalogued here wrote on religious
themes. Bataillon, *Erasmo*, pp. 68–71, 176–179. For some individual studies, see Vicente Beltrán de Heredia, "Directrices de la espiritualidad dominicana en Castilla durante las primeras décadas del siglo XVI," in *Corrientes
espirituales en la España de siglo XVI: Trabajos* (Barcelona: Juan Flors,
1963) pp. 177–202; Ronald E. Surtz, "La Madre Juana de la Cruz (1481–1534)
y la cuestión de la autoridad religiosa femenina," *Nueva Revista de Filología
Hispánica* 33 (1984): 483–491; Mary Elizabeth Perry, "Beatas and the In-

Toward a New Definition of Reform

In mid-sixteenth-century Avila this spirituality was epitomized by the charismatic holy woman Mari Díaz. This illiterate peasant was at one time the city's most revered religious figure; indeed, she was better known than Teresa of Jesus during Teresa's lifetime. Through her holy example and talent as advisor, consoler, and mediator of conflicts, she, too, succeeded in serving the urban community. A person who deeply influenced Teresa by her willingness to suffer and by her unquestioning faith in God's providence, Mari Díaz lent her spiritual prestige to the Jesuits and to the project that symbolized the culmination of the apostolic program of Gaspar Daza and his circle—the foundation of Avila's first Tridentine seminary in 1568.[36]

Mari Díaz was born to prosperous peasants in the village of Vita, near Avila, probably around 1490. She moved to Avila,

---

quisition in Early Modern Seville," in *Inquisition and Society in Early Modern Europe*, ed. and trans. Stephen Haliczer (Totowa, N.J.: Barnes and Noble, 1987) pp. 147–168; Electa Arenal, "The Convent as Catalyst for Autonomy: Two Hispanic Nuns of the Seventeenth Century," in *Women in Hispanic Literature: Icons and Fallen Idols,* ed. Beth Miller (Berkeley and Los Angeles: University of California Press, 1983) pp. 147–183. An important contribution to this field is Electa Arenal and Stacey Schlau, *Untold Sisters: Hispanic Nuns in Their Own Works* (Albuquerque: University of New Mexico Press, 1989).

36. Most information concerning Mari Díaz comes from the "Información de la Vida, muerte, y milagros de la Venerable María Díaz," a series of testimonies by people who remembered the holy woman which was commissioned by the bishops of Avila between 1600 and 1623. ADA Cód. 3.345. See also Puente pp. 60–64; Luis Ariz, *Historia de las grandezas de la ciudad de Avila* (Alcalá de Henares: L. Martínez Grande, 1607) pt. 1, 50v–51r; Gil González Dávila, *Teatro eclesiástico de las ciudades e iglesias catedrales de España . . .* (Salamanca: A. Ramírez, 1618) pp. 150–154; Gerardo de San Juan de la Cruz, "María Díaz, llamada la Esposa del Santísimo Sacramento," *El Monte Carmelo* 16 (1915): 174–177, 380–382, 414–418; 17 (1915): 102–105, 166–170, 224–229, 300–304, 410–416; 18 (1916): 56–59; idem, *Julián de Avila* pp. 183–204; Baldomero Jiménez Duque, "Espiritualidad de María Díaz," *Manresa* 46 (1974): 29–42; Jodi Bilinkoff, "The Holy Woman and the Urban Community in Sixteenth Century Avila," in *Women and the Structure of Society: Selected Research from the Fifth Berkshire Conference on the History of Women,* ed. Barbara J. Harris and JoAnn K. McNamara (Durham, N.C.: Duke University Press, 1984): 74–80.

like so many rural dwellers, in the 1530s. In this case, the immigrant moved to the city not in search of work in the wool trade, but "because she had heard it said that there were sermons in the city of Avila."[37] The city, with its many parishes and monastic houses, its festivals and fairs, and its wealthy people being urged ever more frequently to give alms, offered a wide range of support for those who decided to follow the religious life. In the rural setting of Vita, in which all hands were needed for labor-intensive agriculture, Mari Díaz's desire to spend long hours at church and in the distribution of alms was viewed with resentment, especially (and understandably) on the part of her family. Also opposed to the vow of chastity she made, her parents had engaged her to a young man, but she managed to scare off the suitor and retain her commitment to serve God alone.

Mari Díaz moved to Avila only after her parents died. Once in Avila, she lived at first in the humble district of las Vacas, where many newcomers from the country settled. She quickly gained recognition for her life of extreme austerity and prayer. Vowing to live in poverty, she gave most of her possessions to the needy around her.

By the mid-sixteenth century neighborhoods in cities and towns frequently were home to individual women or groups of women who chose an informal religious vocation as beatas. Sometimes these women who prayed together, attended church services together, and engaged in charitable activities formed the basis for a convent. A 1561 survey of households in Avila mentioned several beatas who lived alone or with others in various parts of the city, women such as Juana Gutiérrez and María de Henao, in the districts of el Cocuelo and San Esteban, a certain Inés, too poor to pay taxes, who lived near the monastery of Santo Tomás, and an unnamed beata who worked as the servant of a notary in the neighbor-

37. "Información de la Vida," testimony of Ana Reyes.

hood of San Juan. Beatas lived this way in other areas of Spain, as well.[38] Mari Díaz distinguished herself by the extent and intensity of her asceticism and devotion. The neighborhood women of las Vacas noticed how she once spent six consecutive hours at church and another time became so engrossed in prayer that she let her chickens fly away. They marveled at her fervent, though undisciplined, piety.

Mari Díaz sought spiritual directors, exhausting, as one witness claimed, "several monasteries with her pleas that they confess her."[39] The foundation of a Jesuit college in Avila in 1553 changed her life. The enthusiastic young Jesuits of San Gil, committed to developing programs of systematic prayer and mortification and indifferent to the social status and potential for donations of their penitents, agreed to direct the pious woman. On the orders of her confessors, particularly Baltasar Alvarez, she went to live at the palace of the devout widow Doña Guiomar de Ulloa, located opposite the College of San Gil. Here her humility was put to the test. Taken from her poor but free and respected life in the neighborhood, she now worked, like so many rural immigrants, as a domestic servant. Doña Guiomar's employees, probably without the knowledge of their mistress, taunted and tormented the aging woman.

Nevertheless, Mari Díaz's six-year stay at this house had long-lasting consequences. Through Doña Guiomar the holy

38. AGS Exp. Hac. 50–3. William A. Christian, Jr., *Local Religion in Sixteenth Century Spain* (Princeton: Princeton University Press, 1981) pp. 15–17. Bartolomé Bennassar, "Medina del Campo: Un example des structures urbaines de l'Espagne au XVIe siècle," *Revue d'Histoire Economique et Sociale* 4 (1961): 474–495. Mary Elizabeth Perry, *Crime and Society in Early Modern Seville* (Hanover, N.H.: University Press of New England, 1980) pp. 214–215. Richard L. Kagan, "The Toledo of El Greco," in *El Greco of Toledo*, ed. Jonathan Brown et al. (Boston: Little, Brown, 1982) pp. 59–61.

39. "Información de la Vida," testimony of Bartolomé Díaz de Luján (not a relative).

life and edifying words of Mari Díaz became known throughout Avila, especially to members of the aristocracy, and her neighborhood reputation for homespun wisdom and piety grew to citywide recognition and respect. At the house of Doña Guiomar de Ulloa in the late 1550s Mari Díaz first met Peter of Alcántara, the renowned Franciscan reformer, as well as Teresa de Ahumada. Teresa, who often visited the house, once asked the old woman, "Mother, do you not have a great desire to die? . . . Because I do, in order to see my [celestial] husband." The beata replied, "No, daughter, I do not desire to die, but rather to live longer, in order to suffer for Christ, which I won't be able to do after death, and then there will be plenty of time to enjoy Him."⁴⁰

In 1564 or 1565 Bishop Alvaro de Mendoza gave Mari Díaz permission to move from Doña Guiomar's palace to a small chamber (tribuna) in front of the main altar of the church in San Millán, where she lived until her death in 1572. Her decision to remain cloistered in a tiny space, surviving on alms, subsisting on one meal a day, wearing rags, sleeping on a board with a stone for a pillow, and spending hours in prayer before the Blessed Sacrament recalls the heroic asceticism of the stylite saints and desert hermits of late antiquity.⁴¹ In fact, male writers described her as manlike, just as male writers had the female warrior Jimena Blázquez, of Avila's medieval past. The early Christian monks built a city in the desert, and Mari Díaz, by living like a hermit in a church located right off Avila's main marketplace, succeeded

40. Montalva and Steggink 1:356. "Madre Maridíaz, ¿no tiene gran deseo de morirse? Porque yo grande le tengo por ver a mi esposo." "Yo, hija, no me deseo morir, sino vivir mucho para padecer por Cristo, lo cual no podré hacer después de muerta, que después nos queda tiempo harto para gozarle." This exchange recalls the theme of Teresa's most famous poem, which begins "Vivo sin vivir en mi / Y tan alta vida espero / Que muero porque no muero." (I live without living in myself / And in such a way I hope / I die because I do not die.)

41. Peter Brown, "The Rise and Function of the Holy Man in Late Antiquity," Journal of Roman Studies 61 (1971): 80–101.

in bringing the desert to the city. Her presence sacralized this corner of worldly bustle and activity. The beata played an integral part in the city's social life. The "Mother" Mari Díaz offered consolation and counsel to the many people who regularly came to talk with her. Witnesses at pre-beatification hearings held after her death recalled how supplicants often approached the holy woman with pleas to intercede for them in her prayers. Bartolomé Díaz de Luján claimed that the faithful not only of Avila but "from many leagues away came to beg her to commend to God affairs of great importance."[42] Both he and Luis de Victoria recounted cases in which the prayers of Mari Díaz restored the sick to health. On other occasions she comforted mourners and advised a young widow to remarry. When a couple who had been infertile for many years finally bore a daughter, many abulenses attributed the event to the intercession of the beata.[43]

A villager who had come to the city, a woman who refused to conform to society's rules regarding personal appearance, an old person concerned for the problems of the young, and a peasant who had lived in the palace of an aristocrat, Mari Díaz occupied a social category all her own—sexless, ageless, and classless. Like the stylite saints described by Peter Brown, she represented "objectivity personified" and was, thus, successful in mediating conflicts and settling disputes. The seventeenth-century historian Gil González Dávila eulogized the beata, claiming that "she commanded such au-

42. "Información de la Vida," testimony of Bartolomé Díaz de Luján. "Pero que de muchas leguas venían a pedir encomendarse a Dios negocios de grande ynportancia." On this point see also testimonies of Francisco Diez and Julián de Avila.
43. Ibid. testimonies of Bartolomé Díaz de Luján (for his sick brother), Luis de Vitoria (for the case of the sick son of barber-surgeon Bartolomé López). For childless couple, testimonies of Juan de Villanueva and Francisco Dávila y Ulloa, the grandson of Doña Guiomar de Ulloa. González Dávila p. 299. "Llevaba el afligido consuelo, el perseguido paciencia, favor el pobre, ámparo el huérfano y todos buenos consejos." See 150–154 for widow.

thority with her good and holy life among the residents of [Avila] that they would leave the most important affairs in her hands, and they were so satisfied with her responses that, as if it were law, they would obey her decisions." Punning on the Spanish term for her little room in San Millán, González Dávila continued: "Her *tribuna* was a tribunal where all were served."[44]

On at least one occasion Mari Díaz mediated a conflict between generations, a situation to which her own experiences perhaps made her particularly sensitive. Luis Pacheco, who entered the Premonstratensian house of Sancti Spiritus in his early twenties, almost immediately began to suffer the doubts and temptations common to young clerics unsure of their calling. When Luis left the monastery before the end of the first year of his novitiate, his father at first would not let him back into the house. Finally the older man appealed to the Mother Mari Díaz, to whom he was much devoted. Luis went to San Millán and discussed his problems with the venerable old woman, and then quickly resolved to return to the monastery. He spent the rest of his life there as a respected preacher.[45]

The beata could not exercise certain forms of spiritual leadership, for only men were permitted to preach, celebrate mass, and absolve sins. She could, however, offer advice and set an example, expressing in a less formal way the virtues of penitence and mortification emphasized by the Jesuits. Many held up the holy woman—pious, patient, and humble—as a model for female behavior. She also influenced male behavior, in particular, male clerical behavior, which, as we have seen, in this period was undergoing careful scrutiny and

44. González Dávila p. 299: "Tuvo tanta autoridad, con su buena y santa vida, con los de aquesta ciudad que los mayores negocios los dejaban en sus manos, y quedaban tan compuestos con las respuestas que daba, que, como si fuera ley, obedecían sus acuerdos. La tribuna era el tribunal donde despachaban todos."

45. "Información de la Vida," testimonies of Luis Pacheco and Diego de Espinosa.

redefinition. For example, Mari Díaz helped the young Baltasar Alvarez upon his arrival in Avila through her lofty example and her many connections. "For what she did," wrote de la Puente, "he came to be well-known and esteemed by all in the city."[46] Alvarez's biographer recalled a conversation between the priest and Mari Díaz concerning "the five sources of suffering," namely, the effects of climate, bodily pains, adverse conditions, dishonor and disdain, and the temptations of the spirit. The beata, de la Puente commented, "spoke from experience." Many years later Baltasar Alvarez raised these same points in discussions with young Jesuits.[47] Mari Díaz also influenced Julián de Avila, whose family she had known since her early days in las Vacas.

Although advanced in years during her period of cloister at San Millán, Mari Díaz maintained a special relationship with young people. The complex at San Millán housed los Niños de la Doctrina Cristiana, so she had many opportunities to interact with children. Like Juan de Avila, she taught the city's children their basic prayers. Years after Mari Díaz's death, many of Avila's priests recalled that they had had uplifting conversations with her during their years as seminarians. She also gathered around her a group of young women who came to the beata for their moral education and formed the core of a network of female spiritual support and communication which spanned two generations. Ana Reyes, whose parents brought her to Mari Díaz so that she might learn virtue at "such a good school," was a popular holy

46. Puente p. 60. This interesting passage indicates that the confessor-penitent relationship was often a mutual one: "Tuvo esta santa mujer buena dicha en topar con el Padre Baltasar, que le ayudó mucho en esta subida [to spiritual perfection]; y el Padre la tuvo en topar con ella, porque se ayudó mucho de su grande ejemplo; y por lo que ella hizo vino a ser muy conocido y estimado de todos en aquella ciudad."

47. Ibid. pp. 62–64. "Pero será de mucho provecho y consuelo poner aquí lo que yo oí contar al Padre Baltasar en una plática que hizo exhortándonos al padecer, por los grandes bienes que en ello había; y entre otras cosas nos dijo una conferencia que había tenido con la Madre Mari Díaz, sobre cinco fuentes que había de padecer sin culpa propia."

woman in the 1590s and in the early years of the seventeenth century.[48]

Like the Jesuits of San Gil, Mari Díaz served and taught "all the estates in Avila . . . from the great lords and prelates and ladies, down to the most humble."[49] Her life of radical austerity and enclosure at a time of genuine scarcity of food, space, and shelter linked her to the poor and homeless who flocked to Avila during the course of the sixteenth century. But the simple peasant and neighborhood holy woman also became the object of devotion for members of the city's highest aristocracy, especially noblewomen. The need of elite women for consolation and reassurance in a world filled with strict rules of etiquette, concern over reputation, and the death of loved ones was apparently boundless, as Teresa de Ahumada would discover. Mari Díaz—disinterested, otherworldly ascetic on the one hand and sympathetic "City Mother" on the other—was well suited to be a confidant to aristocratic women. At first the beata would leave her room in San Millán to visit the city's "principal ladies." When Alvarez ordered her to remain cloistered at the church, the noblewomen complained of his rigor but left their homes to visit her there. Her highborn devotees saw to it that her modest need for food was always fulfilled.

The death of Mari Díaz in November 1572 unified abulenses, ordinarily divided by social status and neighborhood. Although she died in total poverty, the holy woman was given one of the grandest funerals anyone in Avila could remember. The city council held a special session in which the regidores hailed her as a woman "so Christian and exemplary" and ordered that she be embalmed and buried in the

48. Fernández Valencia 1:285–289.
49. In eulogy to Mari Díaz, by cathedral chapter of Avila, quoted in Gerardo de San Juan de la Cruz, *Julián de Avila*, p. 202. Ana Reyes also testified that the beata gave "sanísimos consejos a todos a cada uno según su condición, estado y capacidad" (in "Información de la Vida").

church where she had lived with Christ as her "neighbor."[50] Individual gentlemen donated the wax, casket, and ornaments. In a truly amazing moment of fervor, the members of the cathedral chapter agreed to perform an elaborate funeral service completely free of charge. Huge crowds of people from all social levels attended the nine days of services and sermons and literally stormed the burial in an attempt to snatch pieces of the beata's clothing and body as relics. She was popularly acclaimed a saint.[51]

Even in death, Mother Mari Díaz provided the focus for a community-wide urban spirituality that emphasized service, charity, and Christian education and downplayed the stratification of the city along class lines. The same qualities that caused people to revere the beata in life and death had attracted Gaspar Daza and his supporters and led to her involvement with the programs for sacerdotal reform. In 1568 the trio of Gaspar Daza, Julián de Avila, and Mari Díaz made a proposal to the bishop of Avila, Alvaro de Mendoza. As los Niños de la Doctrina occupied only a small part of the complex at San Millán, they suggested converting the remainder of the buildings to a seminary for the training of the bishopric's priests, a provision mandated by the recent Council of Trent. Mendoza felt a deep personal devotion to Mari Díaz, influenced, perhaps, by that of his sister Doña María. In addition, as a prelate imbued with the Tridentine sense of the dignity of the bishop's office, he no doubt understood the

50. AHPA Actas Consist. libro 15, November 17, 1572. For Mari Díaz's references to Christ or to the Host as "vecino," see Puente p. 61; Gerardo de San Juan de la Cruz, *Julián de Avila*, p. 190. For a brilliant analysis of the meaning of this kind of eucharistic piety for late medieval women, see Bynum.

51. For the popular acclamation of saints, see Donald Weinstein and Rudolph M. Bell, *Saints and Society: The Two Worlds of Western Christendom, 1000–1700* (Chicago: University of Chicago Press, 1982) pp. 4–5, 141–163. For miracles of curing attributed to Mari Díaz after her death, see "Información de la Vida," testimonies of Julián de Avila, Gonzalo Pérez, and Pedro de Arteaga.

advantages to be gained by founding a seminary under direct episcopal jurisdiction. He therefore enthusiastically supported the project and allocated certain benefices in the bishopric of Avila for its completion. By 1572, although still awaiting papal approval, the College of San Millán operated with a rector and six poor boys.[52]

Daza and Julián de Avila had long been involved in educational and clerical reform and probably conceived of the College of San Millán. But to ensure the success of their project they needed the prestige, the popular appeal, and the connections with the city's aristocracy which their illiterate penitent Mari Díaz could provide. By 1568 the beata who spoke familiarly with God from her little space at San Millán distinguished the church as the site of direct religious experience. The involvement of a figure widely known and identified with youth, education, and clerical formation added legitimacy to an enterprise precisely designed to further these ends. Mari Díaz, mystic and holy woman, played a fundamental role in the creation of the first Tridentine seminary in Avila (and one of the first in all Spain), completing the drive for formalized clerical education begun some forty years earlier by Maestro Juan de Avila.

Between 1540 and 1570 religious innovation and experimentation flourished in Avila, as new ideas, some external, some indigenous, charged the city's spiritual atmosphere. Urban growth and social change over several decades set the stage for the emergence of an alternative vision of the religious life which developed alongside an older view, one that linked religious patronage and liturgical practice to the consolidation and perpetuation of the city's great dynasties. The institutions supported by Gaspar Daza and his circle and

---

52. Mendoza's letter asking for a relic of Mari Díaz's at the time of her death is reproduced in Gerardo de San Juan de la Cruz, *Julián de Avila*, p. 200. For College of San Millán, see Hernández pp. 136–144. AHN Clero leg. 245. ASA leg. 8, núm. 6.

the charismatic holy woman Mari Díaz, namely, the Children of Christian Doctrine, the Jesuit College of San Gil, and the Seminary of San Millán, envisioned a clergy dedicated to the ideal of providing service to a wide community through public preaching, poor relief, and the education of youth. The Society of Jesus in particular also stressed the spiritual formation of the individual through confession, penitence, and a program of systematic mental prayer. These new institutions received significant support from members of certain non-noble and recently ennobled families whose mercantile and ethnic backgrounds may previously have excluded them from political power and the system of religious patronage dominated by the city's traditional landed elite.

Teresa de Ahumada was deeply affected by Avila's reform movements of the mid-sixteenth century. She attempted to adapt the features of apostolic service, religious autonomy, mental prayer, and asceticism, and the reception of direct religious experience, to a female, monastic, and contemplative context. Her ability to combine the structure and discipline of institutional reform with the emotion and spiritual authority of the beata resulted in the reform of the Carmelite order, one of the great achievements of the Counter-Reformation, and Avila's most enduring legacy.

5

Saint Teresa of Jesus and
Carmelite Reform, 1560–1580

On August 24, 1562, Teresa de Ahumada and four other women officially entered the convent of San José as nuns of the primitive Carmelite rule. Gaspar Daza presided over the ceremony, reserving the Blessed Sacrament in the convent and bestowing upon the nuns their habits of coarse wool. Also present were other members of Avila's "reform party" who had helped to realize this foundation: Julián de Avila, Gonzalo de Aranda, and Francisco Salcedo.[1] It was entirely fitting that these people, some of whom had supported local reform institutions for the preceding fifteen years, be in attendance at the birth of a monastic order that emphasized many of their goals and values. Carmelite reform was deeply influenced by religious movements that had active represen-

1. *The Book of Her Life* (hereafter *Life*) [chapter] 36:[paragraphs] 1–6. Unless otherwise indicated, all English quotations are taken from the three-volume *Collected Works of St. Teresa of Avila*, trans. Kieran Kavanaugh and Otilio Rodríguez, 3 vols. (Washington, D.C.: Institute of Carmelite Studies, 1976–85). For original Spanish texts I have used Santa Teresa de Jesús, *Obras completas*, ed. Efrén de la Madre de Dios (Montalva) and Otger Steggink (Madrid: Editorial Católica, 1977). I use chapter and paragraph citations to facilitate reference to other editions. For a good recent biography in English see Stephen Clissold, *St. Teresa of Avila* (New York: Seabury, 1982).

tatives in mid-sixteenth century Avila. Ultimately, this reform proved compatible with the designs of the Council of Trent. In order to understand this, we must examine the life and conventual experience of the remarkable woman we now call Saint Teresa of Avila, and the social and liturgical principles by which she lived and which she came, eventually, to reject.

Early Years

Teresa de Ahumada y Cepeda was born in Avila on March 28, 1515, the daughter of Alonso Sánchez de Cepeda and his second wife, Doña Beatriz de Ahumada. Her paternal grandfather, Juan Sánchez, had been a wealthy converso merchant and tax farmer in Toledo. In 1485 the Inquisition of Toledo prosecuted him as a *judaizante*, a secret practitioner of Jewish customs. He was found guilty and sentenced to walk, along with his children, in penitential processions to Toledo's churches on seven consecutive Fridays. This information, long suppressed by biographers and Teresian scholars, became public only in the 1940s.[2]

Soon after this humiliating experience Juan Sánchez moved

2. Efrén de la Madre de Dios (Montalva) and Otger Steggink, *Santa Teresa y su tiempo* vol. 1 (Salamanca: Universidad Pontificia, 1982) pp. 45–48. The authors admit in a note that in the first edition of their book (*Tiempo y vida de Santa Teresa*, 1951) they suppressed this information "in order to mitigate the moral effect of this news on our surprised readers." Today the saint's converso origin is one of the most prevalent topics in Teresian scholarship. See, for example, Alonso Cortes, "Pleitos de los Cepeda," *Boletín de la Real Academia Española* 25 (1946): 85–110; Homero Serís, "Nueva genealogía de Santa Teresa," *Nueva Revista de Filología Hispánica* 10 (1956): 365–384; Francisco Márquez Villanueva, "Santa Teresa y el linaje," in his *Espiritualidad y literatura en el siglo XVI* (Madrid: Alfaguarra, 1968) pp. 141–152; José Gómez-Menor Fuentes, *El linaje familiar de Santa Teresa y de San Juan de la Cruz* (Salamanca: Gráficas Cervantes, 1970) pp. 25–37. See also Teófanes Egido, "The Historical Setting of St. Teresa's Life," *Carmelite Studies* 1 (1980): 122–182, and other works by this author.

his family from Toledo. By 1493 he was living in Avila, maintaining a "rich shop of woolens and silks" in the Cal de Andrín, the heart of the city's converso commercial district. The energetic and astute merchant worked to recover his fallen dignity, using his wealth and business connections to establish relations with Avila's important families, particularly ones whose members held positions on the city council. He lived in great luxury, like a gentleman, and arranged good marriages for his children. Around 1500 Juan Sánchez won a pleito de hidalguía entitling him to the status of gentleman and exemption from taxes.[3]

Few abulenses, however, were fooled as to the real, and "unclean," origins of "el toledano." In the value system of sixteenth-century Castile the possession of "honor," that complex set of qualities connoting gentle birth, purity of blood, reputation, and the attainment of certain social graces, ranked far above the possession of wealth. Money could buy the descendants of Juan Sánchez access to many of the privileges of upper-class society in Avila, but not necessarily full social acceptance. As several authors have noted, Teresa de Ahumada's identification of the features of "honor," especially obsession with one's family, as undue "attachment to the things of this world," and her rejection of these values as incompatible with the religious life, probably stemmed, at least in part, from her own problematic position as a member of a "tainted" parvenu family.[4]

Teresa and her eleven siblings and half-siblings grew up in an atmosphere of strict Catholic orthodoxy, raised by parents who were "virtuous and God-fearing."[5] There is no reason to doubt the sincerity of Alonso de Cepeda's devotion, despite his ethnic background. Doña Beatriz was from an Old Christian family in the province of Avila. As a girl Teresa loved popular chivalric novels and saints' lives. Her love of reading,

3. Cortes pp. 85–110. Montalva and Steggink 1:48–54.
4. For example, Egido pp. 142–154.
5. *Life* 1:1.

somewhat unusual for a woman of her day, remained with her for the rest of her life.[6] Tales of chivalry and romance from books, and perhaps also from the oral traditions of Avila's Reconquest history, influenced her early ideas. In one of the most famous anecdotes recounted in her autobiography, she told how she and her brother Rodrigo walked out of the city, determined to die as martyrs in the "land of the Moors," only to be met and brought home by one of their uncles. Military imagery and a sense of mission informs much of Saint Teresa's writing, as it does that of another great lover of chivalric novels, Ignatius Loyola.[7]

Her mother died in 1528, when Teresa was 13 years old, and her oldest sister married soon afterward. At this critical juncture between childhood and womanhood, Teresa, an outgoing and vivacious girl, fell in with female companions devoted to enhancing their own "honor." Teresa succumbed to peer pressure and also began to concern herself with her appearance, her dress, and her reputation. Forty years later the memory of this period of "sins" and "vanities" would still torment her. After Teresa had a brief flirtation with a male cousin, her worried father sent her to the Augustinian convent of Nuestra Señora de Gracia, which took in the daughters of well-to-do families as students. At this time Teresa "was strongly against . . . becoming a nun."[8]

6. *Life* 2:1: "I was so completely taken up with this reading that I didn't think I could be happy if I didn't have a new book." Victor García de la Concha, *El arte literario de Santa Teresa* (Barcelona: Ariel, 1978) pp. 47–54. Sara T. Nalle, "The Unknown Reader: Women and Literacy in Golden Age Spain" (Paper presented at the Fifth Berkshire Conference on the History of Women, Vassar College, Poughkeepsie, N.Y., June 1981).

7. *Life* 2:4. Egido p. 129. *The Way of Perfection* (Valladolid edition; hereafter *Way*) 3:1 offers one example among many of her use of military imagery: "It has seemed to me that what is necessary is . . . the approach of a lord when in time of war his land is overrun with enemies and he finds himself restricted on all sides. He withdraws to a city that he has well fortified and from there sometimes strikes his foe." Recall that Teresa spent her life in a walled city.

8. *Life* 2:8.

The eighteen-month stay at Nuestra Señora de Gracia changed her mind. Don Alonso probably selected the convent because it was the smallest and strictest in Avila, housing only fourteen professed nuns in 1532. This group of women, so different from her fashionable companions, impressed Teresa by their virtue and commitment to a life of prayer. The nun in charge of the novices and lay-pupils, Doña María Briceño, an intelligent and kind person who was much devoted to the religious life, provided a role model. However, the austerity and strict cloister practiced at Nuestra Señora de Gracia repelled Teresa as "altogether excessive."[9] When she decided to enter a convent, she chose the Carmelite house of la Encarnación. Some thirty years later, Teresa would leave la Encarnación to take up a religious life much like that of Nuestra Señora de Gracia, which she had rejected in her youth.

At la Encarnación

Doña Teresa de Ahumada entered the convent of la Encarnación on November 2, 1535, at the age of 20. One year later she made her formal profession as a nun of the Order of Our Lady of Mount Carmel. She would remain in this house for twenty-seven years.[10] La Encarnación was very different from Nuestra Señora de Gracia. Housing over one hundred nuns, it was one of the largest religious houses in Avila and a center for the city's upper classes. Teresa had a good friend in this convent, as well as several relatives and acquaintances. Most of the nuns at la Encarnación descended from the "hon-

9. Montalva and Steggink 1:149–154. Silverio de Santa Teresa, *Historia del Carmen Descalzo en España, Portugal, y América* vol. 1 (Burgos: El Monte Carmelo, 1935) pp. 103–111. Miguel Cerezo, "Santa Teresa de Jesús y la Madre María Briceño," *La Ciudad de Dios* 100 (1915): 107–120.
10. Montalva and Steggink 1:179–184.

ored and principal men of the city." While entering the religious life, they remained women of privilege.[11]

The "half-monastic, half-hidalgo world" of la Encarnación essentially reproduced in microcosm the conditions of abulense society and perpetuated the issues of class, caste, and "honor" which Teresa had thought to avoid by entering a convent. The nuns upheld distinctions of social rank and lineage, addressing one another by family names and, when appropriate, the title *Doña*. Officially nuns were ranked, like cathedral canons, by seniority, but in fact doñas enjoyed higher status within the convent than lower-born women. For example, whereas women of more limited economic means slept together in a common dormitory, the wealthy lived in their own quarters, enjoying both relative comfort and privacy. Many elite nuns had their own servants, or even slaves. These social differences, coupled with the pressures of rapid demographic expansion between 1540 and 1560, periodically produced bitter conflicts, such as the one settled by the Jesuit Miguel de Torres in 1550.[12]

Nuns took with them into the convent the values and codes of behavior of the aristocratic milieu in which most of them had been raised. Frivolous talk, character judgments, rumors, and petty intrigues filled the halls of la Encarnación. One's reputation stood paramount. Teresa would later confess that she, too, enjoyed "things that are usually esteemed in the world." She loved the religious life but "didn't like to suffer anything that seemed to be scorn."[13] She had assimilated the contemporary concern for prestige and reputation, although not completely, perhaps recognizing the shallow-

11. Nicolás González y González, *El monasterio de la Encarnación de Avila* vol. 1 (Avila: Caja Central de Ahorros y Préstamos, 1976) pp. 125–142.

12. Egido pp. 152ff. González 1:197–198. Otger Steggink, *La reforma del Carmelo español: La visita canónica del general Rubeo y su encuentro con Santa Teresa (1566–1567)* (Rome: Institutum Carmelitarum, 1965) pp. 289–311.

13. *Life* 7:2, 5:1.

ness of her claims to "honor" in the dynastic and ethnic senses. After a series of conversion experiences her ambivalence and guilt would explode in an intense and systematic reaction against *la honra negra*, "black honor." Teresa ultimately traced the social problems found in the convent of la Encarnación to the relaxation of the primitive Carmelite rule. Pope Eugenius IV had moderated the thirteenth-century rule of strict poverty, chastity, and obedience in a Bull of Mitigation of 1432. The modified rule did not require that nuns renounce their worldly possessions upon entering the convent, and in fact some nuns received considerable revenues from rural and urban property and other sources. The communal funds of the convent of la Encarnación were severely limited, and nuns without private incomes lived in a state of near destitution while other nuns maintained a style of life not very different from that enjoyed in the houses of their fathers and husbands.[14]

Teresa de Ahumada fully participated in this "laxity," but it was a participation that would eventually traumatize her. Cepeda money and connections guaranteed for her the title of *Doña*. Her father agreed to provide twenty-five fanegas of grain or two hundred gold ducats a year, a substantial if not lavish income, and pay the costs of entrance and profession at the convent. Perhaps the most notable feature of Doña Teresa's dowry was the profusion of items of cloth, including a bed with mattress and bedspread, blankets, sheets, pillows, cushions, and a rug, as well as habits, mantles, and cloaks of the choice woolens from which the Cepeda family derived much of its income.[15] Eventually fabric became for Teresa a tangible symbol of the vanities of the world. She would refer to unreformed Carmelites as religious "of the cloth" (del paño").

14. González 1:143–175. He makes distinctions between a wealthy and a poor convent, and between wealthy and poor nuns, pp. 268–269.

15. Silverio de Santa Teresa 1:154–155, for Teresa's dowry. She had enough income to sponsor celebrations on the feast of St. Joseph, her personal patron. *Life* 6:6–7.

Teresa had a large private apartment at la Encarnación, as befit a woman of the station to which her family aspired. Situated on two levels and connected by a staircase, it included facilities for cooking and eating. Her youngest sister, Doña Juana, and several other relatives lived with her there. The witty and popular Teresa de Ahumada attracted a circle of friends and kin members in the convent, and her parlor became their meeting place. It was here that this group would first discuss plans to restore the order's primitive rule.[16]

"In the convent where I was a nun," wrote Teresa in her autobiography, "there was no vow of enclosure."[17] This situation was not unique to la Encarnación. In sixteenth-century Avila, as elsewhere, nuns engaged in many forms of social intercourse even after entering a convent. Often they stayed with family members during periods of illness or financial necessity. Economic resources at la Encarnación became so strained that as many as fifty nuns at a time would live away from the convent.[18]

Teresa de Ahumada herself was absent from the convent for prolonged periods. Soon after professing, she fell ill with a terrible, crippling disease that kept her out of the convent for about two years. In other years she nursed her father during his final illness, made a pilgrimage to the shrine of Nuestra Señora de Guadalupe, and (from 1556 or 1557 to 1558) stayed in the house of Doña Guiomar de Ulloa.[19] In addition, monastic officials, recognizing her innate good humor, tact, and verbal skills, sent her on special assignments. "Some persons to whom the superiors couldn't say 'no' liked to have me in their company, and when urged the superiors urged me to go," she remembered.[20] We know from other sources that the aristocratic ladies of Avila often requested nuns as confi-

16. Silverio de Santa Teresa 1:173–174. González 1:244–245.
17. *Life* 4:5.
18. González 1:201.
19. Montalva and Steggink 1:239–268, 295–300, 311–317.
20. *Life* 32:9. For Teresa's visit with the recently widowed Doña Luisa de la Cerda in Toledo, see *Life* 34:1.

dants and companions, especially in times of distress such as after the death of a husband or child. These women, actual or potential benefactors of convents, undoubtedly came to expect certain services from female religious in exchange for needed donations. On several occasions Teresa fulfilled the role of consoling bereft or lonely ladies and acting as fundraiser for la Encarnación. She found herself deep within the web of patronage and clientage relations which bound together Avila's religious institutions and its oligarchy.

Conversion

The transformation of Doña Teresa de Ahumada to Teresa of Jesus occurred gradually, over a period of nearly twenty years. She did not undergo one dramatic experience of conversion, but rather took a series of steps by which she reached an understanding of God and self, culminating in the call to restore the original Carmelite rule. This process entailed a rejection of the social and religious system by which she lived at la Encarnación and, in its most intense stages, coincided with Avila's urban reform movements of the 1550s.

In 1538, afflicted with a paralyzing disease, Teresa left the convent she had recently entered and traveled to a mountain village in search of a cure. On the way she stayed with a pious uncle who gave her a copy of Francisco de Osuna's *Third Spiritual Alphabet*. This served as her introduction to the ideas and values of the *devotio moderna*, the spiritual flourishing of the late fifteenth and early sixteenth century, and the movement for spiritual renewal of the Church which had influenced Juan de Avila and so many others. The Franciscan Osuna's book, published in 1527, brought together many of the currents of northern European and Mediterranean spirituality then flowing through Spain. It introduced Teresa to the concept of recollection (*recogimiento*), which, broadly speaking, is a method of prayer based upon a passive or quiet negation of self in order to attain a pure reception of God's will.[21] Teresa's encounter with Osuna inspired her to begin upon a path of interior, mental, prayer which would bring her to a full commitment to God. It also redirected her love of reading away from adventure books and toward the abundant devotional literature of her day. Her autobiography is filled with references to the books she read over the years, which included the *Confessions* of St. Augustine, the *Vita Christi* of Ludolph of Saxony, the *Dialogue* of Catherine of Siena, and *The Ascent of Mount Zion* by Bernardino de Laredo. For many years unable to find a confessor who could understand or sympathize with her, Teresa had only those books as her teachers and directors.[22]

Teresa's return to la Encarnación in 1540, far from confirming her in her new spiritual goals, distracted her from them. She found herself once again concerned with matters of etiquette—correct social behavior with family members, nuns, and benefactors of the convent—and with enhancing her own reputation. "On the one hand, God was calling me," she would recall. "On the other hand, I was following the world."[23]

In the early 1540s Teresa received her first divine revelations; the revelations corresponded to the guilt and dissatisfaction she felt with her way of life, though at the time she was only partly aware of these feelings. During a conversation with a nun who frequently engaged her in gossip and frivolous talk, she saw "with the eyes of the soul" Christ

21. E. Allison Peers, *Studies in the Spanish Mystics* vol. 1 (London: Sheldon Press, 1927) pp. 79–131. Melquíades Andrés Martín, *Los recogidos: Nueva visión de la mística española (1500–1700)* (Madrid: FUE, 1976) pp. 107–167. Fidèle de Ros, *Un maître de Sainte Thérèse, le Père François d'Osuna: Sa vie, son oeuvre, sa doctrine spirituelle* (Paris: G. Beauchesne, 1936).

22. For Teresa's critique of confessors, see, for example, *Way* 4:1–5, *Life* 5:3.

23. *Life* 7:17. For an analysis of the effect of this indecision on her writing style, see Randolph Pope, *La autobiografía española hasta Torres Villaroel* (Bern: Herbert Land, 1974) pp. 47–55.

watching her actions with stern disapproval. Later she perceived this same nun accompanied by a large and hideous toad.[24] These experiences frightened and amazed her, but her attachment to the "things of the world"—honor, possessions, friends, family—remained strong. "It made me fearful to see how . . . bound I became so that I was unable to resolve to give myself entirely to God," she wrote.[25] She continued to suffer many years of frustration and "aridity" in prayer.

Finally, around 1555, Teresa de Ahumada, now 40 years old, began to have frequent and powerful spiritual experiences, hearing voices, seeing visions, and even achieving a coveted state of mystical Union with God. She came to recognize the connection between behavior and prayer and the reception of divine favors. "Now then, when I began to avoid occasions [of sin] and to devote myself to prayer, the Lord . . . started to grant me favors."[26] Within a short time she began to change her life, adopting certain ascetic customs that her fellow nuns regarded as "extreme," just as Teresa had considered the life inside the Augustinian convent of Nuestra Señora de Gracia of her youth.

Teresa's feelings of joy at approaching God were overshadowed by a deep anxiety, shared by many Catholics, that these experiences and visions came not from God, but from the devil. All Spain remembered the case of Magdalena de la Cruz, an abbess from Córdoba who claimed to have received divine revelations but was exposed in 1546 as a fraud.[27] At this point a fearful Teresa decided to call in an expert to examine the state of her soul. She turned to Gaspar Daza, the

24. *Life* 7:6–8.
25. *Life* 9:8.
26. *Life* 23:2.
27. Valentín Vázquez de Prada, "La reforma teresiana y la España de su tiempo," in *Santa Teresa en el IV centenario de la reforma carmelitana,* ed. José María Castro Calvo et al. (Barcelona: Universidad de Barcelona, 1963) pp. 81–96. For a recent examination of a case of fraudulent sanctity in early seventeenth-century Italy, see Judith C. Brown, *Immodest Acts: The Life of a Lesbian Nun in Renaissance Italy* (New York: Oxford University Press, 1986) especially ch. 4.

most respected preacher in Avila and coordinator of a local reform movement whose fame could not have failed to reach the walls of la Encarnación. Ties of kinship helped bring Daza to the Carmelite nun, for his associate Francisco Salcedo was related by marriage to the Sánchez de Cepeda family.

Daza, in fact, proved ill-equipped for the task. Partly because he was very busy at the time, and perhaps also because his pastoral experience consisted mainly of preaching to and hearing the confessions of large groups of people, he found himself unable to deal with this extraordinary case. Teresa's strange visions and voices, her bold statements about prayer followed by guilt-ridden expressions of self-deprecation, disquieted the well-known cleric. Like his colleagues Salcedo and Julián de Avila, he was uneasy with supernatural experience, which he had never known. Daza and Salcedo concluded, sadly, that Teresa de Ahumada suffered from demonic delusion, but they possessed a sufficient degree of perception and self-knowledge to recognize their own inability to treat cases of this sort.[28] Salcedo therefore referred Teresa de Ahumada to the men he acknowledged as master directors of the interior life, the Jesuits of the College of San Gil, the institution co-founded by his brother-in-law Hernando Alvarez del Aguila.[29]

In the Fathers of the Society of Jesus, many of whom were twenty years younger than her, Teresa finally found confessors who could understand her experiences, her emotions, and her method of prayer. The Society's founder, Ignatius Loyola, after all, had read and savored the same books of the European and Spanish *devotio moderna* which she had. Teresa's first Jesuit confessor, Diego de Cetina, immediately reversed Daza and Salcedo's decision, declaring her led by the

28. Montalva and Steggink 1:345–349.
29. *Life* 23:9: "I see that what happened was all for my greater good, that I might get to know and deal with people as holy as are those of the Society of Jesus."

spirit of God and encouraging her to continue on her path of prayer. He insisted, however, on a new behavioral and emotional foundation, introducing her to the Jesuit program of systematic mortification in which Baltasar Alvarez instructed Mari Díaz. Subsequent Jesuit confessors, including Alvarez, exercised a critical influence on Teresa's concepts of prayer and monastic administration.[30]

Thus Teresa de Ahumada became acquainted with the members of Avila's "reform party," Gaspar Daza and his associates and the Society of Jesus. They later became enthusiastic supporters of her reform movement, even the initially skeptical Daza. Baltasar Alvarez introduced her to his penitent Doña Guiomar de Ulloa, and at her house she met the ascetic holy persons Mari Díaz and Peter of Alcántara. They, too, would help to give shape and meaning to her spiritual impulses.[31]

Teresa's supernatural experiences and interactions with influential religious reformers brought about a fundamental transformation of her life. When her attachments to acquaintances at la Encarnación whom Baltasar Alvarez deemed unedifying persisted, the Jesuit suggested that she commend the matter to God, beseeching Him with the hymn "Veni, Creator." After a day spent in fervent prayer, Teresa began the hymn and experienced for the first time ecstatic rapture (arrobamiento). She heard the words "No longer do I want you to converse with men but with angels."[32] This powerful experience was liberating as well as mystical. Teresa de Ahumada, who for years had not dared to challenge the tenets of polite social convention, who had been unable even to heed the warnings of a stern Christ and loathsome toad, now found the strength to cut social ties and to commit herself

30. *Life* 23:16–18. Victoriano Larrañaga, *La espiritualidad de San Ignacio de Loyola: Estudio comparativo con la de Santa Teresa de Jesús* (Madrid: Casa de San Pablo, 1944) pp. 41–131.
31. *Life* 24:3–4. Montalva and Steggink 1:354–357.
32. *Life* 24:5–7.

totally to the service of God. Of the origin of this power she had no doubt: "The Lord gave me the freedom and strength to perform the task. . . . He gave the freedom that I with all the efforts of many years could not attain by myself."[33]

Over the next several years her visions and raptures occurred more frequently. Many who knew her, shocked by the change in her behavior, complained to her confessors. She felt God assure and comfort her, however, and people of undeniable spiritual prestige, notably the famous Jesuit Francis Borgia and Peter of Alcántara, defended her publicly. She received tender visions of the hands and face of Jesus, and, in 1559 or 1560, perceived her heart pierced, or transverberated, by an angel with a burning arrow. (This, the most celebrated of all her mystical experiences, was immortalized by the baroque sculptor Bernini.)[34] As she severed her attachments to things of the world, so her experience of Union with God deepened. She was replacing one form of "friendship" with another.[35]

Up to this point Teresa's experiences of prayer and divine favors had wrought dramatic changes within herself. But in 1561 she received a vision that elicited for the first time an organizational response to the issue of how to serve God and save souls. While at prayer one day she found herself in hell and saw for one terrifying moment "the place the devils had prepared there" for her. Teresa saw as her fate to be placed in a suffocating, constricted crevice, "like an oven," surrounded by foul mud and evil-looking reptiles. Here her body would endure pain but, more importantly, her soul would suffer waves of total and unending despair. Describing this scene nearly six years later, Teresa trembled as she wrote.[36]

Her immediate reaction was missionary in nature, imagin-

33. *Life* 24:7–10.
34. *Life* 29:13.
35. *Life* 8:5: "For mental prayer in my opinion is nothing else than an intimate sharing between friends."
36. *Life* 32:1–5.

ing how to save from even greater torments the "Lutherans" (the name by which many Spaniards referred to the French Calvinist Huguenots). She then began to feel a "pleasant restlessness," considering a way of doing penance for her sins and withdrawing from the world in order to merit God's blessings. Her conclusion would have enormous and unforeseen consequences. "I was thinking about what I could do for God, and I thought that the first thing was to follow the call to the religious life, which His Majesty had given me, by keeping my rule as perfectly as I could."[37] After twenty-five years at la Encarnación, Teresa de Ahumada was ready for a change.

She brought up this idea in discussion with the friends and relatives composing her private clique. They were enthusiastic, especially María de Ocampo, a cousin of Teresa's, who recommended that they establish a convent of discalced, or barefoot, nuns (that is, wearing sandals as a sign of humility), along the lines of the reform organized by Peter of Alcántara among the Franciscans. María de Ocampo later took the discalced habit as María Bautista and eventually served as the prioress of the Valladolid convent.[38] A few days following this discussion with her circle of supporters, after receiving communion, Teresa heard the mandate of God. "His Majesty earnestly commanded me to strive for this new monastery with all my powers, and He made great promises that it would be founded and that He would be highly served in it. He said that it should be called St. Joseph and that this saint would keep watch over us at one door, and Our Lady at the other, that Christ would remain with us, and that it would be a star shining with great splendor."[39] Compelled by divine command, Teresa of Jesus initiated the reform of the Carmelite order. She was reacting, in many ways, to the social and religious world of la Encarnación, and was influ-

37. *Life* 32:9.
38. *Life* 32:9–10. Montalva and Steggink 1:384–388.
39. *Life* 32:11.

enced by contemporary reform movements as experienced in sixteenth-century Avila.

Teresa's Idea of a Convent

The complicated process by which Teresa purchased a house in Avila and established it as a convent, all in strict secrecy, can be gleaned from her *Life* and standard biographies. My purpose here is to analyze the features of Discalced Carmelite reform and suggest the sources of inspiration for its conventual and devotional program in Teresa's response to life at la Encarnación and exposure to certain currents of religious reform.

Despite some initial hesitations, Teresa of Jesus decided to found the convent of San José in strict poverty, following a tradition of monastic reform reaching back at least as far as the mendicant movements of the twelfth and thirteenth centuries.[40] Her understanding of the primitive Carmelite rule led her to reject the regular, fixed incomes, usually tied to investments in land, which financially supported most religious houses. Teresa insisted that she and her nuns rely entirely on the fruits of their own labor and on God to move people to donate alms for their survival.[41]

Her determination to found a house in poverty quickly

40. Lester K. Little, *Religious Poverty and the Profit Economy in Medieval Europe* (Ithaca: Cornell University Press, 1978). Teresa made frequent reference to Saint Francis and Saint Clare in her works, for example, *Life* 33:13. The Poor Clares of las Gordillas, Avila, helped San José with alms. Julián de Avila, *Vida de Santa Teresa de Jesús*, ed. Vicente de la Fuente (Madrid: Antonio Pérez Dubrull, 1881), p. 188.

41. Teófanes Egido, "The Economic Concerns of Madre Teresa," *Carmelite Studies* 4 (1987): 151–172. José Antonio Alvarez Vázquez, "Financiación de las fundaciones teresianas," in *Actas del Congreso Internacional Teresiano* vol. 1, ed. Teófanes Egido Martínez et al. (Salamanca: El Congreso, 1983) pp. 249–285. For Teresa's understanding of the vow of poverty and the primitive Carmelite rule, see Efrén Montalva (de la Madre de Dios), "El ideal de Santa Teresa en la fundación de San José," *Carmelus* 10 (1963): 206–230, especially 219–230.

emerged as the single most controversial aspect of her reform, and consequently was the first issue discussed in *The Way of Perfection*, the fascinating handbook to the religious life she wrote for her nuns in 1565. "When I began to take the first steps toward founding this monastery . . . it was not my intention that there would be so much external austerity or that the house have no income," Teresa recounted. "On the contrary, I would have desired the possibility that nothing be lacking."[42] She undoubtedly recalled the hunger and deprivation suffered by many nuns at the overcrowded la Encarnación.

Her immediate motivation for insisting upon strict poverty and other forms of asceticism was, again, missionary. French Calvinism, on the rise since the death of Henry II in 1559, deeply disturbed Teresa, especially after the outbreak of the Wars of Religion in 1561. Anti-Protestant propaganda in Spain at this time was plentiful. She determined to do what she could to remedy the evil of Calvinism: "To follow the evangelical counsels as perfectly as I could and strive that these few persons who live here do the same. I did this trusting in the great goodness of God, who never fails to help anyone who is determined to give up everything for Him."[43]

Teresa of Jesus found inspiration in the Franciscan concept of voluntary poverty and asceticism and found a representative of this tradition in her own city in the mid-sixteenth century. He was Peter of Alcántara, a friar from Extremadura and a frequent visitor to Avila in the 1550s. He had initiated a reform among the Franciscans in 1540 based upon the austere lifestyle that he identified as the original intention of the saint of Assisi, an ideal that, in his opinion, had since degenerated. Alcántara's great personal sanctity, and the popular *Book of Prayer and Meditation*, a devotional tract he wrote which owed much to the school of Juan de Avila, gained him considerable spiritual prestige. In about 1559, during a trip to

42. *Way* 1:1.
43. *Way* 1:2. Vázquez de Prada p. 89. Egido, "Historical Setting," pp. 128–129.

the city, he stayed at the house of Doña Guiomar de Ulloa, who arranged a meeting with her friend and confidant the nun Teresa de Ahumada.[44]

The two understood each other immediately. Alcántara reassured the doubt-ridden Teresa of the divine origins of her mystical experiences. He frequently received visions and raptures himself, and recognized a kindred spirit. He was able also to convince Daza and Salcedo, who still feared that their penitent was being deceived by the devil. He later interceded with Bishop Alvaro de Mendoza on her behalf as well. From that time on, Peter of Alcántara was one of Teresa's staunchest supporters, first in upholding her personal integrity, and later in defending her idea of reform. He greatly impressed her by his extreme asceticism, surviving with a minimal amount of food, sleep, and shelter, wearing only sackcloth and sandals, and mortifying his flesh in some particularly distasteful ways. Teresa never went to these lengths, adhering more to the Jesuit model of moderate physical mortification. She remained, however, deeply attracted to the notion of primitive Franciscan poverty.[45]

Peter of Alcántara died in October of 1562, a few months after the opening of San José. Before his death he had written to Teresa several times, insisting that she found her convent in complete poverty and receive no fixed income whatsoever. In the winter of 1562–63, as Teresa faced continual pressure to modify her stand and accept rentas, she received a vision of the departed Franciscan: "He looked severe and told me only that I should by no means accept income and asked why I didn't want to take his advice."[46] This experience at first

44. Arcángel Barrado Manzano, *San Pedro de Alcántara (1499–1562): Estudio documentado y crítico de su vida* (Madrid: Editorial Cisneros, 1965). In her *Constitutions* no. 8, Teresa recommended that her nuns read Alcántara's book.

45. *Life* 27:16–18. *Way* 15:3: "I am rather strict when there is question of your doing too many penances. They can do harm to one's health if done without discretion."

46. *Life* 36:20.

startled her, and then strengthened her in her conviction. At that time she would accept no regular income at San José.

Asceticism and complete trust in God's providence also characterized the saintly Mari Díaz, whom Teresa of Jesus greatly admired. As she had Peter of Alcántara, Teresa met the holy woman through Doña Guiomar de Ulloa in the late 1550s, when Mari Díaz was working as a servant at the house of the aristocratic widow and steadily gaining prestige for her piety and wise words of advice. Teresa alluded to the edifying example set by Mari Díaz several times in her *Life* and letters.[47]

Once she had attained the beata's degree of confidence in God, Teresa found herself liberated from the burden of pleasing benefactors in order to secure donations for the convent, an activity in which she frequently engaged while at la Encarnación. She felt certain that God would move people's hearts to give alms to His religious. "Don't think, my sisters, that because you do not strive to please those who are in the world you will lack food," she assured the nuns of San José. "Leave this worrying to the One who can move all, for he is the Lord of money and of those who earn money."[48] And not having to "strive to please those who are in the world" gave Discalced Carmelites an autonomy from the world and from the social niceties that engulfed the nuns at la Encarnación. Like the Jesuits, they could achieve *santa libertad* (holy freedom). "True poverty brings with it overwhelming honor. Poverty that is chosen for God alone has no need of pleasing anyone but Him," she maintained. "It is clear that in having need of no one a person has many friends."[49]

47. *Life* 27:17. *Cartas* nos. 13 (1568), 58 (1574), 424 bis (1582), in *Obras completas*.
48. *Way* 2:1–2. This translation does not identify precisely, as does the original Spanish, the source of the money that usually supported religious houses: "Dejad ese cuidado al que los puede mover a todos, al que es *Señor de las rentas y de los renteros*" (emphasis mine). *The Book of Her Foundations* (hereafter *Foundations*) 3:48. *Constitutions* no. 9.
49. *Way* 2:6.

Teresa also quickly realized that any policy other than one of strict poverty would jeopardize her plans for an egalitarian convent in which the social differences that fragmented la Encarnación would never take hold. She welcomed but did not require dowries. The *Constitutions* she composed for the new convent stated explicitly that a novice whose personal qualities were acceptable "should not be turned away because she had no alms to give the house."[50] Eventually many wellborn women would take the discalced habit, but Teresa of Jesus could still proudly declare "I have never refused to accept anyone because of lack of money, provided I was satisfied with all the rest."[51] She rejected the principles of honor and lineage as incompatible with the religious life. For Teresa, obsession with one's reputation was a particularly insidious example of attachment to "things of the world." In her writings she frequently grappled with this issue, a compelling force both in social relations at la Encarnación and in her own life before her "second conversion."

"[The sister] who is from nobler lineage should be the one to speak least about her father. All the sisters must be equals."[52] At San José, Teresa abolished all distinctions based on social rank. In sharp contrast to the system at la Encarnación, nuns used only the title *Sister*, or *Mother*, in the case of the prioress. They abandoned all forms of polite address and family names. Even nuns from distinguished families adopted names in religion, consciously obscuring their origins as they collectively devoted themselves to God.

50. *Constitutions* no. 21. Otger Steggink, *Experiencia y realismo en Santa Teresa y San Juan de la Cruz* (Madrid: Editorial de Espiritualidad, 1974) pp. 93–98. Egido, "Historical Setting" p. 131.

51. *Foundations* 27:13.

52. *Way* 27:6. This chapter is titled "Deals with the great love our Lord showed us in the first words of the Our Father and how important it is for those who truly want to be children [literally, *daughters*] of God to pay no attention whatsoever to lineage." Also, *Way* 12:4: "Take careful note of interior stirrings, especially if they have to do with the privileges of rank (*mayorías*)."

A dramatic recognition of Teresa's own transformation from *señora* to humble, discalced nun appears in a statement by the Dominican Pedro Ibáñez, an influential supporter: "This lady is now known as Teresa of Jesus: formerly she was Doña Teresa de Ahumada."[53] Ibáñez recognized, as did Teresa, that through conversion she had "become" a different person.

The nun who had lived more than twenty-five years in private quarters, surrounded by servants and kin, now insisted that all the convent's property and resources be held in common. As a young nun at la Encarnación, Teresa de Ahumada had resented being assigned menial tasks. The new woman, Teresa of Jesus, prescribed manual labor for all and gladly participated in the chores of the convent, even as prioress. She gaily reminded her nuns that a life of devotion takes place in the kitchen as well as in the choir: "The Lord walks among the pots and pans."[54]

For Teresa, the key to the proper observance of the religious life lay in one's total indifference to the things of this world. She recognized that for many the most difficult aspect of "detachment" (*desasimiento*) involved severing ties with family members. In a society in which the concerns of kin and dynasty played a ubiquitous role in an individual's existence and even identity, this was a genuine sacrifice. After her conversion, Teresa, who herself shared strong bonds of affection with her numerous relatives, bitterly criticized the pervasive obsession with lineage. Her position as *conversa* may well have partly inspired her strong preference for merit above pedigree.[55]

53. "Documents illustrative of the Life, Works, and Virtues of Saint Teresa," published in *The Complete Works of Saint Teresa of Jesus*, trans. E. Allison Peers, vol. 3 (New York: Sheed and Ward, 1946) p. 313. *Life* 28:13: "For I saw clearly that by these experiences I was at once changed."
54. *Foundations* 5:8. *Constitutions* no. 22: "The Mother Prioress should be the first on the list for sweeping so that she might give good example to all." Later the Discalced Carmelites accepted lay sisters to help with the manual labor, but no more than three per convent.
55. Márquez Villanueva pp. 160–171. Egido, "Historical Setting" pp. 133–134, 150–158, 160–167.

Teresa explained some of her reasons for restricting intercourse between nuns and family members in her *Constitutions*. "As much as they can, the sisters should avoid a great deal of conversation with relatives [for] . . . they will find it difficult to avoid talking to them about worldly things."[56] The nuns at la Encarnación (including Teresa de Ahumada) had spent many hours chatting and gossiping with their kin, and she had witnessed the unedifying results. In addition, she believed that inordinate regard for one's family led to the love of honor and the creation of bonds between convent and dynasty which inhibited nuns from dedicating themselves wholly to the service of God. For her it was essential that Carmelites maintain their autonomy. This entailed a departure from the system in which religious engaged in a series of obligations with benefactors in exchange for donations. "You are removed from this here," she commented in *The Way of Perfection*. "Since everything is held in common and no one can have any special comfort . . . you are freed from trying to please [relatives] on this account, for you know that it is the Lord who provides for all in common."[57] For Teresa, the connection between a convent's reception of fixed incomes and accommodation of kin members, and a convent's loss of spiritual freedom, was all too apparent.

In a society that exalted the attributes of birth and blood, Teresa of Jesus proposed an alternative system of values which was religious and fundamentally egalitarian. Nobles might brag of their honors and privileges in sixteenth-century Castile, but as true contemplatives realized, "in the kingdom without end they [would] have nothing to gain from this."[58] Genuine honor resided in a person's moral virtues and willingness to serve God. This included, of course, those whom the world considered "lowly" or "tainted," such as the descendants of Jews. "Well, it could not be because I am from

56. *Constitutions* no. 19.
57. *Way* 9:1. This chapter is titled "On how good it is for those who have left the world to flee from relatives and how they find truer friends."
58. *Way* 36:10.

the nobility that He has given me such honor," she once concluded briskly.[59]

Perhaps the most dramatic expression of Teresa's rejection of lineage occurred during her foundation of a discalced convent in Toledo in 1570. She had met with considerable opposition in the city because of the converso background of her principal backers there. A divine command resolved the conflict in her own mind. "While I was at the monastery in Toledo and some were advising me that I shouldn't give a burying-place to anyone who had not belonged to the nobility the Lord said to me, 'You will grow very foolish, daughter, if you look to the world's laws. Fix your eyes on me, poor and despised by the world. Will the great ones of the world, perhaps, be great before me? Or, are you to be esteemed for lineage or for virtue?' "[60]

Like many of the great religious reformers, Teresa replaced honor with its reverse, humility, as the value most appropriate to the spiritual life. This concern influenced many of her decisions involving the organization of San José. For example, anxious to avoid the development of a grand but unmanageable institution like la Encarnación, she placed limits on the number of nuns at her convent, restricting acceptance to thirteen. Like Francis of Assisi she envisioned a humble and ascetic lifestyle in the imitation of Christ. "The houses must be poor and small in every way," she insisted. "Let us in some

59. *Foundations* 27:12. Here the original Spanish is (intentionally?) more ambiguous: "Pues no sería por ser de sangre ilustre el hacerme honra." "Illustrious blood" could refer to either class or ethnicity. This passage is one of several cited as evidence that Teresa was aware of her converso heritage.

60. *Spiritual Testimonies* no. 5. See also *Foundations* 15:15. Rosa Rossi, *Teresa de Avila: Biografía de una escritora* (Barcelona: Icaria, 1984) pp. 54–59, 64, 84, 232, 272, 280, 286, 288. Américo Castro suggested that Teresa's writings reveal "el anhelo de compensar con un linaje espiritual la carencia de uno socialmente estimable" (the desire to compensate with a spiritual lineage the lack of a socially respectable lineage); *Teresa la Santa y otros ensayos* (Madrid: Alianza, 1982) pp. 26–28. A similar point about her ability to "transcend honor" is made by Daniel de Pablo Maroto, "Resonancias históricas de 'Camino de Perfección,' " in *Actas del Congreso Internacional Teresiano* 1:51–58.

manner resemble our King, who had no house but the stable in Bethlehem where He was born and the cross where He died."[61] Like the Jesuits, she opted for a small but select group of religious chosen for their virtues, detachment from worldly things, maturity, ability to read, and commitment to the religious life. But Teresa also had personal reasons for insisting on a small house. She had seen how unchecked expansion at la Encarnación had rendered the convent nearly impossible to administer, a problem she would directly confront as its prioress from 1571 to 1574.[62]

Even more disturbing to her was the degeneration of the large convent into cliques or factions of nuns. Fear of factionalism and "special friendships" informs much of her writing. She warned that excessive love between nuns could lead to greater dangers than those posed by too little love. Her *Constitutions* state bluntly: "The sisters should not have particular friendships but should include all in their love for one another, as Christ often commanded His disciples."[63] It is important to recall that Teresa de Ahumada had led one of the many cliques at la Encarnación. She now viewed suppression of special affections as an effective form of penance.

In keeping with the tradition of imitating the humility and poverty of Christ, the Carmelites of San José were required to wear simple brown habits of the coarsest and cheapest cloth. Doña Teresa de Ahumada had entered la Encarnación with many fine articles of fabric. Teresa of Jesus now stipulated, "Straw-filled sacks will be used for mattresses. . . . No hangings should be used except, in cases of necessity. . . . Let there be no carpeting or cushions, except in the church."[64] Again, she completely rejected the features of her former life of comfort and "worldliness."

As she stressed voluntary poverty and the ascetic lifestyle

61. *Way* 2:9. The number was later increased but kept under twenty.
62. González 1:251–294.
63. *Constitutions* no. 28. *On Making the Visitation* no. 19.
64. *Constitutions* nos. 12–13.

it entailed, Teresa also emphasized the fulfillment of the other traditional monastic vows according to the original Carmelite rule. In one of the most striking departures from her life at la Encarnación she insisted upon enclosure, fundamental to a strict interpretation of the vow of chastity, and limited the opportunities for nuns to receive visitors at the convent.[65] While this policy may seem repressive and patriarchal, for Teresa voluntarily chosen enclosure had a potentially liberating effect. Her years of experience at la Encarnación convinced her that the communication of nuns with secular society inevitably brought "worldliness" and temptations of various sorts. More critically, "freedom" of movement and intercourse led to a loss of the most important type of "freedom," spiritual autonomy from social obligations and special interests. Nuns who remained cloistered were, paradoxically, more "free" than those who interacted with, and thereby became entangled in the demands of, the world. Thus, she came to the same conclusion as the Council of Trent regarding enclosure for female religious, but for different reasons.[66]

65. *Constitutions* nos. 15–20. On questions of chastity and enclosure for women in this period see Ruth P. Liebowitz, "Virgins in the Service of Christ: The Dispute over an Active Apostolate for Women during the Counter-Reformation," in *Women of Spirit: Female Leadership in the Jewish and Christian Traditions,* ed. Rosemary Ruether and Eleanor McLaughlin (New York: Simon and Schuster, 1979) pp. 131–152.

66. For Teresa's use of the term *libertad* see, for example, *Life* 7:3, *Way* 9:4. Rossi pp. 140, 212, 238. A. D. Wright, *The Counter-Reformation: Catholic Europe and the Non-Christian World* (New York: St. Martin's Press, 1982) pp. 47–49. For a similar analysis of the social function of chastity among learned women in Renaissance Italy, see Margaret L. King, "Book-Lined Cells: Women and Humanism in the Early Italian Renaissance," in *Beyond Their Sex: Learned Women of the European Past,* ed. Patricia H. Labalme (New York: New York University Press, 1984) pp. 66–90. King suggests that "when learned women (or men for that matter) themselves chose a celibate life, they did so at least in part because they sought psychic freedom; when, on the other hand, men urged chastity upon learned women, they did so at least in part to constrain them. . . . In the first case, chastity is a source of pride and independence; in the second, it is an instrument of repression" (p. 78).

Teresa's own experience of the third monastic vow, obedience, was a complex one. She worked hard over the years to maintain the appearance of obedience to church officials, monastic superiors, and confessors, even when their directives seemed to contradict one another, what she believed to be the will of God, or her own common sense and understanding of the religious life. In an age that, as we shall see, was fraught with dangers for charismatic spiritual people, especially women, Teresa's efforts to fulfill her mission as monastic reformer, writer, and advocate of mental prayer while preserving the appearance of obedience to traditional religious authorities may have been her most difficult endeavor.[67]

Nevertheless, Teresa stressed obedience as an authentic foundation of the monastic life and urged her nuns to surrender their wills as an effective form of mortification and self-discipline. Here, too, the acceptance of an externally imposed obligation could have an internal, spiritually cleansing, and liberating quality, in her formulation. The prologue to her *Book of Foundations*, written toward the end of her life, offers a glimpse of Teresa's thinking on the virtue of obedience:

> I have seen through experience the great good that comes to a soul when it does not turn aside from obedience. It is through this practice that I think one advances in virtue and gains humility. In obedience lies security against that dread . . . that we might stray from the path to heaven. Here one finds the quietude that is so precious in souls desiring to please God. For if they have truly resigned themselves through the practice of this holy obedience and surrendered the intellect to it,

67. For what follows, see the penetrating study by J. Mary Luti, "Teresa of Avila, Maestra Espiritual" (Ph.D. diss., Boston College, 1987) pp. 212–259. Luti describes Teresa's performance of obedience as "often characterized by tension, ambiguity and a high degree of strategic manipulation" (p. 218). See also Tomás Alvarez, *Santa Teresa y la Iglesia* (Burgos: El Monte Carmelo, 1980) pp. 34–59.

not desiring any other opinion than their confessor's (or, if they are religious, their superiors') the devil will cease attacking with his continual disturbances. . . . Those who practice obedience remember that they resolutely surrendered their own will to God's will, using submission to the one who stands in God's place as a means to this surrender.

She concluded the prologue by recounting that, because of ill health—she was 58 years old when she began the work— she never expected to be able to finish the book. But God assured her, telling her in prayer, "Daughter, obedience gives strength."[68]

In the mid-sixteenth century, male clerical reformers such as Juan de Avila and his followers in Avila and the Jesuits responded to pastoral needs by developing apostolic programs based upon public preaching, confession, poor relief, and religious education. Teresa of Jesus envisioned her task as no less apostolic or missionary. As we have seen, Teresa defended her decision to found San José in strict poverty in missionary terms. She sought to rectify the Calvinist religious violence in France and the Low Countries, using the means available to her as a woman and a contemplative, namely, prayer and penitence. If secular clergymen engaged in active apostolates, Discalced Carmelite women maintained an apostolate of prayer, which to Teresa was as powerful a weapon against heresy as preaching, and more effective than the sword.[69] Complete observance of the primitive Car-

68. *Foundations* Prologue:1–2, also 5:5–13. *Way* 18:7. "Where there is no obedience there are no nuns."
69. *Way* 1:2: "Human forces are not sufficient to stop the spread of this fire caused by these heretics [even though people have tried to see if with the force of arms they could remedy all the evil that is making such progress]." The passage in brackets, with its implicit criticism of Philip II's policies, was censored out of some editions. Jodi Bilinkoff, "Private Prayer, Public Apostolate: The Mission of Teresa of Avila" (Paper delivered at the Seventh Berkshire Conference on the History of Women, Wellesley College, Wellesley, Mass., June 1987). Luti pp. 116–120, 141–149. Not coincidentally, the first Discalced Carmelite convents founded outside the Iberian peninsula

melite rule made for the more perfect service of God, which would in some way compensate for the insults dealt Him by the "heretics."

A lover of religious images and pictures, she was deeply shocked by Calvinist iconoclasm. "It indeed appears that they do not love the Lord," she reasoned, "for if they loved Him they would rejoice to see a portrait of Him."[70] For Teresa, the foundation of a new convent or monastery, especially once the house was sanctified for worship, directly countered the Protestant campaign of destruction. "It is the greatest consolation to see one church more where the Blessed Sacrament is preserved," especially "at a time so dangerous, on account of those Lutherans."[71] A clear sense of mission motivated the almost incredible activity of her last twenty years, during which she founded seventeen religious houses.

Teresa conceived her foundational program as a response to Calvinist destruction, but also as a support system for the clerical reformers of her day. She saw as one of the most important tasks of Discalced Carmelites continual prayer for the "servants of God," the men who actively defended the Church but had to work in the world with all its snares and temptations. A testimony written in 1596 by her niece Teresita, who was also a Discalced Carmelite nun, clearly describes the saint's concern for the secular clergy. "Being a woman and prevented from benefiting them [the lost souls in

were established in France and Flanders. Julián Urquiza, *La Beata Ana de San Bartolomé y la transmisión del espíritu teresiano* (Rome: Institutum Carmelitarum, 1977). Emmanuel Renault, *L'Idéal apostolique des Carmélites selon Thérèse d'Avila* (Paris: Desclee de Brouwer, 1981).

70. *Life* 9:6. For Calvinist religious violence, see Natalie Z. Davis, "The Rites of Violence," in her *Society and Culture in Early Modern France* (Stanford: Stanford University Press, 1975) pp. 152–187. For contrasting Catholic and Protestant attitudes toward religious images, see Margaret R. Miles, *Image as Insight: Visual Understanding in Western Christianity and Secular Culture* (Boston: Beacon Press, 1985) pp. 95–125.

71. *Foundations* 3:10.

France] as she would have liked," Teresita said of her aunt, "she determined to undertake this work in order to make war on the heretics with her prayers and her life and with the prayers and lives of her nuns and to help Catholics by means of spiritual exercises and continued prayer."[72] Teresa herself claimed that if the prayers of her nuns bolstered priests in their struggles with the world and encouraged them in the service of God, then the nuns "shall be fighting for Him even though [they] are very cloistered."[73]

The little girl who had dreamed of dying for the faith as a martyr had at last found her life's mission. It depended upon prayer, especially interior, mental, prayer, as its major weapon. As we shall see, Teresa's emphasis on mental prayer became one of the most controversial and, in the eyes of many, one of the most dangerous aspects of her program.

Carmelite reform offered a fundamental critique of the religious system closely associated with the values of honor and family by which Doña Teresa de Ahumada lived for over twenty-five years. As Teresa of Jesus she sought to establish an alternative conventual order, detached from the things of the world. She drew from many religious traditions for her ideas and policies: voluntary poverty and asceticism, egalitarianism, religious autonomy, separation from family and society, strict obedience and enclosure, and an intense sense of mission, and she found models in the clerical and ascetic movements active in Avila in the mid-sixteenth century. Juan de Avila and his local followers, the holy people Peter of Alcántara and Mari Díaz, and the Jesuits of the College of San

72. *Complete Works* 3:363.
73. *Way* 3:5. Vázquez de Prada p. 91. Diego Yepes, in his biography of Saint Teresa, noted that upon hearing of the death of Juan de Avila, the nun began to weep bitterly. When asked the reason for this grief, if she did not think that his soul was now rejoicing in God, she replied, "De eso estoy yo cierto, mas lo que me da pena es que pierde la Iglesia de Dios una gran columna, y muchas almas un grande amparo" (of this I am certain, but what gives me pain is that the Church of God loses a great pillar, and many souls a great source of help). Quoted in *Obras completas del Santo Maestro Juan de Avila* vol. 1, ed. Luis Sala Balust (Madrid: Editorial Católica, 1970) p. 346.

Gil influenced her and became valued supporters. Their support was critical because at its inception, the convent of San José met with stiff resistance.

Carmelite Reform: Controversy and Acceptance

In the early hours of August 24, 1562, Teresa of Jesus left la Encarnación in order to receive, along with four local women, the discalced habit at San José. Carefully selected for their virtue and commitment, they all possessed close connections with Avila's "reform party." Peter of Alcántara sent his penitent Antonia del Espíritu Santo. Ursula de los Santos came through the recommendation of Gaspar Daza. María de la Cruz, like Mari Díaz, had worked in the house of Doña Guiomar de Ulloa as a servant. María de San José was the sister of Julián de Avila. True to Teresa's ideal, none of these "poor orphans" brought with her a dowry, although Antonia del Espíritu Santo donated money as alms.[74] Teresa recorded her feelings at this moment, the culmination of many months of planning, in her autobiography: "I was so intensely happy that I was as though outside myself, in deep prayer."[75] Her sense of contentment and peace was short-lived, however, as within a few hours a commotion (*alboroto*) put the fate of the new convent in doubt.

According to Teresa's biographer Julián de Avila, the residents of the neighborhood around San José greeted the house with joy, but the *principales de la ciudad* demanded its immediate dissolution.[76] The municipal officials of Avila, the corregidor and regidores, firmly opposed the new convent. Their most serious objection stemmed from Teresa's intention to found San José in complete poverty, without rentas, and depend entirely upon alms, donations, and the

74. *Life* 36:5–6.
75. *Life* 36:6.
76. Julián de Avila, *Vida de Santa Teresa de Jesús* pp. 209–210.

Portrait of Teresa of Jesus by Fray Juan de la Miseria, 1576, in convent of San José, Seville. Photograph courtesy of Editorial de Espiritualidad, Madrid.

fruits of the nuns' own labor. They also expressed apprehension over whether the nuns would enclose within their garden a public fountain and whether the nuns would fail to make the mortgage payments due the city. As some historians have suggested, these issues may have been pretexts. Their real interest lay in blocking a religious house founded in poverty.[77]

The regidores, meeting in council the day after San José's inauguration, complained that the city already housed a large number of monasteries and convents, many of them impoverished. If houses of orders "noted for their sanctity, piety, authority and great example to the city" could not maintain themselves, how could this new convent, established with the "novel" idea of accepting no private property ("no tener ni poder tener propios algunos")? They claimed that another convent would place too great a strain on already limited municipal resources. The city simply could not meet the *demandas* made by the nuns of San José.[78]

But perhaps another factor accounted for the vehemence with which the authorities opposed Teresa's idea of a convent. City councilors and other principales de la ciudad were precisely the kind of people who placed their daughters in la Encarnación and the other aristocratic convents of its type. Some of the regidores serving in 1562 (notably Pedro del Aguila and Alonso Guiera) descended, in fact, from families that had long associations with this house.[79] As we have seen, while communal funds at la Encarnación were limited, on an individual basis, nuns often lived very well. Rich and powerful men provided their daughters with lavish dowries and fixed incomes that ensured their support for the remainder of their lives. Elites frequently founded capellanías in

77. AHPA Actas Consist. libro 12, 1562–1563. See also Jesús Molinero, "Actas municipales de Avila sobre la fundación del monasterio de San José por Santa Teresa," BAH 66 (1915): 155–185. Fidel Fita, "El gran pleito de Santa Teresa contra el ayuntamiento de Avila," BAH 66 (1915): 266–281.

78. Molinero pp. 156, 161.

79. González 1:127ff. AHPA Actas Consist. libro 12, 1562–1563.

exchange for prayers for their souls, or entered into other forms of mutual obligations with the convent. Their wives and widows came to rely upon nuns, frequently released from cloister, as advisors, confidants, and companions. Avila's principales, in short, possessed a vested interest in perpetuating the socio-religious system that Teresa of Jesus had come to reject. Elites undoubtedly realized that if upper-class women accepted the discalced reform, they might see their daughters starve or, perhaps even worse in their eyes, sever the bonds of family and honor essential to the ordering of life as they knew it. The twice-yearly payments they made to a convent guaranteed its continued association with, even dependence on, the world—that is, on *them*. Teresa's idea of a convent further threatened the exclusive rule of Avila's aristocracy by representing both religious poverty and religious autonomy. The city fathers were prepared to begin legal proceedings against the nuns of San José.

Opposition to Carmelite reform also emerged from several quarters because of Teresa's emphasis on mental, as opposed to vocal, prayer, and because of her claims to divine revelations. As Teresa recognized, she was operating during particularly "rough times" ("tiempos recios").[80] Teresa's conversion experiences and reform activities coincided with an intense reaction in Spanish society against any form of expression associated with religious heterodoxy, especially on the part of women. That Carmelite reform managed to survive and even flourish in this period of repression is due, in large part, to the sheer force of personality of the woman called Teresa of Jesus.

In the early decades of the sixteenth century Spain remained open to the manifold spiritual movements originating in northern Europe and Italy and from within its own culture. Cardinal Cisneros, who played a critical role in fos-

---

80. *Life* 33:5. Julián de Avila, *Vida de Santa Teresa de Jesús* p. 182: "Andaban los tiempos peligrosos, no fuese menester tratar de ello la Inquisición."

tering the translation, publication, and diffusion of devotional works in Castilian, possessed a particular interest in mystical theology and encouraged writers of mystical tracts and holy people who underwent direct supernatural experiences. Many of these were women.[81] He did much to create an atmosphere receptive to various forms of spirituality and to new styles of religious life, open to both women and men. Beginning around 1555, however, the religious climate within Spain underwent a radical change, due to both internal and external developments.[82] As Protestantism established itself more fully in Germany, the Netherlands, England, and Geneva, Spaniards recognized a greater and more implacable enemy of the faith than had heretofore been imagined. The leaders of the Church gathered at Trent to define and confirm the features of Catholic theology and practice. The rigid Philip II replaced the more cosmopolitan Charles V as head of the earth's largest empire.

In 1559 groups of so-called Lutherans were discovered in Seville and Valladolid. Members of the Valladolid coterie, led by the famous Dr. Agustín Cazalla, even visited the palace of Doña Guiomar de Ulloa in nearby Avila, though without any apparent success in gaining adherents. This revelation of heresy in the very heartland of Catholic orthodoxy set off a wave of panic throughout Spanish society. As Philip attempted to isolate Spain from external influences, the In-

81. Marcel Bataillon, *Erasmo y España* (Mexico: Fondo de Cultura Económica, 1950) pp. 68–71. Vicente Beltrán de Heredia, "Directrices de la espiritualidad dominicana en Castilla durante las primeras décadas del siglo XVI," in *Corrientes espirituales en la España de siglo XVI: Trabajos* (Barcelona: Juan Flors, 1963) pp. 177–202.

82. For what follows, see Bataillon pp. 699–737; Juan Ignacio Gutiérrez Nieto, "La discriminación de los conversos y la tibetización de Castilla por Felipe II," *Revista de la Universidad Complutense* 22 (1975): 99–129. Ricardo García-Villoslada, "Felipe II y la Contrarreforma Católica," *Historia de la Iglesia en España* vol. 3, pt. 2, ed. José Luis González Novalín (Madrid: Editorial Católica, 1979) pp. 5–106. Joseph Pérez, "Cultura y sociedad en tiempo de Santa Teresa," *Actas del Congreso Internacional Teresiano* 1:31–40.

quisition renewed its efforts to ferret out and punish dissenters, frequently focusing on conversos and women. Teresa, of course, qualified in both categories.

Correctly identifying printing as the most effective means of spreading new and potentially dangerous ideas, the Grand Inquisitor Fernando de Valdés published an Index of Prohibited Books. Within a short time, nearly all religious literature in the vernacular, including many works by Erasmus and the *Audi, filia* of Maestro Avila, had been censored or suppressed. In general, only technical theological works in Latin, inaccessible to women and others without formal education, remained.[83] "When they forbade the reading of many books in the vernacular, I felt that prohibition very much," Teresa recalled in her autobiography. But she heard God comfort her, saying, "Don't be sad, for I shall give you a living book."[84]

Sides now formed in an ongoing, although not always explicitly defined, debate between *letrados*, "learned men" with academic training in theology, and *espirituales* or *experimentados*, spiritual people who exalted the knowledge gained through direct religious experience and prayer.[85] The dominant letrado faction mistrusted any form of spirituality not grounded in a firm understanding of dogma, convinced that the espirituales' emphasis on private mental prayer served as a screen for Protestant pietism and other forms of heterodox belief, and as a means of avoiding the control of the Church hierarchy. They stressed the outward ceremonies and duties of the Church and, for members of religious orders, vocal choral prayer as the appropriate and traditional manner of praising God. Dominicans, firmly in

83. Luis Sala Balust, "Vicisitudes del 'Audi, filia,'" in Juan de Avila, *Obras completas* 1:186–213. For Valladolid heretics in Avila, see José Luis González Novalín, "Teresa de Jesús y el Luteranismo en España," *Actas del Congreso Internacional Teresiano* 1:351–387.
84. *Life* 26:6.
85. For this section I am much indebted to Alvarez pp. 115–145.

control of the theology faculty at the University of Salamanca and of the Inquisition, figured prominently in the letrado group.[86] Teresa had responded to the same fears of heresy which motivated the inquisitors, her desire to defend God against the insults of the "Lutherans" compelling her first to personal and then to organizational goals. The forms that her response took, however—visions, voices, raptures, and the "quiet" experience of God through recollection and mental prayer—provoked the intense suspicion of letrados. They feared that unregulated mystical experience would lead to heterodox opinions, especially on the part of women, widely thought to be weaker, more impressionable, and more vulnerable to the snares of the devil than men.[87] Francisco Salcedo, who had initially traced Teresa's revelations to demonic influences, had studied at the Dominican University of Santo Tomás in Avila.

Teresa of Jesus therefore found herself on the side of the espirituales, people who disdained technical theology as dry and detached from the spirit of religion and considered letrados frankly incapable of understanding supernatural experiences, of which they had no notion. In attempting to explain her method of prayer, for example, she concluded, "As much as I desire to speak clearly about these matters of prayer, they

---

86. For example, Juan de la Cruz, O.P., "Diálogo sobre la necesidad y provecho de la oración vocal," in *Tratados espirituales*, ed. Vicente Beltrán de Heredia (Madrid: Editorial Católica, 1962). I owe this reference to Ronald E. Surtz.

87. The letrado-spiritual conflict and its difficulties for women have been treated extensively, especially by Spanish Carmelite historians. See, for example, Alvarez pp. 115–145; Teófanes Egido, "Santa Teresa y su condición de mujer," *Surge* 40 (1982): 258–275; Otger Steggink, "Teresa de Jesús, mujer y mística ante la teología y los teólogos," *Carmelus* 29 (1982): 111–129; Antonio Comas, "Espirituales, letrados, y confesores en Santa Teresa de Jesús," in *Homenaje a Jaime Vicens Vives* vol. 2, ed. J. Maluquer de Motes (Barcelona: Universidad de Barcelona, 1967) pp. 85–99; Ulrich Dobhan, "Teresa de Jesús y la emancipación de la mujer," in *Actas del Congreso Internacional Teresiano* 1:121–136. See also Luti pp. 94–157.

will be really obscure for anyone who has not had experience."[88] Her indefatigable supporter in this position was Peter of Alcántara, the author of popular devotional works of the type disparaged by the inquisitor Valdés as "theology for carpenters' wives."[89]

Teresa's insistence on mental prayer, institutionalized for Discalced Carmelites in her *Constitutions* and eloquently defended in *The Way of Perfection*, caused her as many problems as her refusal to accept fixed incomes.[90] Given the political and religious climate of the times, many members of the Church hierarchy, even those sympathetic to other features of her program, felt intensely uncomfortable with her revelations and methods of prayer, so potentially dangerous, especially for women. Avila's city councilmen, the principales of the city, may have recognized that the emphasis on mental over vocal prayer also undermined the system of capellanías and prayers chanted for the souls of benefactors and their kin. Perhaps like Bernardo Robles and his descendants they wanted to be able to verify the terms of their endowments, to be sure that religious fulfilled their duties to their patrons. Teresa was more interested in her duty to God. The special junta that met on August 30, 1562, to discuss the fate of the convent of San José consisted of Avila's regidores and of the city's leading letrados, two groups almost unanimously opposed to Teresa's decision to live in complete poverty and her devotional program based upon mental prayer. Only the passionate plea for moderation by the young

88. *Life* 10:9. Maximiliano Herraiz, "Teresa de Jesús, Maestra de Experiencia," *El Monte Carmelo* 88 (1980): 270–304.

89. Quoted in Alvarez p. 128. Valdés was referring to the work of Luis de Granada, the disciple and biographer of Juan de Avila and an important source for Alcántara. For Alcántara's fiercely polemical letters to Teresa against the letrados, see pp. 122–123.

90. *Constitutions* no. 7. *Way* 16:1ff. Julián de Avila boasted that Discalced Carmelites "tienen de constitución de tener horas señaladas para la oración mental, lo cual no hay en las demás ordenes" (are required by their constitution to have hours designated for mental prayer, [a requirement] no other religious order has) (*Vida de Santa Teresa de Jesús* pp. 198–199).

Dominican Domingo Báñez restrained city officials from dissolving the convent that day.[91]

In the first six months of San José's existence, as Avila's corregidor attempted to close down the convent, Avila's regidores brought legal proceedings against the convent at the Royal Council in Madrid, and most of the learned members of Avila's established religious orders condemned the convent as a dangerous "novelty," only a few people dared to take the side of the discalced nuns. These people mainly belonged to the city's "reform party," which was active in the foundation of other "novel" religious institutions in the mid-sixteenth century. By 1562 Gaspar Daza and his circle commanded considerable respect in Avila. Peter of Alcántara had attained immense spiritual prestige on the local level. The combined forces of institutionalized apostolic reform and the appeal of the charismatic holy man succeeded in convincing the bishop of Avila of the divine origin of Teresa of Jesus' commission and the righteousness of her reform program. This finally swung the balance in favor of the nuns of San José, although not before a period of "trials and persecution."[92]

Alcántara's most critical task was convincing Teresa's confessor, the Jesuit Baltasar Alvarez, and Gaspar Daza of the correctness of her cause. Once persuaded of the divine, as opposed to demonic, origins of Teresa's revelations, Daza and the members of his circle, particularly Francisco Salcedo, Julián de Avila, and Gonzalo de Aranda, became untiring supporters of her reform.[93] The men so active in contemporary clerical and educational movements realized that Teresa's program had goals that corresponded to many of their own apostolic goals. Like Mari Díaz in her retreat at San

91. Julián de Avila, *Vida de Santa Teresa de Jesús* p. 214. *Life* 36:15. AHPA Actas Consist. libro 12, 1562–1563. Paulino Alvarez, *Santa Teresa y el P. Báñez* (Madrid: Impr. de Lezcano, 1882) pp. 162–164.

92. *Life* 36:18.

93. Montalva and Steggink 1:419–422.

Millán, San José was located in the heart of Avila's commercial district, a "desert in the city." The dramatic contrast between the bustle of the streets and market and the quiet detachment of the "poor little nuns" made for a powerful example to the rest of the population. The nuns of San José remained at once cloistered and highly visible, a living sermon. Gaspar Daza and Julián de Avila knew the value of good sermons.

Teresa's reform found early support and drew recruits among conversos, including members of her own family. This was true in Avila and also in other places in which she founded convents between 1567 and her death in 1582.[94] Some conversos may have been attracted by the inherent egalitarianism of the discalced message and its emphasis on private internalized prayer. Others may have seen an opportunity to participate in the values of Old Christian society— values they had assimilated from a society from which they had often been barred. Over time Teresa reluctantly allowed some convents, particularly those located in rural areas and less likely to receive alms, to accept rentas and the capellanías and family chapels that so often accompanied them. She refused, however, to demand proof of *limpieza de sangre*

94. The *Foundations* provide several cases of converso benefactors of Discalced Carmelite houses, and describe the difficulties they and Teresa encountered from the Old Christian establishment. In Toledo she negotiated with the merchant Alonso Alvarez and faced many critics "since that family was not from the nobility [*no eran ilustres y cavalleros*], although the family was very good, regardless of its social status" (15:15). The patroness of the Alba de Tormes convent, Teresa de Laíz (or Layz), was the wife of Francisco de Velázquez, the accountant and estate manager of the duke of Alba, a typical position for a converso. Nevertheless, Teresa hastened to assure her readers that the benefactress was "a daughter of noble parents, hidalgos of pure blood" ("de padres nobles, muy hijos de algo y de limpia sangre") (20:2). She almost slipped when describing the fortitude of her Burgos patroness, Catalina de Tolosa, commenting, "How much more courage for doing great things do the servants of God have than do those of high nobility if they are not His servants." She then quickly added, "Although she, being of noble descent, is not without much nobility in her background" ("Aunque ella no le falta mucha limpieza en el suyo, que es muy hija de algo") (31:30).

from prospective nuns. Conversos thus had the chance to place their daughters in convents and endow chaplaincies for family members, social and spiritual privileges denied them by most other religious orders, which by the mid-sixteenth century required the infamous purity of blood statutes for entrance.[95]

When Teresa began to extend her reform movement throughout Castile she gravitated toward commercial centers such as Medina del Campo, Toledo, Segovia, and Seville, which possessed the population and economic resources to support religious houses, and the type of people—merchants, professionals, bureaucrats—to whom her programs appealed. This is not to imply that only middle-class conversos became Discalced Carmelites or supported the reform. As time went on and Teresa first gained acceptance and then popularity, more and more aristocrats became involved, sometimes to her chagrin. But during her lifetime her movement remained to a considerable extent bourgeois and urban in nature.[96] In Avila by this time, Gaspar Daza and his associates had been involved in such movements for over fifteen years.

Ultimately, however, the most important supporter of Teresa of Jesus and her reform, especially during those critical early years, was the bishop of Avila, Alvaro de Mendoza. Julián de Avila once stated bluntly, "If the bishop of Avila had not been so disposed towards the Mother, I do not doubt that [city officials] would have closed down [the convent] that

95. The unreformed or Calced Carmelites adopted measures prohibiting entrance to the descendants of Moors and Jews in their *Constitutions* of 1566. Steggink, *Reforma del Carmelo español*, pp. 205, 264; Albert A. Sicroff, *Los estatutos de limpieza de sangre: Controversias entre los siglos XV y XVII* (Madrid: Taurus, 1985) pp. 92–122; Egido, "Historical Setting," pp. 132–133, 158, 166–168; Márquez Villanueva pp. 164–170. Márquez comments that Teresa now had to face a new problem "en evitar que sus monasterios vinieran a constituir monumentos a la vanidad de los conversos" (trying to keep her convents from becoming monuments to the vanity of the conversos) (p. 170).

96. Márquez Villaneuva pp. 152–164. Egido, "Historical Setting," pp. 163–164.

very first day."[97] Bishop Mendoza felt a personal attraction to Teresa of Jesus and her goals but was also much aware of the dignity of his office. In the long run Carmelite reform and other religious movements of the mid-sixteenth century helped to enhance the prestige and power of the episcopacy, an explicit goal of the Council of Trent.

Peter of Alcántara initially had difficulty dispelling Bishop Mendoza's doubts about Teresa of Jesus, particularly in regard to her interpretation of the monastic vow of poverty. However, once convinced by Alcántara and by Daza, one of his closest advisors on the cathedral chapter, as to Teresa's divine inspiration, and after talking with Teresa herself, Mendoza became a steadfast supporter of Carmelite reform. The bishop was much devoted to charismatic holy people. Both he and his pious sister Doña María de Mendoza gave moral and financial assistance to Teresa, Doña María sponsoring the foundation of a discalced convent in their native city of Valladolid in 1568. Although transferred to the see of Palencia in 1577, Don Alvaro requested burial at the main altar of the convent of San José in Avila, whose success he had done so much to ensure.[98]

When Teresa received papal permission to found a convent in February 1562, the house was placed under the jurisdiction of the bishop of Avila rather than the hierarchy of the Carmelite order. This made for uncomfortable and at times violent conflicts between the calced and discalced branches of the order, finally officially separated by the pope in 1580. It did, however, extend the authority of the bishop in the period after the Council of Trent, when prelates began to take an active role in the religious life of their sees. The city council of Avila felt compelled to drop its lawsuit against the convent of San José after six months, claiming lack of funds; the

97. Julián de Avila, *Vida de Santa Teresa de Jesús* p. 216: "Si el Obispo de Avila no estuviera tan de parte de la Madre, no dudo sino de que de hecho la acabaron aquel día."
98. Silverio de Santa Teresa 2:108–132.

Anonymous sixteenth-century portrait of Bishop Alvaro de Mendoza, in convent of San José, Avila. Photograph courtesy of Editorial de Espiritualidad, Madrid.

immense influence of the Mendoza family at the court of Philip II may also have been a decisive factor here.[99] By that time the initial furor had died down and the convent, although continuing to refuse rentas, more or less became an accepted addition to Avila's urban landscape.

Alvaro de Mendoza believed in Teresa, and he believed that her reform movement served the greater glory of God. He may also have recognized that her monastic program expressed many of the values held by the Tridentine Fathers. Independent of the Council of Trent she had insisted upon strict cloister for women. She carefully limited the number of nuns and instituted a long and selective novitiate, and a minimum age for entrance of 17. Teresa was always careful to stress the importance of obedience and orthodox thinking, exalting as an effective form of penance and self-mastery subjugation to the will of monastic authorities, confessors, and prelates, regarded as God's representatives on earth. She enthusiastically embraced all the ceremonies and sacraments of the Church. And, as we have seen, her motivation was fundamentally missionary. She prepared to do battle against the heretics on her own terms, but in tandem with the theologians and the preachers and the soldiers of Philip II, not in conflict with them. Her goals were theirs.[100]

The origins of Teresa's ideas on prayer lay in the religious ferment of late medieval Europe and the Erasmian milieu of early sixteenth-century Spain. She was deeply influenced by the devotional literature disseminated by Cardinal Cisneros. This included works by authors such as Francisco de Osuna and Juan de Avila which described an inner spiritual life oriented toward the quiet reception of God and the progressive disengagement from the world as opposed to the vocal recitation of prayer and accommodation of the dynastic needs of patrons.

99. Montalva and Steggink 1:430–439. The city apparently never completely paid its lawyer Alonso de Robledo for his services in the "pleito de la monjas de San Josef." AHPA Actas Consist. libro 12, 1562–1563.
100. Alvarez, *Santa Teresa y la Iglesia* pp. 36–41.

Saint Teresa of Jesus and Carmelite Reform

By the time Teresa reached spiritual maturity in the mid-sixteenth century, her society, obsessed with the threat of heterodoxy from within and Protestantism from without, regarded these earlier trends with intense suspicion. The mystical experiences and methods of prayer of this nun, who was, after all, a woman and a conversa, remained under close scrutiny during her lifetime, her writings minutely examined, censored, and withheld from publication until after her death.[101]

However, the articulation of her program for a renewed monastic life, inspired in part by clerical and ascetic movements in mid-sixteenth-century Avila, corresponded perfectly to the new, Tridentine, mood. Teresa of Jesus died exclaiming, "At the end, Lord, I am a daughter of the Church."[102] Her church was redefining its values, insisting upon the exclusive control of a newly energized clergy. Carmelite reform contributed to the effort to make female convents "less a particular part of lay society, and more a part of the hierarchical and professional church."[103] Endorsement and integration of these Tridentine goals assured the success of Teresa's monastic reform during her lifetime. Social and economic changes in subsequent generations would modify this view of the religious life, and bring an end to the period of spiritual innovation in Avila.

101. Enrique Llamas Martínez, *Santa Teresa de Jesús y la Inquisición española* (Madrid: CSIC, 1972) pp. 221–488. For publication histories of Saint Teresa's works, see the excellent studies in *Introducción a la lectura de Santa Teresa*, ed. Alberto Barrientos (Madrid: Editorial de Espiritualidad, 1978).

102. Ismael Bengoechea, "¿Por fin, muero hija de la Iglesia?" in *Teresa de Jesús: Mujer, Cristiana, Maestra* (Madrid: Editorial de Espiritualidad, 1982) pp. 243–255. See also Egido's discussion of this quote in the context of Teresa's program for a "praying Counterreformation" ("Historical Setting" pp. 130–131).

103. Wright p. 48. He notes that the attempt to reform female houses in this way did not generally succeed, but he cites the Discalced Carmelites and Poor Clares as exceptions (p. 205). This view is shared by Jean Delumeau, *Catholicism between Luther and Voltaire: A New View of the Counter-Reformation* (Philadelphia: Westminster Press, 1977) pp. 36–37.

6

Avila after Saint Teresa,
1580–1620

By the time of Teresa of Jesus' death in 1582, the character of her native city had already begun to change. In Avila, as elsewhere, a period of dynamic growth and development in the first half of the sixteenth century gave way to a series of economic and demographic crises in the last decades of that century and the first of the next. With economic decline and stagnation as a backdrop, religious life in Avila also underwent fundamental transformations of mood and expression. A return to the traditional, dynastic style of founding monastic institutions by members of Avila's oligarchy, an impressive gain in the power and influence of the city's bishops, and a deepening suspicion of claims to mystical experience and of the exercise of private mental prayer, all signaled a sharp departure from the movements for religious autonomy of the mid-sixteenth century. By 1620, the majestic walls of Avila served as a cruel metaphor for a city closing ranks. Its population declining, its economic structure shaken, its noble families on the move to Madrid, Avila was destined never again to experience a golden age like that of the sixteenth century, the age of Saint Teresa.

Avila after Saint Teresa

"La Necesidad de la Ciudad:"
Economic and Demographic Crises

The litany of economic and demographic ills plaguing Castile in the late sixteenth and early seventeenth centuries is well known to those familiar with the history of Spain. Crises in the wool trade, drought, famine, and plague took their toll in Avila as in neighboring cities and regions.[1] My purpose in this section, therefore, is not to provide a detailed analysis of Avila's economic problems, but rather to describe the atmosphere of dearth and disease in which certain social and religious changes took place.

Avila's population reached its peak in 1572, when the city was home to between twelve thousand and thirteen thousand people. Hard times began in the late 1560s, as the overcrowded city began to feel the effects of a series of severe droughts. Shortage of water in this dry, rocky zone was a perennial problem, but in these years the situation seems to have worsened. Appeals for aid became strident and frequent, as individuals and religious institutions petitioned the city council for water. At San Gil, for example, situated on top of a hill, the Jesuits had trouble retaining water and suf-

---

1. Of the extensive literature on this topic, see J. H. Elliott, "The Decline of Spain," *Past and Present* 20 (1961): 52–75; idem, "Self-Perception and Decline in Early Seventeenth Century Spain," *Past and Present* 74 (1977): 41–61; Henry Kamen, "The Decline of Spain: A Historical Myth?" *Past and Present* 81 (1978): 24–50, and a rejoinder by J. I. Israel, *Past and Present* 91 (1981): 170–180; Pierre Vilar, "El tiempo del Quijote," in his *Crecimiento y desarrollo: Economía e historia, reflexiones sobre el caso español* (Barcelona: Ariel, 1964) pp. 332–346. For similar conditions in neighboring cities, see Michael Weisser, "The Decline of Castile Revisited: The Case of Toledo," *Journal of European Economic History* 2 (1973): 614–640; Angel García Sanz, *Desarrollo y crisis del Antiguo Régimen en Castilla la Vieja: Economía y sociedad en tierras de Segovia de 1500 a 1814* (Madrid: Akal, 1977). For a recent formulation of the theory of a "general crisis" that affected all of Europe in this period, see the introduction by Geoffrey Parker to *The General Crisis of the Seventeenth Century*, ed. Geoffrey Parker and Lesley M. Smith (London: Routledge and Kegan Paul, 1985) pp. 1–25.

fered terribly.[2] The regidores desperately sought remedies for the parched city, authorizing committees of experts to find new wells and springs, build new pipes, requisition privately owned fountains, and even construct a reservoir for snow.[3] Most of these measures proved ineffective.

In the midst of these dry years, Avila experienced the first in a series of agricultural crises. Avila's demographic growth, like that of most European cities at the time, depended upon the city's ability to feed an expanding population with food-stuffs, particularly cereals, from the surrounding country-side. In the spring of 1571, locusts attacked the crops in the province of Avila. The city's regidores, who usually decided policy only after exhaustive debate, on this occasion moved quickly, sending money and representatives to the belea-guered villages (including a priest to "conjure" the locusts). Despite the government's efforts, the pests destroyed most of that year's harvest. Faced with widespread famine, munici-pal officials moved to place ceilings on the price of bread. Ultimately, they spent most of the money they had received from the Royal Council for this emergency on food distribu-tion and relief for the poor.[4] As the bad times continued, Avila's city councilors would find themselves increasingly called upon to play the role of dispensers of charity. And as municipal revenues diminished, they were often hard-pressed to accomplish this task.

Avila's poor felt the effects of food shortages more swiftly

2. AHN Jesuitas leg. 489–1, núm. 23. AHPA Actas Consist. leg. 278, June–September 1567, September 1568.

3. AHPA Actas Consist. libro 12, 1563; leg. 278, 1567–1568; leg. 279, 1589; libro 32, 1616–1617.

4. Ibid. libro 15, April 1571. For "conjuring" of insect pests, see William A. Christian, Jr., *Local Religion in Sixteenth Century Spain* (Princeton: Princeton University Press, 1981) pp. 28–31. For economic relations be-tween Castilian cities and their hinterlands, see Weisser, "Decline"; and García Sanz, *Desarrollo*; and Bartolomé Bennassar, *Valladolid en el Siglo de Oro: Una ciudad de Castilla y su entorno agrario en el siglo XVI* (Vallado-lid: Ayuntamiento, 1983). Carla Rahn Phillips, *Ciudad Real, 1500–1700: Growth, Crisis, and Readjustment in the Spanish Economy* (Cambridge: Harvard University Press, 1979).

and keenly than anyone else. In addition, depression in the Castilian wool trade dealt a crushing blow to the city's large merchant and artisan classes. As many historians have noted, the Castilian manufacture of wool, centered in Segovia, faced serious challenges from foreign competitors beginning in the late 1580s. Entrepreneurs, especially from the Low Countries, exported large quantities of raw wool from Castile, produced textiles more cheaply abroad, and then flooded Spain with imported cloth, effectively destroying the country's native industries. Avila's wool economy, tied to that of Segovia, also experienced severe contraction. For the hundreds of abulenses, male and female, employed in the carding, combing, fulling, spinning, weaving, dyeing, shearing, marketing, and transport of wool, this could mean social and economic disaster, a descent into the ranks of the urban poor.[5]

When plague hit Avila in 1599–1600 as part of a terrible epidemic that ravaged most of Castile, an underemployed, undernourished population lay particularly vulnerable to its effects. Disease first broke out in nearby villages in the spring of 1599, and municipal authorities worked frantically to keep it from entering the city. They closed the city gates and refused admission to outsiders, especially those from infected areas. They ordered the city to be cleaned "with much care." But these measures failed to keep out a variety of illnesses: bubonic plague, tertian fevers, typhus.[6] By August

5. For abulenses employed in the wool trade, see Serafín de Tapia, "Estructura ocupacional de Avila en el siglo XVI," in *El pasado histórico de Castilla y León* vol. 2, *Edad Moderna*, ed. Jesús Crespo Redondo (Burgos: Junta de Castilla y León, 1983) pp. 201–223. AGS Exp. Hac. leg. 50–3. For crises in the Castilian wool trade, see works cited above by Elliott, Israel, Vilar, Weisser, García Sanz, Bennassar, Phillips, and the particularly informative article by Jean-Paul Le Flem, "Vraies et fausses splendeurs de l'industrie textile ségovienne (vers 1460–vers 1650)," in *Produzione, commercio e consumo dei panni di Lana (nei secoli XII–XVIII)*, ed. Marco Spallanzani (Florence: Olschki, 1976) pp. 525–536.

6. Bartolomé Bennassar, *Recherches sur les grandes épidémies dans le nord de l'Espagne à la fin du XVIe siècle: Problèmes de documentation et de méthode* (Paris: SEVPEN, 1969) pp. 112–129. See Serafín de Tapia, "Las

of that year, the corregidor reported the rapid spread of disease in the city, almost exclusively among the poorest of the urban population. He identified the causes of their miserable state very precisely. These "greatly impoverished people" suffered from hunger "because in the preceding year bread was so scarce and because they lack[ed] work due to the halt in production of cloth."[7]

Through the winter of 1599–1600, Avila's city councilors, having organized a board of health, tried to control the contagion. Municipal doctors isolated the sick in homes or in hospitals, and buried the dead outside the city gates. At the suggestion of the regidor Luis Pacheco, officials began to collect and burn the clothing and blankets of the ill. This action necessitated the distribution of new clothing, for these wretched people had been left naked on their beds "and the weather [was] so cold that many [died] from this cause." Death and emigration resulted in a decrease of some 12 percent in the city's population during these dreadful plague years.[8]

At the turn of the seventeenth century Avila's demographic decline accelerated. The establishment of a permanent court in Madrid gradually lured away many of Avila's merchants, professionals, and, especially, nobles. Philip II's 1562 decision produced dire consequences for many Castilian cities, especially ones such as Valladolid, Segovia, and Toledo, in which the cortes had met and other functions of royal government had previously taken place. As hard times continued in Avila,

fuentes demográficas y el potencial humano de Avila en el siglo XVI," *Cuadernos Abulenses* 2 (1984): 74–75, for population loss in poor neighborhoods.

7. Bennassar, *Grandes épidémies* pp. 123ff: "Gente pobrísima que con el año pasado que fue tan esteril y corto de pan y faltándoles en que trabajar por haber cesado el obraje de los paños padescen anbre."

8. AHPA Actas Consist. libro 25, January 27, 1600. "Son gente tan pobre y miserable que dando la ropa que les cogió el mal se van desnudo a la cama y otros quedan sin ellos y sin cama y el tiempo es tan frío como se ve muchos morir de el."

its aristocrats increasingly opted for the charm, the glitter, and the opportunities for political advancement offered by the capital, and moved there with their families, servants, and retainers.[9] Wills and pious endowments written in Madrid and deposited in Avila during the seventeenth century indicate that for many nobles, Avila still represented their *patria chica*, the land of their ancestors, where they wished to be buried and to commend their souls. But they preferred to spend their lives, and their money, at court.[10]

Avila lost another important segment of its population at the expulsion of the moriscos in 1610–11. This ethnic minority of nominally Christianized Moors had grown considerably since the arrival in the province of some nine hundred families from Granada in December 1570. Their relocation at that time was part of a royal effort to resettle Granada's large morisco population after an abortive uprising in the Alpujarras region. Of these moriscos, many moved to the city of Avila, most settling in the southern district of la Trinidad, joining the smaller and older community of *convertidos* who had converted en masse from Islam to Catholicism in 1502. The Crown's decision in April 1609 to expel from Spain all persons of Moorish descent exacerbated Avila's already precarious financial and demographic situation. While the Granadan moriscos worked mainly in humble transport jobs and as artisans, many of the more integrated *convertidos* played a crucial role in the city's economy, owning shops and businesses and supporting a disproportionate share of the munic-

9. On the growth of Madrid see José del Corral, *El Madrid de los Austrias* (Madrid: Avapiés, 1983) pp. 71–86; Fernand Braudel, *The Mediterranean and the Mediterranean World in the Age of Philip II* vol. 1 (New York: Harper and Row, 1972) pp. 344–345, 351–352. Antonio Domínguez Ortiz, *La sociedad española en el siglo XVII* vol. 1 (Madrid: CSIC, 1963) p. 150: "La decadencia de Avila era también antigua ... para una ciudad eminentemente nobilaria, de escasa base económica, el éxodo de una parte de su nobleza a la Corte tuvo que resultar fatal." See Tapia, "Estructura" pp. 216, 222–223, for declining numbers of domestic servants in Avila during the seventeenth century.

10. See, for example, AHN Clero libro 562.

ipal tax burden. Avila thus lost hundreds of hard-working and, in some cases, wealthy citizens at its moment of greatest economic need. The 350 morisco families that left the city in 1610–11 composed about 14 percent of Avila's total population.[11]

A look at Avila in the years 1616–17 reveals the once proud fortress city in full decline. For these two years the city suffered from intense drought. During May of both 1616 and 1617, the city council and the cathedral chapter pooled their resources in order to sponsor processions with the Marian image of Nuestra Señora de Sonsoles, "because of the great lack of water" ("por la gran necesidad que hay de agua").[12] In 1616, municipal officials appealed to the king for a contribution of two hundred ducats, as they could not afford to hire a doctor for the city. Neither did they have the funds to clean the streets or repair fountains for that year's Corpus Christi celebrations. Traditionally, this holiday had offered an occasion for opulent display and great civic pride.[13]

March 1616 found Avila's regidores fully recognizing a major source of the city's economic woes and proposing measures to reverse an already well-established trend. The licentiate Palacios reported that certain individuals representing "outsiders" ("personas forasteras") were buying up wool in that city and its environs. This made supplies so scarce, he said, "that we have come to lose completely the production

11. Tapia, "Fuentes" pp. 71, 78–79; idem, "Estructura" pp. 209–210, 217–219. See also Henri Lapeyre, Geographie de l'Espagne morisque (Paris: SEVPEN, 1959) pp. 162–164. He estimates that an additional 460 families were expelled from the province of Avila in January 1611.

12. AHPA Actas Consist. libro 32, 1616–1617. Processions were also made with the image of Nuestra Señora de la Soterraña, housed in the basilica of San Vicente, in cases of drought and disease. Bartolomé Fernández Valencia, Historia y grandezas del insigne templo . . . de . . . San Vicente vol. 2 (Avila, 1676) pp. 167–183. AHPA libros 2454–2455.

13. AHPA Actas Consist. libro 32, December, March 1616. For the elaborate Corpus Christi celebrations taking place in Madrid around this time, see José Deleito y Piñuela, La vida religiosa española bajo el cuarto Felipe (Madrid: Espasa-Calpe, 1963) pp. 168–180; del Corral pp. 103–116.

of the coarse and fine cloth that was made in this city, which sustained many poor people." The councilors agreed to prohibit, on pain of fine and a year of exile, the sale of wool to anyone not authorized by the city government to buy it.[14] But Avila's economic problems continued. On October 3, 1617, the city councilors discussed preparations for the feast day of their own Blessed Teresa of Jesus, who had been beatified three years earlier. They planned some torch-lit processions and dances but warned that all this would have to occur at moderate cost, "given the hardship of the city and its great poverty."[15] The municipality of Avila, thus, had become too poor even to celebrate its own saints properly. The city that had bustled with some twelve thousand inhabitants in the 1560s counted around six thousand in 1632.[16] Avila soon descended to the rank of small, provincial town.

A Return to Dynastic Foundation

In this atmosphere of social and economic contraction, aspects of religious life in Avila underwent some significant changes. The city's aristocracy now reemerged as a major force in the establishment and control of religious institutions, particularly monastic houses. In the mid-sixteenth century, innovative foundations such as the Children of

14. AHPA Actas Consist. libro 32, March 26, 1616. "Se ha venido a perder totalmente el trato de la labor de las rajas y paños que se hacían en esta ciudad en lo cual sostenaba mucha gente pobre."

15. Ibid. October 3, 1617. "Todo a poca costa supuesto la necesidad de la ciudad y estar tan pobre." Contrast this with the huge celebrations for the canonization of St. Teresa in Madrid in June 1622. Deleito y Piñuela pp. 138–141. Avila did manage to stage a week of festivities on the occasion of her beatification in 1614, but only by pooling together the resources of the city council, the cathedral chapter, and many monastic houses. Diego de San José, *Compedio de las Solenes fiestas que en toda España se hicieron en la beatificación de N.B.M. Teresa de Iesus, en prosa y verso* (Madrid, 1615) 3r–8r.

16. Tapia, "Fuentes" pp. 70–88.

Christian Doctrine, the Jesuit College of San Gil, and Teresa of Jesus' Discalced Carmelite convent of San José had drawn financial backing from a group of merchants, professionals, and lower clergy committed to the goals of apostolic service and spiritual autonomy which these institutions represented. By the end of the century, economic crisis in the wool trade and other sectors, plague, and emigration had reduced the resources and the influence of this segment of Avila's population. Nobles who owned land possessed one of the few even relatively secure sources of income in this period.[17] Some aristocrats also gained fortunes through service at the court. Thus, the wellborn soon became virtually the only laymen capable of providing significant economic support for religious institutions.

Perhaps in this period of insecurity and stagnation people returned to the values of order and hierarchy from which they had strayed somewhat in the decades of rapid growth and development. This new mood may have encouraged the deference to secular and ecclesiastical authorities which is characteristic of the post-Tridentine world. Whatever the cause, by 1620 most of the reform institutions established in mid-sixteenth-century Avila had lost their religious autonomy to either noble patrons or the episcopacy. These institutions were replaced by new foundations, often endowed by abulenses residing in Madrid. The new institutions signaled a return to the traditional, dynastic style of endowment, which featured capellanías, family tombs, and vocal prayers chanted for benefactors and their clients, and a shift away from reformist ideals and toward hard economic, social, and ecclesiastical realities.

Even as early as 1577 Don Rodrigo del Aguila, the principal heir of a distinguished aristocratic family, founded a monastery of Discalced Franciscans, dedicated to Saint Anthony, in his palace at Avila. He had no personal need of the house, as this knight of Santiago, corregidor of Madrid, and steward of the empress resided, like many of his peers, in the capital.

17. Phillips makes this point for Ciudad Real, on pp. 65–75.

"Being so virtuous and zealous in regard to the Divine Cult," in 1583 Don Rodrigo transferred the friars to a new monastery located on an impressive tract of land he owned outside the city walls. His family would exercise considerable economic control over this institution.[18] Through an intensive building program and numerous donations made by the Aguila family and other noble families, San Antonio soon became one of the largest and wealthiest male religious foundations in Avila. City residents particularly admired its parklike grounds, beautifully landscaped with trees and roses, pools and fountains. Bringing water to the drought-stricken city in sufficient quantities to maintain this setting, of course, required large sums of money. In 1617, for example, Francisco Guillamás Velázquez, who owned land in the province of Avila but served the king in Madrid, donated one hundred ducats for this purpose.[19]

The monastery of San Antonio with its ornate chapel and luxurious gardens gained popularity among local residents as a place for socializing in the early seventeenth century. Evidently few of them considered the irony of building such an elaborate foundation for the order established in the 1550s by the radically austere Peter of Alcántara. As so often happened in extreme ascetic movements, the efforts of a holy person to return to the religious order's pristine origins simply paled beside the determination and the resources of powerful noble families.[20]

18. Luis Ariz, *Historia de las grandezas de la ciudad de Avila* pt. 1 (Alcalá de Henares: L. Martínez Grande, 1607) 56r. Juan Martín Carramolino, *Historia de Avila, su provincia y obispado* vol. 1 (Madrid: Librería Española, 1872) pp. 522–523.

19. Ariz pt. 1, 56r–v, for description of the gardens and the fountain, still standing, in the shape of a serpent. According to one local historian, the monastery was "la frequentación de Avila." Antonio de Cianca, *Historia de la vida, invención, milagros, y translación de San Segundo*... bk. 2 (Madrid: Luis Sánchez, 1595) 134v. AHPA libro 2902. AHN Clero libro 562 lists contributions made to the monastery.

20. For this trend among the medieval Cistercians and mendicant orders, see R. W. Southern, *Western Society and the Church in the Middle Ages* (Harmondsworth: Penguin, 1970) pp. 250–272, 289–292.

The Jesuits of the College of San Gil began to experience severe economic problems in the 1580s, and by the early seventeenth century the institution had been transformed. A dispute with a new Jeronimite monastery named San Jerónimo resulted in relocation for the Jesuits. The Jeronimite community, established around 1606 by Rodrigo del Aguila (who also founded San Antonio), originally resided at the nobleman's estate in La Serrada. In 1616 the Jeronimites and their powerful patron decided the monks should move to a suitable location within the city of Avila.[21] They chose the old church of San Gil, strategically situated at the city's center, and offered the impoverished Jesuits the enormous sum of 6,200 ducats to make a trade. They proposed that the Jesuits take the money and occupy houses owned by the Aguila family outside the city walls, and that the Jeronimites relocate to San Gil. The Jesuit fathers appealed to the city council, arguing that they needed to reside within the city "in order to communicate their doctrine" to its residents, but they had no choice at that time but to accept the Aguila money and make the move.[22] They compromised their mission somewhat in order to ensure their survival during these difficult years.

Seven years later, in 1623, a new endowment ended the economic difficulties of the Jesuit college but in the process completely changed an institution that in the mid-sixteenth century had promoted the Ignatian concept of *santa libertad,* religious autonomy from patrons and private interests. In this year, Don Diego de Guzmán, formerly a missionary to the Indies and chaplain of the king, renamed the Jesuit college in Avila for the recently canonized founder of the Society. Don Diego pledged one thousand ducats a year in rentas, as well as his personal library, to the College of San Ignacio, but stipulated a long series of obligations in return.

21. Carramolino 1:524. Fernández Valencia 1:132–134.
22. AHN Clero leg. 528, 529. AHPA Actas Consist. libro 32, August–October 1616.

He insisted upon his clear recognition as the college's "founder and patron," a distinction that would pass on to his nephews after his death and then to their heirs in perpetuity. For one of his nephews, Don Juan de Guzmán, he reserved an ecclesiastical benefice worth five hundred ducats a year. The college's rector and all students and priests were to celebrate annual anniversary masses for the soul of their patron, as well as a special mass on the Feast of Santiago, a saint to whom, as a knight of this order, Don Diego was particularly devoted. The noble cleric left money for a magnificent tomb of marble and jasper, which was to be placed in the college's main chapel, where he and his nephews would receive burial. His family's coat of arms would adorn the chapel's walls.[23]

In 1553, a small group of reform-minded clerics and laymen had founded the College of San Gil, one of the first and most innovative of a cluster of institutions dedicated to apostolic service to the urban community, clerical formation, and the maintenance of religious autonomy. Seventy years later, in a period of dearth and uncertainty, the Jesuits had little choice but to accept the terms of a rich patron, and to satisfy his spiritual and dynastic needs.

Even Saint Teresa's Discalced Carmelites were not exempt from the shift in monastic foundation in the late sixteenth and early seventeenth centuries toward accommodating aristocratic values. While essentially able to maintain the ascetic and independent character of Carmelite reform at her original convent of San José in Avila, Teresa of Jesus was forced to make compromises in many of the other houses she established between 1567 and 1582.

The most important departure from her ideals concerned the issue of accepting fixed incomes for her convents. Teresa's intention of founding all her houses in complete poverty had caused great controversy in 1562. By 1568, however, she realized that the situation was altered, and she agreed to

23. AHN Jesuitas leg. 489–1, núm. 37. José María Quadrado, *Salamanca, Avila, y Segovia* (Barcelona: D. Cortezo, 1884) p. 422.

accept a property donated by the aristocratic devotee Doña Luisa de la Cerda, in the small rural town of Malagón. A convent that was remote from an urban population disposed to give alms and purchase the articles spun or embroidered by the nuns simply had to have a secure source of income, or the sisters would starve. Teresa was finally persuaded to deviate from the ascetic program she and Peter of Alcántara had championed several years earlier.[24] She recognized the threat to Carmelite autonomy inherent in this move, however, and insisted, in 1571, that if houses were to receive incomes they be large ones, so that the houses had "enough to keep the nuns from dependence on relatives or on anyone." She went on to comment, "In founding many monasteries in poverty . . . I never lack courage or confidence . . . [but] in founding them with an income that is small, everything fails me; I find it better that they not be founded."[25] Nevertheless, Teresa of Jesus founded seven houses with rentas, all located in rural areas, and nine in poverty, all in cities. As Teresa grew older (and, some would say, more realistic or pragmatic) and the economic situation worsened, she became more concerned with financial matters. She now actively encouraged prospective nuns to enter convents with dowries—the bigger the better—although she still refused to make this a requirement for acceptance to the order. At the end of her life, with Castile's economic decline well under-

24. *The Book of Her Foundations* 9:2–3. *The Collected Works of St. Teresa of Avila*, trans. Kieran Kavanaugh and Otilio Rodríguez, vol. 3 (Washington, D.C.: Institute of Carmelite Studies, 1985). "I in no way wanted to accept since the town was so small that we would be forced to have an income in order to support ourselves—something to which I was very much opposed. . . . My confessor [the Dominican, Domingo Báñez] . . . told me that I was wrong, that since the holy council [of Trent] had given permission to have an income, I shouldn't, because of my own opinion, fail to found a monastery where God could be so much served. To this were added the many urgings of this lady which I could not resist." *The Canons and Decrees of the Council of Trent*, trans. H. J. Schroeder (Rockford, Ill.: TAN Books, 1978) p. 219.

25. *Foundations* 20:13 (on Alba de Tormes house).

way and the level of donations perilously low, she considered beginning even urban foundations with fixed incomes.[26]

In 1587, only five years after Teresa's death, male Discalced Carmelite officials established a minimum dowry payment for novices, which, of course, selected for nuns from well-to-do families. While perhaps "something very foreign to our Holy Mother," as the policy was bitterly condemned by María de San José, one of Teresa's closest associates, this policy faithfully reflected the conservative spirit of the times.[27] In an even more dramatic departure from the idealistic goals of Teresa of Jesus, the Discalced Carmelites in 1597 at last bowed to social pressure from Old Christian elites and instituted strict statutes of purity of blood. In an ironic twist, the *Constitutions* adopted by the Spanish Chapter in that year blocked entrance to the descendants of conversos extending back four generations, a proviso that would have prevented Teresa de Ahumada from joining the order she founded.[28]

Thus, in Avila, as elsewhere, aristocrats regained their control of monastic institutions, and they, in turn, came to reflect their patrons' needs and values. The concern for family, prestige, and continuity on the part of noble men and women ultimately outweighed their interest in religious reform. Even Doña Guiomar de Ulloa, the old friend and

26. Introduction to *Foundations* by Kieran Kavanaugh, pp. 38–40. Teófanes Egido, "The Economic Concerns of Madre Teresa," *Carmelite Studies* 4 (1987): 156–162. José Antonio Alvarez Vázquez, "Financiación de las fundaciones teresianas," in *Actas del Congreso Internacional Teresiano* vol. 1, ed. Teófanes Egido Martínez et al. (Salamanca: El Congreso, 1983) pp. 249–285. Efrén de la Madre de Dios (Montalva), "El ideal de Santa Teresa en la fundación de San José," *Carmelus* 10 (1963): 221–227. Houses founded with rentas: Malagón, Pastrana, Alba de Tormes, Beas, Caravaca, Villanueva de la Jara, Soria; houses founded in poverty: Avila, Medina del Campo, Valladolid, Toledo, Salamanca, Segovia, Seville, Palencia, Burgos.

27. Egido pp. 156–158. Alvarez Vázquez pp. 278–279. Introduction to *Foundations* p. 41.

28. Teófanes Egido, "The Historical Setting of St. Teresa's Life," *Carmelite Studies* 1 (1980): 169, 182 n. 198. These applied to Discalced Carmelites in Spain, Portugal, and Mexico.

supporter of Teresa of Jesus, requested and received burial around 1585 in the fashionable new monastery of San Antonio, revealing herself, in the final analysis, to be a true representative of her class.[29]

The Rise of the Bishop

While monastic patronage remained largely private, in the hands of elite families, many other aspects of religious life in Avila in the late sixteenth and early seventeenth centuries came under the control of the city's bishops. This signaled a fundamental break with the past. Before the mid-sixteenth century, the men who held Avila's highest ecclesiastical offices were by and large unable to influence the daily workings of the diocese. Frequently absent from the city, at court or in Rome, these prelates would delegate the responsibilities of administration to the cathedral chapter and its powerful deans. They simply failed to impress their personalities upon the city.

In the final decades of the century, however, legislation from the Council of Trent designed to buttress the power of the episcopacy, and the Crown's appointment of strong-willed men prepared to take up the Tridentine challenge, combined to alter the situation. These "new" bishops quickly learned that by associating themselves with the city's popular devotions they could style themselves abulenses and gain considerable spiritual prestige. They achieved a degree of power and influence over the local ecclesiastical hierarchy unknown by their predecessors.

The Council of Trent, the great European conference to define doctrine and bring needed reforms to the Catholic

29. Fernández Valencia 1:345–352. In 1578 Doña Guiomar de Ulloa attempted to enter San José as a nun but quickly found its austerities too much for her health (and ego?). See E. Allison Peers, *Handbook to the Life and Times of St. Teresa and St. John of the Cross* (London: Burns Oates, 1954) pp. 227–228.

Church, ended in 1563. The canons and decrees promulgated in the following years included many that were designed to "restore reality and substance to episcopal power."[30] The new, Tridentine, bishop, for example, was strictly enjoined to reside continuously within his diocese. He was to ensure that priests gave sermons in all the parishes within his jurisdiction. He would exercise complete control over the secular clergy in his diocese, overseeing the education and ordination of priests and personally monitoring the performance of their duties through frequent diocesan visitations. Bishops now claimed authority over the regular clergy in many matters as well, enforcing the strict enclosure of nuns, inspecting orders suspected of laxity, and compelling monks to observe the diocese's feast days. These measures in principle substantially broadened the scope of episcopal power; putting them into practice proved difficult, however.[31] Bishops of Avila, as in other places, often found themselves confronting local elites, capitular, monastic, and lay, who were unwilling to relinquish control over religious institutions they had appropriated during the decades of episcopal absence and weakness. In Avila, the process of building the power of the bishop took several decades to complete.

As early as 1557, the Basque bishop Diego de Alava y Esquivel, a participant in the first session of the Council of Trent and great benefactor of the Jesuits, attempted to enact legislation in support of the episcopacy. The edicts of the diocesan synod over which he presided that year required clerics to receive the bishop's license before celebrating mass, called for yearly visitations, and sternly ordered cathedral canons to reside in the diocese.[32] Alava, however,

30. Jean Delumeau, *Catholicism between Luther and Voltaire: A New View of the Counter-Reformation* (Philadelphia: Westminster Press, 1977) p. 18.

31. Ibid. pp. 1–23. Bernardino Llorca, "Participación de España en el Concilio de Trento," in *Historia de la Iglesia en España* vol. 3, pt. 1, ed. José Luis González Novalín (Madrid: Editorial Católica, 1979) pp. 385–513.

32. *Libro de las constituciones synodales del obispado de Avila . . .* (Salamanca: Andreas Portonaris, 1557). ADA núm. 27.

held the important post of president of the court (*chancillería*) of Granada during his ten-year tenure (1548–58) at the see of Avila. He spent most of his time fulfilling his political duties outside the diocese rather than cementing his authority within it.[33]

Alvaro de Mendoza, bishop from 1560 to 1577, did much to enhance the spiritual prestige of the episcopacy in Avila. During his long term as bishop, he gained the admiration of many abulenses for his generosity toward the poor and his pious devotion to the local holy people Mari Díaz, Peter of Alcántara, and, eventually, Mother Teresa of Jesus. Mendoza, in turn, developed a strong affection for his adopted city, and although a native of Valladolid and later bishop of Palencia, he requested burial at Avila's convent of San José.[34] But even this esteemed ecclesiastic did relatively little to consolidate the power of the episcopal office, rarely presiding over the cathedral chapter, often away at court, and frequently delegating authority to others. For example, once he gave his permission to the establishment of San José in 1562, and of the College of San Millán in 1568, he left subordinates, notably his trusted advisor, Gaspar Daza, to take charge of the practical details.

Not until the 1580s did Avila receive a bishop intent upon imposing his personal authority to the fullest degree, as stipulated by the Council of Trent. In this instance, his vigor and personality served only to alienate Avila's elites, especially those in the cathedral chapter and the city council. Pedro Fernández Temiño, bishop from 1581 to 1590, appears to have been a man of strong will and quick temper. These qualities gained for him very little cooperation in the battle for ecclesiastical jurisdiction in Avila.

In December of 1581, several months after taking office,

33. Constancio Guitérrez, *Españoles en Trento* (Valladolid: CSIC, 1951) pp. 226–232.

34. Peers p. 203. Mendoza also left a generous donation to the cathedral of Avila. AHN Clero Cód. 914-b. Antonio de Cianca commented that the bishop was brought back to Avila for burial "como si muriera siendo su perlado" (2:134v).

Bishop Temiño, as he was known, submitted himself to a ceremony in which he swore, on his knees, to uphold the "statutes and laudable customs" of the cathedral chapter of Avila. But in making an inspection of the chapter the following month, the determined prelate followed the guidelines established at the Council of Trent, although they conflicted with the chapter's own book of statutes.[35]

Debate arose over the issue of punishing and correcting cathedral clergy guilty of wrongdoing. Avila's canons, led by longtime dean Don Diego de Bracamonte, a member of one of the city's most powerful families, claimed that time-honored custom dictated that canons and prebendaries choose judges from among their ranks to investigate and punish the abuses of their colleagues. In the face of the bishop's challenge, they clung to this privilege, recounting recent cases in which they had censured fellows for various crimes, including immorality, embezzlement of capitular funds, insulting canons during chapter meetings, and selling wheat above the government's ceiling price.[36] Temiño, however, claimed that canons seldom enforced this principle of self-regulation, and

35. AHN Clero leg. 373, 374. Tomás Sobrino Chomón, *Episcopado abulense: Siglos XVI–XVIII* (Avila: Institución "Gran Duque de Alba," 1983) pp. 21–26. "Ruidosas debieron de ser sus tiranteces y diferencias con el cabildo catedral a la hora de aplicar las reformas tridentinas" (p. 22). In Burgos, Bishop Francisco de Mendoza, upon taking office in 1557, also swore to "guardar los statutos, privilegios, libertades, inmunidades, usos y costumbres desta sancta iglesia de Burgos," and came into serious conflict with his canons when he attempted to extend his jurisdiction over the chapter. Nicolás López Martínez, "El Cardenal Mendoza y la reforma tridentina en Burgos," in *Miscelánea conmemorativa del Concilio de Trento (1563–1963): Estudios y documentos* (Madrid: CSIC, 1965) p. 79.

36. AHN Clero leg. 373, 374. López Martínez p. 81. On the important subject of conflicts of jurisdiction between bishops and chapters, especially in the wake of the Council of Trent, see also Demétrio Mansilla, "Reacción del Cabildo de Burgos ante las visitas y otros actos de jurisdicción intentados por sus obispos (siglos XIV–XVII)," *Hispania Sacra* 10 (1957): 135–159; Feliciano Cereceda, "El litigio de los cabildos españoles y su repercusión en las relaciones con Roma (1551–1556)," *Razón y Fe* 13 (1944): 215–234; Tomás Marín, "Primeras repercusiones tridentinas: El litigio de los cabildos españoles, su proceso en la diócesis de Calahorra," *Hispania Sacra* 1 (1948): 325–349.

that they left many faults unpunished. He insisted that inspection and correction of abuses was an exclusive right of the bishop, and he proceeded to make his own *visita*. The bishop could cite the Council of Trent in his defense, but Avila's canons retorted that their appointed judges "never said that in their proceedings they would uphold the orders of the Council and not of the Statute."[37]

The conflicts between bishop and chapter over precedence and jurisdiction lasted until 1588, that is, during most of Temiño's tenure as bishop. At one point relations between the two parties became so strained that, according to one document, "no canon or other persons of the cathedral would deal with, talk to or associate himself with the bishop." Both sides appealed to the pope, generating a great deal of paper and bad feelings. Finally, a papal nuncio, swayed by the chapter's allegations of arbitrariness in Temiño's investigations of and accusations about clerics, ruled against the bishop, prohibiting him from making capitular visitations without the presence of witnesses.[38]

Almost as soon as Temiño's dispute with the chapter ended, however, another dispute began, this time between the bishop and the city council, over the College of San Millán. In 1568, at the instigation of Gaspar Daza, Julián de Avila, and other prominent members of Avila's "reform party," Bishop Alvaro de Mendoza had approved the foundation of a *colegio* at the old church of San Millán. Within a few years, the school had begun to operate with a rector and six poor boys, and the matter seemed settled. But in May 1589, the ambitious Temiño found a new opportunity to assert his authority. He proposed replacing the old *colegio* with a new institution that would bear the official title *seminary*. In his

37. AHN Clero leg. 373, 374: "Los jueces del cabildo nunca dieron que en el proceder se guardase la orden del Concilio y no el statuto." *Canons and Decrees* pp. 49, 193–194.

38. AHN Clero pergamino carpeta 37: "Ningún capitular ni otra persona de la Iglesia tratase, comunicase ni comendase con el sr. obispo." AHN Clero leg. 367, 445–2.

opinion, ambiguous wording of the original papal bull, the failure of Mendoza to endow San Millán with income from his own estate, and certain financial problems suffered by the school in recent years made it a less than "genuine" Tridentine seminary. Temiño wanted to go on record as having founded Avila's first authentic training school for priests.[39]

A surprised and none too pleased city council expressed opposition to the bishop's plan, bringing suit against him at the Royal Council in Madrid. The regidores insisted that the institution established by Mendoza served the city well, and that this proposed "novelty" would only contradict the intentions of the founder and donors. The councilors, several of whom at this time had relatives on the cathedral chapter, accused Temiño of speaking merely out of "passion and hatred and enmity." "If the said bishop feels he has such a strong obligation to found a seminary in accordance with the Council of Trent," the exasperated regidores exclaimed, let him do it "without undoing the foundations and works that others have made."[40]

In October 1589 the Royal Council ruled that the bishop of Avila should receive his bulls and could proceed with his project. The city council, using legal stalling tactics, appeals, and a great deal of ill-afforded money, managed to drag out the affair well into 1590, delaying a final decision. On August 23 of that year, Pedro Fernández Temiño died. His attempts to increase the power of Avila's bishop had borne little fruit, in large part because of his own difficult personality. His plans pointed the way of the future, however. His successor,

39. ASA leg. 7, núm. 29: "Sobre erección de este colegio." Francisco Martín Hernandez, "Fundación de los primeros seminarios españoles," in *Miscelánea conmemorativa del Concilio de Trento (1563–1963): Estudios y documentos* (Madrid: CSIC, 1965) pp. 5–24. He mentions this case in Avila (p. 18 n. 18).

40. ASA leg. 2, núm. 10: "Se ve claro ser pasión y odio y enemistad . . . si al dicho obispo le parece que tiene tanta obligación de hacer seminario conforme al Concilio de Trento le podía el hacer como bién visto le fuere sin deshacer las fundaciones y obras que otros hicieron." AHPA Actas Consist. leg. 279, November 4, 1589.

Jerónimo Manrique de Lara, a man of consummate diplomatic skill, would succeed where Temiño had failed.

Manrique, a native of Madrid, a man of wealth, distinguished lineage, cosmopolitan tastes, and appreciation of the arts, became bishop of Avila in April 1591, having already been appointed an inquisitor general by Philip II.[41] The see had remained vacant for over seven months after the death of Temiño, the many years of conflict undoubtedly rendering the post a sensitive one. In his four-year term as bishop (1591–95), Manrique worked to reconcile offended parties and to consolidate the position of the bishop, which had in fact been weakened by the choleric Temiño. The new bishop, for example, brought an end to the dispute over San Millán. The school would remain in the same location and would now be designated by the term *seminary*. A new set of Constitutions (published in 1613) made it clear that the institution had been founded by order of the Council of Trent and placed under the direct control of the bishop. It is Manrique, therefore, who receives credit in ecclesiastical histories of Avila as having started the diocese's first Tridentine seminary, although Gaspar Daza and his "sacerdotal team" had helped to establish a school for priests almost thirty years earlier.[42]

Next Manrique moved to accommodate the cathedral chapter. He accomplished this by acceding to the wishes of the canons on an issue that worked to his advantage very well, an improvement in the status of Avila's cathedral and its clergy. In principle, the cathedral was the most important church in the diocese, superior to all others in wealth, size, power, and spiritual prestige. The Council of Trent supported this concept, and documents of the period often referred to

41. On Manrique de Lara see Cianca bk. 3, 1r–2v; Sobrino Chomón pp. 43–49.

42. ASA leg. 7, núm. 38. ASA leg. 8, núm. 6: "Constituciones del Colegio Seminario de San Millán de Avila." Tomás Sobrino Chomón, "Avila," in *Diccionario de la Historia Eclesiástica de España* vol. 1, ed. Quintín Aldea Vaquero et al. (Madrid: CSIC, 1972) pp. 158–162.

Avila's cathedral simply as *la iglesia mayor*, the city's main church.

But while the Cathedral of San Salvador exceeded other churches in terms of economic resources, until the late sixteenth century it suffered from a shortage of "spiritual resources" in the form of relics. In this it was inferior to the exquisite Romanesque basilica of San Vicente, the site of many of Avila's most prized relics and shrines. This church was named for the young martyr Vincent, executed with his two sisters by the emperor Diocletian in the fourth century A.D. The basilica contained the relics of the three martyrs, and their elaborately carved tombs attracted many pilgrims and donations. Abulenses revered San Vicente as their patron saint.[43] The cathedral housed no relics of note. Its canons participated in the cult of San Vicente by making annual processions to the smaller church on his feast day to perform a special ancient rite, but many of them regarded the cathedral as the only proper location for devotion to the city's patron saint.[44] Soon after Bishop Manrique took office in 1591, the chapter petitioned him to authorize celebration of the Feast of San Vicente inside the cathedral. The ceremony as it presently was celebrated lacked the necessary "solemnity," the canons argued, and because of bad weather, they could not always get to San Vicente for the processions. These were pretexts, of course. The real issue at stake involved the cathedral's claims to hegemony within the city's ecclesiastical hierarchy.[45]

Manrique agreed, and promptly approved the change. It offered him a chance to show good will toward the chapter. It also helped to enhance the role of Avila's cathedral as *iglesia mayor*. But spiritual prestige still demanded relics. Avila's

43. Fernández Valencia vol. 1, especially pp. 421–472.
44. Ariz bk. 1, 30r–32v.
45. AHN Cód. 914-b: "No se celebrarán con la solemnidad que requería y también muchas veces el temporal era tan áspera que no se iba allá y se quedaba la procesión." Gabriel María Vergara y Martín, *Estudio histórico de Avila y su territorio* (Madrid: Hernández, 1896) p. 178.

new bishop and canons knew exactly where to look: they cast their eyes on the relics of San Segundo, which had been kept in the small church on the river Adaja since their discovery in 1519. The presence of the remains of this important figure in an obscure chapel in the city's "industrial" end must have caused bitter embarrassment to the aristocratic cathedral canons. They attempted on several occasions, most notably at the discovery in 1519 and again in 1543, 1547, and 1572, to have the relics transferred to the cathedral. The canons claimed that the relics were isolated, neglected, and vulnerable to crime in their current location and that only the chapter could provide the "decency, sumptuousness and security owed to such a holy body." However, the members of the neighborhood Confraternity of San Segundo, self-appointed guardians of the relics, successfully opposed these plans. The confraternity's patrones, influential merchants and manufacturers of woolen cloth, some probably of converso origin, consistently maintained that their church served as a respectable repository for the relics and attracted numerous pilgrims, especially from the surrounding countryside.[46]

By 1593, however, the efforts of a determined bishop and the encouragement of a king with a passion for relics (and, perhaps, the relatively weak position of the brothers of the San Segundo confraternity and other laymen due to economic crises in the wool trade) made possible the canons' long-held dream of translating the remains of San Segundo to Avila's cathedral.[47] The sequence of events was described in lov-

46. Cianca bk. 1, 101r–103v, 106r–109r, 109v–113r, 125v–129r: "Diciendo pertenecerle, como por primero obispo suyo, y para tenerla en ella con la decencia, sumptuosidad y custodia a tan santo cuerpo debida." AHN Clero leg. 345.

47. Phillips p. 56: "By the end of Phillip III's reign . . . the guilds of textile workers, which had been strong enough to oust the corregidor during the revolt of the comuneros in 1520, dwindled to merely nothing." In Avila a decree of the diocesan synod held by Bishop Francisco de Gamarra on April 16, 1617, prohibited confraternities from writing ordinances without prior

ing detail by the ecclesiastical notary and spokesman for Bishop Manrique, Antonio de Cianca, in a book commissioned by the cathedral chapter in 1595. According to Cianca, Manrique fell ill with heart palpitations in September of 1593. Despairing of the bishop's life, the cathedral chapter quickly organized processions to the tiny church of San Segundo and celebrated mass there. At the precise moment of elevating the Host, the bishop experienced a complete and miraculous cure. Attributing his recovery to the intercession of San Segundo, the prelate readily agreed to the chapter's request to bring the saint's relics to the cathedral, "where there would be more decency and authority."[48] In rapid order, the bishop and canons won approval for their project from various secular and ecclesiastical authorities. They convinced Avila's city council (despite complaints from the San Segundo brotherhood), resurrected a papal bull issued by Leo X in 1520 but never acted upon, and solicited enthusiastic letters from Philip II, whose only request was that they save him a bone for his burgeoning collection of relics at El Escorial.[49]

The long-awaited event finally took place in September 1594. Residents of Avila witnessed the transfer of the relics of San Segundo from the church on the Adaja to the cathedral amid week-long celebrations that included processions, jousts, dances, displays of fireworks, and enactment of the liturgical drama *San Segundo de Avila*, written by Manrique's young protégé, the playwright Lope de Vega.[50]

episcopal approval. *Constituciones synodales del obispado de Avila . . . libro primero* II.5 (Madrid: Juan de la Cuesta, 1617) BN 2/46320. For the post-Tridentine preference for placing the activities of confraternities under episcopal control, see John Bossy, "The Counter-Reformation and the People of Catholic Europe," *Past and Present* 47 (1970): 58–60. A. D. Wright, *The Counter-Reformation: Catholic Europe and the Non-Christian World* (New York: St. Martin's Press, 1982) pp. 50–53, 254–255.

48. Cianca bk. 3, 3r–4r: "Donde estaría con más decencia y autoridad."

49. Christian pp. 135–137. Juan Manuel del Estal, "Felipe II y su archivo hagiográfico de El Escorial," *Hispania Sacra* 23 (1970): 193–333.

50. Lope's *San Segundo de Avila* has been published in the Biblioteca de Autores Españoles series, vol. 177. In his preliminary study, Marcelino

It is clear that the bishop exercised a critical influence in all this. When on previous occasions the canons had expressed the desire to move the relics of San Segundo, the prelates had not exhibited much enthusiasm for the idea. Perhaps they retained greater loyalty to the religious traditions of their native cities than to those of Avila. But Manrique, with his strong personal devotion to the local cult of San Segundo and his determination to enhance the power and dignity of the episcopal office, readily grasped the opportunity. In many ways, the translation of the relics of San Segundo became Manrique's own affair, paid for, organized by, and reflecting upon the bishop. For example, Manrique agreed to donate money from his personal estate for the elaborate processions, decorations, and entertainments. This was decisive in persuading the city councilors to approve the transfer during a period of economic hardship. The bishop also offered to build a new chapel for the relics of San Segundo, complete with a hospice for pilgrims. He provided an annual endowment of over two thousand ducats, enough to support six chaplains, who would perform a special liturgy approved by the pope. This sizable addition to the Cathedral of San Salvador required permission to break the city wall and change the course and the name of an adjacent street. The chapel still displays the coat of arms of Manrique de Lara, its "lord and founder."[51]

Menéndez Pelayo referred to it as "un especie de tributo rendido a . . . su primer protector, D. Jerónimo Manrique." For a general discussion of popular saints' lives in Spanish golden age theater, see Julio Caro Baroja, *Las formas complejas de la vida religiosa: Religión, sociedad, y carácter en la España de los siglos XVI y XVII* (Madrid: Akal, 1978) pp. 101–106. On relics and civic ritual in late medieval and early modern Europe see, for example, Charles Pythian-Adams, "Ceremony and the Citizen: The Communal Year at Coventry, 1450–1550," in *The Early Modern Town*, ed. Peter Clark (New York: Longman, 1976) pp. 106–128; Richard Trexler, *Public Life in Renaissance Florence* (New York: Academic Press, 1980) pp. 57–61.

51. Cianca bk. 3, 78r–82r. Manrique also made donations and endowed anniversary masses at the cathedral of Avila. AHN Cód. 914-b. He is buried in "his" chapel of San Segundo.

Antonio de Cianca's book made explicit one of Manrique's most important goals in the San Segundo project, namely, to associate himself with Avila's first bishop. After much discussion, the Fathers at the Council of Trent had decreed the episcopal office divinely ordained and agreed that an unbroken succession of bishops descended from the apostles. Manrique, through his spokesman, Cianca, applied this concept to the case of Avila.

Cianca stated his intentions in the full title of his book: *History of the Life, Discovery, Miracles, and Translation of San Segundo, First Bishop of Avila, and Narration of the Bishops, His Successors, until Don Gerónimo Manrique de Lara, Inquisitor General of Spain.* San Segundo, Cianca reported, was one of the seven companions of Saint James, who first brought Christianity to Spain. San Segundo's evangelistic fervor and death as a martyr gave him almost apostolic standing. "And thus we can very well honor Avila as having been one of the first cities that received the faith of our redeemer and master Jesus Christ," Cianca concluded.[52] While the details of the saint's life remained obscure, Cianca felt certain he could discern aspects of the first bishop's character. San Segundo, he suggested, "would pass the time in high and divine contemplation, combined with an active and exemplary life, which the gospel law requires for its preaching and teaching." In other words, he demonstrated the traits of a good Tridentine bishop. These qualities appear in Lope de Vega's drama, as well.[53]

---

52. Cianca bk. 1, 38r: "Y así Avila se puede muy bien honrar de haber sido de las primeras ciudades que recibieron la Fe de nuestro Redentor y maestro Jesu Cristo."

53. Ibid. 38v: "Bien es piamente de creer, que el bienaventurado San Segundo . . . le pasaría en altas y divinas contemplaciones, con una activa y exemplar vida, cual para la predicación y enseñanza de la divina ley Evangélica requería, como tan buen obrero de ella." Two other cases concerning the relics of bishops in sixteenth-century Spain which are similar to that of Avila have come to my attention. In Cuenca, the relics of San Julián, the diocese's first bishop, were discovered in 1518, only one year before the

For Cianca, the next most important event in Avila's history occurred in 1591 when his patron, Manrique, took office. The bishop soon began to give generous alms to "upstanding widows" and "respectable maidens," for which deeds he was "loved and respected by all his subjects as being one of the best prelates the Church of Avila . . . ever had, *a worthy successor of the blessed San Segundo*."[54] As good shepherd of his people, Manrique effected the transfer of the relics of San Segundo and thus restored the remains of his illustrious predecessor to a position of dignity.

For Manrique, fostering the cult of Avila's first bishop reinforced the claims to episcopal power and authority made at the Council of Trent. His translation of the relics of San Segundo accomplished several objectives. Avila's cathedral now housed the city's most important relics, providing a source of donations, pilgrims, and coveted spiritual prestige for the *iglesia mayor*. The cathedral's canons seemed happy and cooperative, or at least were causing no difficulties, as they had for Bishop Temiño. Furthermore, the episcopal figure of San Segundo replaced San Vicente as the city's patron saint.[55] And Avila's current bishop, the spiritual descendant

discovery of the relics of San Segundo. See Sara T. Nalle, "A Saint for All Seasons," in *Culture and Control in Counter-Reformation Spain*, ed. Mary Elizabeth Perry and Anne Cruz (Minneapolis: University of Minnesota Press, forthcoming). In 1594, the same year as the translation of San Segundo, the abulense Don Sancho Dávila y Toledo, as bishop of Cartagena, arranged for the transfer of the relics of San Fulgencio from a town in Extremadura to the Cathedral of Murcia. See Francisco Candel Crespo, *Un obispo postridentino: Don Sancho Dávila y Toledo (1546–1625)* (Avila: Diputación Provincial, 1968). "Don Sancho Dávila, que estaba convencido de haber sido antecesor suyo en la diócesis cartaginense, San Fulgencio, obtuvo la entusiasta adhesión del Ayuntamiento de Murcia y . . . Felipe II" (p. 47). This prelate, whose mother had been a devotee of Peter of Alcántara in Avila in the mid-sixteenth century (p. 23), was himself a prodigious collector of relics and came to be known as "el obispo de las reliquias" (pp. 48–49).

54. Cianca bk. 3, 11–3r: "Es muy amado y respetado de todos sus súbditos por ser universalmente de los mejores prelados que la iglesia de Avila ha tenido, *digno sucessor del bienaventurado San Segundo*" (emphasis mine).

55. After her canonization in 1622, Saint Teresa of Jesus became the patron saint of Avila.

of the Roman martyr, now exercised a major influence on the city's religious life.

After Manrique's death in 1595, several bishops followed his lead, using the cults of local holy people to enhance their reputations. In fact, in the early seventeenth century, elaborate funerals or ceremonies commemorating the holy dead became relatively common in Avila. Perhaps plague and depression diminished the resources and the will of the city council and of independent religious corporations such as confraternities in this period, accelerating the trend toward centralization of religious affairs initiated by the Council of Trent. Perhaps also, in a time of economic hardship, people welcomed these displays of ecclesiastical pomp as diversions from their daily problems. In any case, bishops and the clerical hierarchy they headed encountered little opposition as they took control of many aspects of religious life in Avila, manipulating the living and the dead.

In this sense, Lorenzo Otaduy, bishop from 1599 to 1612, proved a worthy successor to Manrique. This prelate, for example, resumed the incursion into the "spiritual resources" of the church of San Vicente. As the cathedral had already appropriated a sizable role in the cult of the martyr San Vicente, Otaduy turned to another religious figured buried within the basilica, the local saint Pedro del Barco, a twelfth-century hermit from the western part of the bishopric of Avila.[56]

According to a later chronicler, in 1610 the priest of San Vicente, Pablo Verdugo de la Cueva, requested aid from the bishop in stimulating the worship of San Pedro del Barco. Otaduy needed no second urging. "Seeing how little authority the sepulcher of this saint commanded, whose altar was very small," and desiring to give it "a more ostentatious form," the bishop solicited funds from the city council for this purpose and added more from his own estate. Then, on August 14, 1610, Otaduy, accompanied by several cathedral

56. Fernández Valencia 1:472–511. Carramolino 3:295–299. Sobrino Chomón, *Episcopado* pp. 75–80.

canons, performed a solemn ceremony in which he moved the bones of San Pedro del Barco from one tomb within San Vicente to another.[57] A description of the ritual written for the event provides more information about the bishop performing the ceremony than about the saint being honored. The document begins "In the year of Our Lord Jesus Christ 1610, the illustrious don Laurencio Otaduy y Avendaño, bishop of this city of Avila and of the council of the king, Philip III, revealed the holy body of the glorious San Pedro del Barco." It then records the details of the ritual—how, for example, the bishop rearranged the bones and took them from their decrepit wooden casket and placed them in a new sepulcher of stone. The life, deeds, and miracles of the saint received no mention whatsoever.[58] One suspects that the person enjoying primary homage on this occasion was Bishop Otaduy. The holy man San Pedro del Barco played a secondary role in the drama of expanding episcopal power in Avila.

In 1600, Otaduy initiated a series of hearings on the life and deeds of the beloved holy woman Mari Díaz. The bishop and his assistants enthusiastically collected eye-witness accounts of this "humble peasant woman" who had displayed such "humility, patience and obedience." These hearings, he hoped, would serve as the first stage in the complex process of beatification and, eventually, canonization. The people of Avila had proclaimed Mari Díaz a saint at her death in 1572, but the Council of Trent required bishops to authenticate and approve all saints and miracles in their dioceses. The Church also moved to establish official ecclesiastical channels for the canonization of saints, attempting to suppress the long tradition of popular acclamation.[59] Otaduy did not

57. Fernández Valencia 1:500ff: "Viendo la poca autoridad con que estaba el sepulcro de este santo cuyo altar era muy pequeño."
58. Ibid. pp. 509ff.
59. *Canons and Decrees* pp. 215–217. Caro Baroja pp. 80–82. Donald Weinstein and Rudolph M. Bell, *Saints and Society: The Two Worlds of Western Christendom, 1000–1700* (Chicago: University of Chicago Press,

wish to miss an opportunity to exercise his episcopal prerogatives.

Otaduy died, however, before the long series of testimonies had ended and the canonization process could advance. His successor, Francisco de Gamarra (bishop 1616–23), continued the investigation of Mari Díaz begun twenty years before. By this time, memories of the holy woman had grown hazy, and the highly reverent but realistic reports of 1600 had given way to remembered childhood glimpses, overheard anecdotes, and reputed miracles. Gamarra successfully revived interest in the beata through a ceremony by now familiar to bishops of Avila, the staging of an elaborate reburial. As did Manrique de Lara with San Segundo, and Otaduy with San Pedro del Barco, Gamarra received at least as much attention and respect on this occasion as the holy person he ostensibly came to honor.

In a ceremony in August 1619, Gamarra, a former chaplain of Philip III, opened Mari Díaz's simple tomb in the church of San Millán and laid her remains in a "more decent" lead casket. Unlike her funeral in 1572, which had witnessed a great outpouring of spontaneous popular piety and received funding from the city council and from private individuals, the reburial of the holy woman in 1619 was clearly initiated and sponsored by the bishop and the cathedral chapter. Ironically, only invited members of Avila's elite, clerical and lay, attended this tribute to a humble peasant woman who, in the mid-sixteenth century, had served as "Mother" to the entire urban community. On October 29, 1619, Gamarra reserved the Blessed Sacrament in San Millán's main chapel, and ordered that as long as Mari Díaz's body lay there no one else should receive burial in the chapel. The holy woman's case for canonization was never brought to Rome.[60]

1982) p. 185: "The response of the Counter Reformation church . . . was to assume increasing control of cult formation and then to make it less accessible to popular and spontaneous religious enthusiasm."

60. "Información de la Vida, muerte, y milagros de la Venerable María Díaz," ADA Cód. 3.345. Bishop Gamarra also arranged the reburial of Peter

ESTA MANDADO PORSVS EL SEÑOR OBISPO
DON FRANCISCO DE GAMARA QVE NA...
SE EN TIERE EN ESTA CAPILLA MAYOR DE S
MILIAN MIEN TRAS EN ELLA ES TVBIERE
EL CVERPO DIA BENE...ABLE MADRE MARIA
DIAZ COMO COSTA PORVNA VTO PROBE
DO ANTE IVSTED SA...TIST EVANO TRI...
PERPETVO VNO DLOS QVATRO DEL NV
MERO ANTE QVIEN SE ACABO LA INFOR
MACION DLA VIDA MVERTE YMILAGROS D
DEL A DICHA BENERABLE MDRE MRIA DIA...

VS DS OBISPO DO DFR AND GAMARA A ATENDIE
DO A LA GRANDE VOCIOQ VEL A BENERABLE MDRE
MARIA DIAZ TVVO AL S^{mos} SACRAMENTO POR HORA
SV SEPVLCRO DTERMINO PO...RLE PORSVPERSO
N AEN ESTA CAPILLA DONDEN TIEN PO SPASA
DOS ESTVVO PRECEDIENDO PRIMERO EL ADOR
NO QVE A PRESENTE AY DRE TA LOREJAY D
...S AYVDADO PAR AE L OLA CIVDAD Y TIERA...
...AMISA COGR AF ESTI VIDAD Y MVCHA GETE
...ENTR AMBOS ESTADOS ECLESIASTICO Y SEGLAR
Y PREDICO EL PADRE R ET OR DELA CONPAÑIA D
IESVS Y DIJO GRANDES EXCELENCIAS DSTA INSI
G NE Y BARON IL MVGEREN 29 D OTVBRE 1612

Memorial stones in honor of María Díaz, erected by order of Bishop
Francisco de Gamarra in the church of San Millán, now in Seminario de Avila. Photographs courtesy of Tomás Sobrino Chomón.

First stone:

It is ordered by His Honor the bishop Don Francisco de Gamarra that no one be buried in this main chapel of San Millán as long as in it lies the body of the venerable Mother María Díaz as recorded by an *auto* dictated to you Santiesteban public notary one of the four *notarios del número* before whom was completed the *Información* of the life, death, and miracles of the aforesaid venerable Mother María Díaz.

Second stone:

His Honor the bishop Don Francisco de Gamarra recognizing the great devotion that the venerable Mother María Díaz had for the Blessed Sacrament in order to honor her sepulcher decided to personally reserve it in this chapel where in times past it was first so honored. The adornments at present consist of retable, altar rail, and the rest for which the city and territory helped. The mass was said with great festivity and many people of both estates ecclesiastical and lay and the Father Rector of the Society of Jesus preached and told of the great and excellent virtues of this celebrated and manly woman on 29 October 1612 [*sic:* actually 1619].

Thus, religion in early seventeenth-century Avila, particularly in the aspect of public ritual, increasingly fell within the exclusive domain of the ecclesiastical hierarchy. Avila's bishops, in particular, through their successful application of the canons and decrees of the Council of Trent, their accommodation of members of the cathedral chapter and other elites, and their skillful use of local devotions, came to represent the values of solemnity, decency, and authority in religious life. In many ways, they were the true beneficiaries of religious and social change in sixteenth-century Avila.

Doña María Vela

In 1617, an unusual woman died in Avila. She was Doña María Vela, a Cistercian nun of the convent of Santa Ana, a member of one of the city's most distinguished families, and, for over thirty years, the self-proclaimed recipient of divine favors in the form of visions, voices, trances, and bodily contortions. During Doña María's lifetime, many regarded her as a fraud, a deluded invalid, a heretic, an epileptic, a madwoman, or a victim of demonic possession. Upon her death, she was proclaimed a saint.

In many ways, María Vela simply lived in the wrong place at the wrong time. Her fifty-six years, from 1561 to 1617, spanned a period of profound crisis for her native Avila, as the once-vital urban center succumbed to the effects of plague, famine, emigration, and economic depression. During Doña María's mature years, the city's aristocracy steadily reasserted its control over monastic foundations, and

---

of Alcántara in the monastery the latter had founded in the mountain town of Arenas, today known as Arenas de San Pedro. Sobrino Chomón, *Episcopado* pp. 123–127. His synodal decrees of 1617 stipulated that all parish masses be coordinated with those of the cathedral chapter and that only the cathedral hold the annual Corpus Christi celebrations. *Constituciones synodales* libro tercero XIV.2, XVI.3.

the office of the bishop grew in power and influence. In this post-Tridentine atmosphere, the maintenance of order and hierarchy became a central priority for secular and ecclesiastical elites in Avila (as elsewhere), and a unique individual with claims to divine illumination did not fit into their scheme. In addition, widespread suspicion and fear of heresy and other forms of religious heterodoxy in Spain in the late sixteenth century and the early seventeenth century caused many to view the nun's erratic behavior and claims to mystical knowledge with grave misgivings. The experience of Doña María Vela illustrates many aspects of religious life in Avila in the waning of the city. This extraordinary woman was the last abulense of note to appear for many generations.

Doña María Vela y Cueto was born in the village of Cardeñosa one year before Teresa of Jesus founded the reformed convent of San José. Soon afterwards, her family moved to nearby Avila, and there she remained for the rest of her life. Doña María's parents, Don Diego Alvarez de Cueto and Doña Ana de Aguirre, both belonged to illustrious abulense families that had produced city councilors and ecclesiastics for many generations. A paternal great-uncle, Blasco Núñez Vela, served as Spain's first viceroy in Peru in the early sixteenth century.[61] María Vela's family provided her with a good education, which included Latin and, possibly, music. Like the youthful Teresa de Ahumada, she loved books and "all her life had a great affinity for them."[62]

From early childhood, Doña María experienced both deep spiritual yearnings and poor health. At the age of 15, she decided to embrace the religious life. After some investigation she chose the Cistercian convent of Santa Ana, entering

---

61. María Vela y Cueto, *Autobiografía y Libro de las Mercedes*, ed. Olegario González Hernández (Barcelona: Juan Flors, 1961). Historical introduction by González Hernández, pp. 6–9.

62. Miguel González Vaquero, *La muger fuerte: Por otro título, la vida de Doña María Vela . . .* (Barcelona: Geronymo Margarit, 1627) 65v–66r: "Que toda la vida fue muy aficionada a ellos."

as a novice in 1576. At this time, her father's sister, Doña Isabel de Cueto, held the position of abbess.[63] Santa Ana, Avila's oldest religious house for women, was also one of its wealthiest, owning vast tracts of land in the province and many houses in the city. Its nuns, numbering around seventy in 1576, descended from the city's most powerful noble families. Unlike the sisters of San José, Santa Ana's *señoras* addressed one another by their full names and used the polite title *Doña*. María Vela's decision to affect the style of a humble beata in this thoroughly aristocratic setting would make life particularly difficult for her and provoke a strongly negative reaction from most of her fellow nuns.[64]

After a lengthy novitiate of six years (extended, perhaps, by ill health), Doña María professed as a nun of the Order of Saint Bernard in 1582, the year of Teresa's death. Because of her musical talent, she quickly gained a position of responsibility in the convent's choir, supervising the singers or chanters and playing the organ.[65] For Santa Ana, as for most religious houses of its type, the proper recitation of vocal choral prayer represented the core of its liturgical program.

Not satisfied with the daily rounds of conventual duties, however, María Vela longed for something more. For many years, she reported in an autobiography written at the command of her confessor, "Our Lord in His great goodness" gave her "an immense yearning for perfection."[66] Unlike Teresa of Jesus, whose thoughts had quickly turned to missionary concerns, the young Cistercian began to adopt the style of ascetic spirituality common among late medieval female

63. Vela y Cueto, *Autobiografía* pp. 10–13.
64. Ibid. pp. 44–57. Ferreol Hernández Hernández, "El convento cisterciense de Santa Ana en Avila," *Cistercium* 11 (1959): 136–144.
65. González Vaquero 17v.
66. Vela y Cueto, *Autobiografía*, p. 307: "Comenzó Nuestro Señor por su sola bondad a darme grandes deseos de perfección." English quotes from María Vela y Cueto, *The Third Mystic of Avila: The Self-Revelation of María Vela, a Sixteenth Century Spanish Nun*, trans. Frances Parkinson Keyes (New York: Farrar, Straus and Cudahy, 1960) p. 41.

saints and holy women. She felt called to imitate the sufferings of Christ through extreme penitence and mortification of the flesh. Her comfortable upbringing and the preferential treatment she received in the convent from the abbess, her aunt, now filled her with remorse. "It seemed to me that there was nobody unhappier than I; everyone else had something to endure, either mortification of the flesh, or the scorn of others, or poverty, or disease, any one of which I would gladly have undergone."[67]

Inspired by heavenly voices, María Vela took up a rigorous penitential program that included long hours of private prayer, nocturnal vigils, fasts, wearing a hair shirt, and flagellating herself three times a day. Perhaps she recalled as a model the austere Mari Díaz, who had died when María Vela was 11 years old, or had heard stories from her mother, one of the holy woman's devotees.[68] The convent's abbess and chaplains soon became disturbed by these extreme habits. Doña Isabel, aware of her niece's delicate health, tried to distract her from these practices by assigning to her menial or mindless tasks, such as counting the tiles of the roof. Her confessor restricted her hours of prayer. Although she felt that God called her to greater feats of mortification, monastic authorities "clipped the wings of [her] flight and the freedom of [her] spirit."[69]

67. Vela y Cueto, *Autobiografía* p. 308: "Me parecía que no había persona más desdichada que yo pues todos tenían en qué padecer: ya con penitencias, ya con menosprecios, ya con pobreza, o con enfermedades, que cualquier cosa de estas tomaría yo de buena gana." Idem, *Third Mystic*, p. 42. For spirituality of Cistercian nuns of Helfta in the thirteenth century, see Caroline Walker Bynum, *Jesus as Mother: Studies in the Spirituality of the High Middle Ages* (Berkeley and Los Angeles: University of California Press, 1982) pp. 170–262. For general phenomenon of female ascetic spirituality, see idem, *Holy Feast and Holy Fast: The Religious Significance of Food to Medieval Women* (Berkeley and Los Angeles: University of California Press, 1987) pp. 13–30.

68. "Información de la vida," testimony of Fray Lorenzo de Cueto, Doña María's brother.

69. Vela y Cueto, *Autobiografía* p. 309: "Me cortaba las alas para volar a la libertad del espíritu." Idem, *Third Mystic* p. 43.

During the next twenty years, María Vela struggled to reconcile an inner conflict between obeying her superiors, as stipulated by her monastic vows, and following what she considered to be the direct commands of God. She often refused to eat meat, appeared for matins in a hooded habit of coarse sackcloth, and fell into ecstatic fits, all to the dismay of her fellow nuns.[70] She looked in vain for guidance. Much of her autobiography concerns her relations with a long string of confessors: monks and secular priests, clerics from Avila and from outside the city, old men and young. A few viewed her impulses as divinely inspired and tried to persuade the convent's abbesses to allow her to follow her own way. Other confessors regarded her as suffering from delusions. Many remained undecided, bewildered by a woman who, like Teresa of Jesus, claimed to enjoy divine favors, but who, unlike her illustrious predecessor, could not describe them or express herself very coherently or forcefully. Many of the mystical experiences she recounted essentially duplicated those of the great figures of spirituality she enthusiastically read, notably Saint Catherine of Siena, Saint Bernard, Juan de Avila, and the recently published Teresa of Jesus.[71] Few confessors agreed to direct her for more than a short period of time. María Vela accepted all these trials with characteristic resignation. "I was left with inner quietude and peace in the belief that the Lord desired me to be so tested," she later wrote.[72]

A particularly sharp debate arose over the then controversial question of frequent communion. Doña María heard God

70. Vela y Cueto, *Autobiografía* pp. 312–352.
71. See, for example, ibid. pp. 314–315, where María Vela models her devotions on those of Saint Catherine of Siena and begs God to grant her the same favors, and pp. 385–386, for her description of receiving milk from the suckling Virgin, like St. Bernard. See González Vaquero 65v–66r, for her absorption of the *Audi, filia* of Juan de Avila. She made constant references in her writings to "la Santa Madre Teresa de Jesús."
72. Vela y Cueto, *Autobiografía* p. 323: "Yo quedé con quietud y paz interior, pareciéndome quería el Señor que padeciese aquel trabajo." Idem, *Third Mystic* p. 55.

order her to receive communion daily, assuring her that the Host would provide her with sufficient nourishment. She should, therefore, take no food before attending mass. Whenever the alarmed abbess or María's confessors ordered María Vela to eat before communicating, her jaws would mysteriously lock as she approached the altar, rendering her incapable of communicating. Neither clerics nor doctors could pry her mouth open on these occasions. But, if she fasted, she found that she could receive communion unhindered and felt happy and fulfilled for the rest of the day.[73] At this point, shocked monastic officials, fearing demonic possession, summoned a priest to exorcise her. He could find no devils within the nun calmly kneeling before him, however, and departed, leaving the nuns of Santa Ana more scandalized, and Doña María's confessors more confused, than ever. News of her sensational behavior soon became the talk of Avila.[74]

What caused so many abulenses to regard María Vela, a solitary, if unusual, nun, with such stern disapproval? For one thing, her adoption of an ascetic style of life, with fasts, wretched clothing, and bodily mortifications, offended the aristocratic nuns of Santa Ana. This posture, they felt, implied their own moral inferiority, implied that only those willing to humble themselves in this way merited salvation.

---

73. Vela y Cueto, *Autobiografía* pp. 312–335. Donald H. Marshall, "Frequent and Daily Communion in the Catholic Church of Spain in the Sixteenth and Seventeenth Centuries" (Ph.D. diss., Harvard University, 1952). He discusses briefly the case of María Vela (pp. 274–275) and cites a Jesuit critic of frequent communion in Baeza (late sixteenth century?) who complained of "women having feigned weakness and faints at the time of confession and clamping their teeth or emitting extraordinary sighs or cries and letting themselves fall on the floor at the time of communion" (p. 128). For food asceticism and eucharistic piety among late medieval women, including Catherine of Siena, see Bynum, *Holy Feast*, and idem, "Fast, Feast, and Flesh: The Religious Significance of Food to Medieval Women," *Representations* 11 (1985): 1–25, where she mentions several cases of women who were unable to swallow (pp. 17–18 n. 10).

74. Vela y Cueto, *Autobiografía* pp. 342–343.

Unlike Teresa of Jesus, who made strenuous efforts to pla-
cate the nuns of la Encarnación and even served as that
convent's prioress, María Vela, due to her mental and physical infirmities and her "desire to be despised," kept to herself. The residents of Santa Ana interpreted this as pure
diffidence.[75]

Perhaps, also, class considerations entered here. The ascetic exercises of beatas such as Mari Díaz and her disciple Ana
Reyes merely carried to extremes the material conditions of
the social class from which they actually derived. While
wellborn ladies such as María Vela's mother visited and patronized such holy women and felt themselves edified, few
would propose actually imitating their example. The nuns of
Santa Ana, too, placed a premium on conforming to codes of
behavior thought appropriate to their class, even within the
religious life. As María Vela recorded in her autobiography,
in the midst of her visions and fasts, her colleagues firmly
maintained that "it would be better for [her] to act like the
rest."[76]

Many of her confessors doubted Doña María's claims of
submission and obedience, and accused her of pride and self-
will. "It was said of me that I was stiff-necked and proud, that
I desired to be saint and esteemed as such," she would later
recall.[77] Here she differed from Teresa of Jesus, who was
always careful to give the appearance, at least, of total and
unconditional submission to the will of monastic and ecclesiastical superiors as God's representatives on earth. The
stories she told of exemplary Discalced Carmelites in *The*

75. "Gossip was rife within and without the convent, as if I had clothed
myself like a scarecrow." Vela y Cueto, *Third Mystic* pp. 81–83.
76. Vela y Cueto, *Autobiografía* p. 325: "Mejor fuera hacerlo que todas."
Idem, *Third Mystic*, p. 58.
77. Vela y Cueto, *Autobiografía* p. 343: "A mí por soberbia y altiva y que
quería parecer santa y ser estimada por tal." Idem, *Third Mystic* p. 73. This
recalls the experience of the early fourteenth-century English holy woman
Margery Kempe, who was often accused of pride and hypocrisy. Clarissa W.
Atkinson, *Mystic and Pilgrim: The Book and the World of Margery Kempe*
(Ithaca: Cornell University Press, 1983).

Book of Her Foundations and other sources often highlighted acts of heroic obedience.

For María Vela, however, God's grace at times set her apart from all others, in effect exempting her from society's rules. During the controversy over her desire for frequent communion, Doña María appealed to God in prayer, beseeching, "Since You are such a great advocate of obedience, my failure to obey is the worst charge which they could bring against me." She heard and accepted his reply: "What if I wish to remove thee from the common rule?"[78] Authorities considered this antinomian attitude particularly dangerous, because it not only seemed to connote excessive pride on her part but also resembled views held by the *alumbrados*, or Illuminati. This pietistic sect, which had first appeared in Spain in the 1520s, had reemerged, after a long period of repression, in the 1570s and 1580s, evoking an intense inquisitorial reaction.[79] In this charged atmosphere, the suspicion of heresy on the part of María Vela would bring shame to the nun, her convent, and the city of Avila as a whole. Many of her confessors, notably the aging Julián de Avila, tried to suppress her impulses and persuade her that the voices she heard came from her own imagination.[80]

Some ecclesiastical authorities may have perceived in

78. Vela y Cueto, *Autobiografía* p. 325: "'Mirad, Señor, que la peor señal que hallan es ésta, que no pueda obedecer siendo vos tan amigo de obediencia.' Entendí: '¿Y si yo quiero sacarte a tí de las reglas comunes?'" Idem, *Third Mystic* p. 57. "I turned to the Lord and said, 'Lord, Lord, What has now been aroused?' And the Voices said, 'Do not be afflicted; follow My Divine guidance and pay no heed to what is said by others.'" *Third Mystic* pp. 51–52.

79. Antonio Márquez, *Los alumbrados: Orígenes y filosofía, 1525–1559* (Madrid: Taurus, 1972). Alvaro Huerga, *Historia de los Alumbrados (1570–1630)* 4 vols. (Madrid: FUE, 1978–88). Vicente Beltrán de Heredia, "Un grupo de visionarios y pseudoprofetas que actúa durante los últimos años de Felipe II: Repercusiones de ello sobre la memoria de Santa Teresa," *Revista Española de Teología* 7 (1947): 373–534. Marshall also discusses charges of fraud and diabolism brought against women (pp. 50–76, 109–142, 266–293).

80. González Vaquero 139v–142r. Could it also be that Julián de Avila was trying to discourage any rivals to "his" saint, Teresa of Jesus?

María Vela's actions and opinions a challenge to the resurgent dynastic system of monastic religion based on the recitation of vocal prayers for the souls of benefactors and their clients. Her fits and trances almost always occurred *in choir*, disrupting the program of chanted prayer. She spent long hours away from communal duties, engaging in private mental prayer, which was seen as a dangerous step toward religious heterodoxy, especially for women.[81] In addition, her rigorous fasts often prevented her from joining the other nuns in the refectory.

When Doña María succeeded in persuading others to follow her ascetic example—when several young sisters joined her one day in entering the choir in sackcloth—the nuns of Santa Ana were outraged. To them, this suggested an organized threat to their way of life, a more serious threat than that posed by a single disturbed individual. Rumors spread that María Vela's uncle Don Cristóbal de Vela, the bishop of Burgos, was ready to finance a reformed convent of Cistercians on the model of the Carmelite house of San José, with Doña María as prioress. Although the other nuns quickly succumbed to pressure from the abbess and chaplains to conform, and María Vela never mentioned (nor, in all probability, entertained) plans to found a new convent, resentment ran high.[82]

In 1603, despite efforts to keep her case quiet, certain parties denounced María Vela to the Inquisition. These included the Dominican friars of Santo Tomás, longtime enemies of espirituales, and several nuns within Santa Ana. The accusations made against the 42-year-old nun reveal many of the religious attitudes causing concern among abulenses and other Catholics in this period. María Vela's accusers claimed that she expressed the following beliefs: "Since God inspired me with knowledge or whatever He wished me

81. Marshall demonstrates that mental prayer and frequent communion were often linked in the minds of critics (pp. 160, 168).
82. Vela y Cueto, *Autobiografía* pp. 348–349.

to do, I needed counsel from no one else"; "I did not wish to submit myself to obedience because God, who is above obedience to superiors and confessors, governed me Himself"; "My works were not to be done in secret, but publicly, so that everyone could see them"; and, perhaps most significantly, "I did not care about praying aloud because silent prayer sufficed."[83] María Vela's calm replies to the inquisitors (probably supplemented by the influence of her important family) convinced the authorities of her innocence, and they dropped all charges against her.

Soon after her acquittal by the Inquisition, Doña María Vela met a young priest, Miguel González Vaquero, and began to make her confessions to him. Dr. Vaquero, as he was known, a former chaplain at San José, had heard of the extraordinary nun of Santa Ana through his penitent the beata Ana Reyes. Through an informal but effective network of communication and support among religious women in Avila, Ana Reyes had learned of Doña María's tribulations and her difficulties with confessors. The holy woman begged her own spiritual director to take on this challenging case.[84] Doña María's piety and patience quickly impressed the young cleric, and he became convinced of her divine inspiration. He agreed to have her as a penitent. For María Vela, Vaquero's understanding and affection elicited an overwhelming sense of relief. Vaquero served as her spiritual director for the remaining fifteen years of her life.

As often occurred in these cases, a relationship of mutual commitment, even dependence, developed between director and directed. A mere word from Dr. Vaquero could arrest María Vela's fits or open her capricious jaws. For his part, Vaquero felt certain that the nun's prayers had once saved him from a serious illness. Doña María's final years at Santa

83. Vela y Cueto, *Third Mystic* pp. 86–90.
84. González Vaquero 1911–194v, 218v–219v. Ana Reyes knew about María Vela through Doña María Dávila, her closest friend and confidant within Santa Ana.

Ana were among the calmest and most fulfilling in her stormy monastic career. To the end, however, her fellow nuns found in her a subject for gossip, now suggesting that her relations with Vaquero exceeded the limits of behavior thought proper between clerics and their penitents. Controversy and censure accompanied her to the end of her life.[85]

On September 24, 1617, Doña María died after a long bout of pneumonia and pleurisy. Within an astonishingly short time, the public image of this woman, that of a strange and possibly dangerous eccentric, changed dramatically. Many now regarded her as a saint. The interest and intervention of the bishop of Avila in the case of María Vela made the critical difference.

Anxious to establish his prestige and authority, Francisco de Gamarra, who obtained the see of Avila in June 1616, quickly set out to acquaint and identify himself with the city's particular devotions. When he heard glowing reports, probably circulated by Vaquero, of an extraordinary nun of Santa Ana who received divine visions and revelations, Gamarra arranged for an assistant to visit the convent and examine María Vela personally. In a public statement, the bishop warmly praised Doña María's virtue and contended "God . . . brought her to this city in order to honor it with her life and death."[86] This was the first time that an explicit connection had been made between a highly cloistered and guarded nun and the general populace of Avila. The cult-making process had begun.

At María Vela's "happy death," amid rumors of miracles, mysterious cures, and "the odor of sanctity," crowds of cu-

85. Ibid., for example, 205v, 244r–v, 256v, 261v. A critical Jesuit decried "penitents being in such a state of vassalage to their confessors that it is deemed a great infidelity or sacrilege to confess or hear the sermons of anyone else." Marshall p. 128. John W. Coakley, "Female Saints and Male Confidants in Medieval Dominican Hagiography" (Paper delivered at the Barnard Medieval/Renaissance Conference "Images of Sainthood in Medieval and Renaissance Europe," Barnard College, New York, November 1987).

86. González Vaquero 264v–265v: "Parece la trajó Dios a esta ciudad para honrarla en vida y muerte."

rious and devout people gathered at Santa Ana for a glimpse of the body. In this year of depression and drought, they gratefully greeted reports of a new saint. As the nuns of Santa Ana watched in disbelief, law officials restrained these overnight devotees who seemed intent on stealing pieces of Doña María's clothing and body as relics.[87]

The enterprising Gamarra moved swiftly to gain control of the chaotic situation. In true episcopal form, he arranged a series of burials and commemorative services, working hard to associate his name with that of the little-known nun. Now rendered "harmless" through death, María Vela was to be "his" saint. First, the bishop persuaded the nuns of Santa Ana to allow him to perform an elaborate funeral inside the convent. Arriving in procession with his canons and accompanied by a large crowd of people, "in particular, all the nobility," Gamarra presided over the deposition of Doña María's remains in a grand sepulcher. (Cistercians usually were buried in simple graves, wrapped only in a shroud.)[88]

Two years later, in 1619, the bishop, noting how "it falls upon the pastoral office . . . to bring to light and make manifest the great and heroic deeds of the saints," initiated beatification proceedings for María Vela. Like the documentation relating to Mari Díaz, which was begun by Bishop Otaduy and completed under Gamarra, this series of testimonies featured reports by many witnesses as to the virtue and holiness of the nun of Santa Ana. The name and office of the bishop appears frequently in these pages. As in the case of Mari Díaz, these proceedings never reached Rome.[89]

Finally, in 1623, the last year of Gamarra's episcopacy, the

---

87. Ibid. 264v–271v. Fernández Valencia 1:265–269.

88. González Vaquero 272v. Vela y Cueto, *Autobiografía* pp. 41–42.

89. "Porque importa, al oficio pastoral de su Señoría averiguar si es verdadera virtud y santidad, y saber de quanta importancia sea para la gloria de Dios y edificación de las almas sacar a la luz y que se manifiesten los grandes y heroicos hechos de los Santos." In documents published by Francisco Esteban, the local priest of Doña María's birthplace of Cardeñosa, on the occasion of the three hundredth anniversary of her death, in a pamphlet also called *La muger fuerte* (Avila, 1917) pp. 129–137.

prelate ordered the reburial of Doña María Vela, only six years after her death. As municipal officials opened the tomb, a committee of clerics and physicians examined the body, declaring it completely intact and emitting a "sweet odor." The bishop then rearranged Doña María's corpse and clothing in a new tomb, manipulating her body as he had controlled her cult.[90] The inscription carved on this new sepulcher, placed in a wall of Santa Ana's main chapel, provides as much information about the bishop and other ecclesiastical and secular authorities as it does about the holy woman it was meant to commemorate:

> Here lies the body of the venerable "Strong Woman" doña María Vela, nun of this holy house and native of this city, who died September 24, 1617, and was translated from her first sepulcher to this one by don Francisco de Gamarra, bishop of Avila, formerly of Cartagena, with the approval of the Faculty of Theology of the University of Salamanca, on August 5, 1623, the pope being Urban VIII, and king of Spain don Philip IV and *corregidor* of this city don Juan de Beaumont y Navarra and the abbess of this convent doña María Dávila.[91]

In this *Who's Who* of prelates and politicians, María Vela's name is almost lost.

Doña María's confessor and confidant, Dr. Vaquero, published his penitent's biography shortly after her death, in 1618. He entitled it *La muger fuerte (The Strong Woman)* and explained in its opening pages, "Divine providence, which wanted to bring authority and honor to this city of Avila, with such noble lineages, so that among them might be born men valiant ... for their deeds in the exterior war in defense of law and king, wanted also to enrich it in our times with strong women ... who in the interior war of the spirit might become

90. Ibid. pp. 138–144. Her tomb was reopened on three other occasions, in 1664, 1808, and 1942. Vela y Cueto, *Autobiografía* p. 42.
91. Fernández Valencia 1:268–269.

Doña María Vela, frontispiece to *La muger fuerte* by Miguel González Vaquero, 1618, in convent of Santa Ana, Avila. Photograph courtesy of Cistercian Community of Santa Ana, Avila.

famous for their works."[92] In this formulation, María Vela, battling the devil and temptation through patience, prayer, and sacrifice, becomes a female warrior, recalling Jimena Blázquez of medieval legend. There was an important difference, however. Women such as the heroic Jimena and Mari Díaz played public roles of leadership in their respective societies. By the early seventeenth century the place of even "strong women" was conceived strictly in private and spiritual terms.

Vaquero's book apparently enjoyed popularity in the seventeenth century, for new editions were published in 1627, 1640, and 1674. But neither he nor anyone else published María Vela's own works, her *Autobiography* and *Book of Mercies*, in which she described the favors she received from God. For over three hundred years, the manuscripts of this fascinating woman remained locked in the strongbox of Avila's convent at Santa Ana, their contents unknown, their author forgotten, until, by a strange destiny, the investigations of an American writer led to their discovery in 1959.[93]

Unlike those of Mari Díaz and Teresa of Jesus a generation earlier, the intense spiritual experiences of Doña María Vela failed to attract the attention of reform-minded clerics and laymen or to fulfill the needs of the urban community. Repressed by ecclesiastical authorities during her life, utilized

92. González Vaquero 11-v: "La dicha providencia que quiso autorizar y honrar esta ciudad de Avila con tanta nobleza de linajes, para que de ella naciesen hombres valerosos, de ánimo invencible, como han resplandecido por sus hazañas en la guerra exterior en defensa de su ley, y de su Rey: quiso también enriquecerla en nuestros tiempos de mujeres fuertes (que así las llama el espíritu de Dios) que en la guerra interior del espíritu fuesen famosas en sus obras, y Dios admirable en ellas."

93. Frances Parkinson Keyes came across the manuscripts as she was researching a biography of Isabella the Catholic. The famous and socially prominent writer secured permission from the nuns of Santa Ana to bring the documents back with her to the United States and translate them there. She left her jewelry as collateral. For this remarkable story see Vela y Cueto, *Third Mystic* pp. 3–14. Olegario González Hernández published María Vela's works in Spanish in 1961, one year after Keyes's book appeared.

by them after her death, she represents the last effort to establish an independent religious style in early modern Avila. With priorities now placed on decorum, conformity, and deference to authority in religious as well as political affairs, spirituality, public ritual, and monastic foundation increasingly fell into set and predictable patterns. In the seventeenth century, Avila's religious life, like its economic situation, entered a prolonged period of stagnation. The city's golden age had come to an end.

Epilogue

In 1622 the woman who during her lifetime experienced a transformation of identity from Doña Teresa de Ahumada to Teresa of Jesus underwent a final name change. Canonized by the Roman Catholic church as Saint Teresa of Avila, she attained a cultic prestige accorded few other female saints. In the baroque, post-Tridentine world of the seventeenth century, biographers and propagandists of the faith strove to depict Teresa of Avila in certain prescribed ways that emphasized the agenda of the Counter-Reformation Church and the roles it assigned to women. Thus emerged the image of Teresa as the ecstatic mystic, the miraculous healer, the humble proponent of absolute orthodoxy and absolute obedience.[1] Virtually forgotten were her flesh-and-blood experiences in the world, especially those regarded as controversial. Hagiographers downplayed her insistence upon monastic poverty and autonomy and mental prayer, her struggles with inquisitors and censors and the odds against which she had to fight to establish her vision of the religious life. They were particularly effective at burying all references to Te-

1. J. Mary Luti, "Teresa of Avila, Maestra Espiritual" (Ph.D. diss., Boston College, 1987) pp. 53–56.

Epilogue

resa's Jewish extraction. "Tainted" blood simply would not do for the "Seraphic Virgin" now elevated to the altars.[2]

As Saint Teresa the cult figure rose in popularity, the fortunes of her native city fell precariously low. By 1622 the once proud Avila of the Knights had fallen on hard times. Plague, famine, emigration, and the collapse of the Castilian wool trade decimated its population and substantially reduced its economic base. In this atmosphere of prolonged dearth and depression, the social climate underwent significant changes as well. Avila's aristocratic families and its ecclesiastical hierarchy, headed by increasingly powerful bishops, now firmly controlled the organs of political and religious life. During the first half of the sixteenth century, as the city grew and prospered, a group of merchants, professionals, and minor clerics had challenged the exclusive rule and dynastic style of religion of the hereditary oligarchy. They supported innovative religious institutions that served the social and spiritual needs of the urban community as a whole. It was in this context that Teresa of Jesus founded the reformed convent of San José.

The economic and demographic crises of the late sixteenth century and early seventeenth century greatly reduced the strength and influence of this group, clearing the way for a resurgence of aristocratic dominance in the dwindling city. Then, for 350 years, Avila was little more than an impoverished provincial backwater. However, its very isolation, and its continued identification with a beloved saint, sowed the seeds of the city's revival in the second half of the twentieth century. Avila, which had hardly changed in appearance since the sixteenth century, was discovered as an unspoiled artistic treasure. The Spanish government declared the entire city a National Historic Landmark. Improved highway and rail connections facilitated day trips to Avila from Madrid for

2. Teófanes Egido, "El tratamiento historiográfico de Santa Teresa," in *Perfil histórico de Santa Teresa* (Madrid: Editorial de Espiritualidad, 1981) pp. 13–22.

the growing crowds of visitors and pilgrims. And, thus, tourism has become as vital to the economy of late twentieth-century Avila as wool production was in the sixteenth century.

The historical Teresa of Avila has become more accessible, as well. In the aftermath of the Second Vatican Council, Catholic scholars and lay persons have begun to view Teresa and other saints as real people who lived in identifiable times and places, not merely as disembodied celestial beings.[3] The current interest in ecumenism places an entirely new light on Teresa's Jewish roots. This previously forbidden topic is now among the most popular in Teresian research, a trend accelerated in Spain by the death of Francisco Franco in 1975.[4] Feminist scholarship has also yielded significant insights into Teresa of Avila and her world.[5]

Far from breeding contempt, the process of revision and reevaluation has brought about a deeper understanding of this remarkable woman who lived during the golden age of Avila. Only by considering Saint Teresa in the context of her city and her century can one fully appreciate the meaning of her mission and the magnitude of her achievement.

3. Ibid. pp. 22–31.

4. See Efrén de la Madre de Dios (Montalva) and Otger Steggink, *Santa Teresa y su tiempo* vol. 1 (Salamanca: Universidad Pontificia, 1982) pp. 45–48, for a recent overview by historians who had previously suppressed information relating to Teresa's ethnic origins.

5. See, for example, Luti, "Teresa of Avila," Rosa Rossi, *Teresa de Avila: Biografía de una escritora* (Barcelona: Icaria, 1984), and Alison Weber, *The Golden Pen: Teresa de Jesús and the Rhetoric of Femininity* (Princeton: Princeton University Press, forthcoming).

Selected Bibliography

Primary Sources

Ariz, Luis. *Historia de las grandezas de la ciudad de Avila.* 4 pts. Alcalá de Henares: L. Martínez Grande, 1607.

Avila, Juan de. *Obras completas del santo maestro Juan de Avila,* ed. Luis Sala Balust and Francisco Martín Hernández. 6 vols. Madrid: Editorial Católica, 1970–71.

Avila, Julián de. *Vida de Santa Teresa de Jesús,* ed. Vicente de la Fuente. Madrid: Antonio Pérez Dubrull, 1881.

Ayora, Gonzalo de. *Epílogo de algunas cosas dignas de memoria pertenecientes a la . . . ciudad de Avila.* Salamanca, 1519.

The Canons and Decrees of the Council of Trent, trans. H. J. Schroeder. Rockford, Ill.: TAN Books, 1978.

Cianca, Antonio de. *Historia de la vida, invención, milagros, y translación de San Segundo . . .* 3 books. Madrid: Luis Sánchez, 1595.

Constituciones synodales del obispado de Avila . . . Madrid: Juan de la Cuesta, 1617.

The Constitutions of the Society of Jesus, trans. George E. Ganss. St. Louis: Institute of Jesuit Sources, 1970.

Crónica de la población de Avila, ed. Amparo Hernández Segura. Valencia: Textos Medievales, 1966.

Selected Bibliography

Fernández Valencia, Bartolomé. *Historia y grandezas del insigne templo . . . de . . . San Vicente.* 2 vols. Avila, 1676.

González Dávila, Gil. *Teatro eclesiástico de las ciudades e iglesias catedrales de España . . .* Salamanca: A. Ramírez, 1618.

González Vaquero, Miguel. *La muger fuerte: Por otro título, la vida de Doña María Vela . . .* Barcelona: Geronymo Margarit, 1627.

Libro de las constituciones synodales del obispado de Avila . . . Salamanca: Andreas Portonaris, 1557.

Puente, Luis de la. *Vida del Padre Baltasar Alvarez.* Madrid: Ediciones Atlas, 1958.

Santa Teresa de Jesús. *Obras completas,* ed. Efrén de la Madre de Dios (Montalva) and Otger Steggink. Madrid: Editorial Católica, 1977.

———. *The Collected Works of St. Teresa of Avila,* trans. Kieran Kavanaugh and Otilio Rodríguez. 3 vols. Washington, D.C.: Institute of Carmelite Studies, 1976–85.

———. *Complete Works,* trans. E. Allison Peers. 3 vols. London: Sheed and Ward, 1946.

Vela y Cueto, María. *Autobiografía y Libro de las Mercedes,* ed. Olegario González Hernández. Barcelona: Juan Flors, 1961.

———. *The Third Mystic of Avila: The Self-Revelation of María Vela, a Sixteenth Century Spanish Nun,* trans. Frances Parkinson Keyes. New York: Farrar, Straus and Cudahy, 1960.

Secondary Sources: Books and Dissertations

Actas del Congreso Internacional Teresiano, ed. Teófanes Egido Martínez et al. 2 vols. Salamanca: El Congreso, 1983.

Alvarez, Tomás. *Santa Teresa y la Iglesia.* Burgos: El Monte Carmelo, 1980.

Andrés Martín, Melquíades. *Los recogidos: Nueva visión de la mística española (1500–1700).* Madrid: FUE, 1976.

Arenal, Electa, and Stacey Schlau. *Untold Sisters: Hispanic Nuns in Their Own Works.* Albuquerque: University of New Mexico Press, 1989.

Astraín, Antonio. *Historia de la Compañía de Jesús en la asistencia de España.* 3 vols. Madrid: Razón y Fe, 1909.

Selected Bibliography

Ballesteros, Enrique. *Estudio histórico de Avila y su territorio.* Avila: Tip. de M. Sarachaga, 1896.

Barrado Manzano, Arcángel. *San Pedro de Alcántara (1499–1562): Estudio documentado y crítico de su vida.* Madrid: Editorial Cisneros, 1965.

Barrientos, Alberto, ed. *Introducción a la lectura de Santa Teresa.* Madrid: Editorial de Espiritualidad, 1978.

Barrios García, Angel. *La catedral de Avila en la edad media: Estructura socio-jurídica y económica.* Avila: Caja Central de Ahorros y Préstamos, 1973.

Bataillon, Marcel. *Erasmo y España.* Mexico: Fondo de Cultura Económica, 1950.

Bennassar, Bartolomé. *Recherches sur les grandes épidémies dans le nord de l'Espagne à la fin du XVIe siècle: Problèmes de documentation et de méthode.* Paris: SEVPEN, 1969.

———. *The Spanish Character: Attitudes and Mentalities from the Sixteenth to the Nineteenth Century.* Berkeley and Los Angeles: University of California Press, 1979.

———. *Valladolid en el Siglo de Oro: Una ciudad de Castilla y su entorno agrario en el siglo XVI.* Valladolid: Ayuntamiento, 1983.

Braudel, Fernand. *The Mediterranean and the Mediterranean World in the Age of Philip II.* 2 vols. New York: Harper and Row, 1972.

Brown, Peter. *The Cult of the Saints: Its Rise and Function in Latin Christianity.* Chicago: University of Chicago Press, 1981.

Bynum, Caroline Walker. *Holy Feast and Holy Fast: The Religious Significance of Food to Medieval Women.* Berkeley and Los Angeles: University of California Press, 1987.

Caro Baroja, Julio. *Las formas complejas de la vida religiosa: Religión, sociedad, y carácter en la España de los siglos XVI y XVII.* Madrid: Akal, 1978.

Carramolino, Juan Martín. *Historia de Avila, su provincia y obispado.* 3 vols. Madrid: Librería Española, 1872–73.

Castro, Américo. *Teresa la Santa y otros ensayos.* Madrid: Alianza, 1982.

Castro, Manuel de. *Fundación de "las Gordillas" (convento de clarisas de Santa María de Jesús de Avila).* Avila: Caja Central de Ahorros y Préstamos, 1976.

Chauchadis, Claude. *Honneur, morale, et société dans l'Espagne de Philippe II.* Paris: CNRS, 1984.

205

Selected Bibliography

Christian, William A., Jr. *Local Religion in Sixteenth Century Spain*. Princeton: Princeton University Press, 1981.

Clark, Peter, ed. *The Early Modern Town*. New York: Longman, 1976.

Clissold, Stephen. *St. Teresa of Avila*. New York: Seabury, 1982.

Danvila y Collado, Manuel. *Historia crítica y documentada de las Comunidades de Castilla*. In *Memorial histórico español*, vols. 35–38. Madrid: Est. tip. de la viuda e hijos de M. Tello, 1897–99.

Davis, Natalie Z. *Society and Culture in Early Modern France*. Stanford: Stanford University Press, 1975.

Deleito y Piñuela, José. *La vida religiosa española bajo el cuarto Felipe*. Madrid: Espasa-Calpe, 1963.

Delumeau, Jean. *Catholicism between Luther and Voltaire: A New View of the Counter-Reformation*. Philadelphia: Westminster Press, 1977.

Domínguez Ortiz, Antonio. *Los judeoconversos en España y América*. Madrid: Ediciones Istmo, 1978.

——. *La sociedad española en el siglo XVII*. 2 vols. Madrid: CSIC, 1963.

Egido, Teófanes. *El linaje judeoconverso de Santa Teresa (Pleito de hidalguía de los Cepeda)*. Madrid: Editorial de Espiritualidad, 1986.

Elliott, J. H. *Imperial Spain*. New York: New American Library, 1966.

Esteban, Francisco. *La muger fuerte*. Avila, 1917.

Fernández Mayoral, José. *El municipio de Avila: Estudio histórico*. Avila: Diputación Provincial de Avila, Institución "Alonso de Madrigal," 1958.

García Oro, José. *Cisneros y la reforma del clero español en tiempo de los Reyes Católicos*. Madrid: CSIC, 1971.

García Sanz, Angel. *Desarrollo y crisis del Antiguo Régimen en Castilla la Vieja: Economía y sociedad en tierras de Segovia de 1500 a 1814*. Madrid: Akal, 1977.

Gerardo de San Juan de la Cruz. *Vida del Maestro Julián de Avila*... Toledo: Impr. de la viuda e hijos de J. Peláez, 1915.

Gómez-Menor Fuentes, José. *El linaje familiar de Santa Teresa y de San Juan de la Cruz*. Salamanca: Gráficas Cervantes, 1970.

González y González, Nicolás. *El monasterio de la Encarnación de Avila*. 2 vols. Avila: Caja Central de Ahorros y Préstamos, 1976.

Selected Bibliography

Guibert, Joseph de. *The Jesuits: Their Spiritual Doctrine and Practice*. St. Louis: Institute of Jesuit Sources, 1964.

Haliczer, Stephen H. *The Comuneros of Castile: The Forging of a Revolution, 1475–1521*. Madison: University of Wisconsin Press, 1981.

Historia de la Iglesia en España. Vol. 3, *La Iglesia en la España de los siglos XV y XVI*, ed. José Luis González Novalín, pts. 1 and 2. Madrid: Editorial Católica, 1979.

Klein, Julius. *La Mesta: Estudio de la historia económica española, 1273–1836*. Madrid: Alianza, 1981.

Larrañaga, Victoriano. *La espiritualidad de San Ignacio de Loyola: Estudio comparativo con la de Santa Teresa de Jesús*. Madrid: Casa de San Pablo, 1944.

León Tello, Pilar. *Judíos de Avila*. Avila: Diputación Provincial de Avila, Institución "Gran Duque de Alba," 1963.

Llamas Martínez, Enrique. *Santa Teresa de Jesús y la Inquisición española*. Madrid: CSIC, 1972.

López Arévalo, Juan Ramón. *Un cabildo catedral de la Vieja Castilla: Avila, su estructura jurídica s. XIII–XX*. Madrid: CSIC, 1966.

Lunenfeld, Marvin. *Keepers of the City: The Corregidores of Isabella I of Castile (1474–1504)*. Cambridge: Cambridge University Press, 1987.

Luti, J. Mary. "Teresa of Avila, Maestra Espiritual." Ph.D. diss., Boston College, 1987.

Marcos Martín, Alberto. *Auge y declive de un núcleo mercantil y financiero de Castilla la Vieja: Evolución demográfica de Medina del Campo durante los siglos XVI y XVII*. Valladolid: Universidad de Valladolid, 1978.

Marshall, Donald H. "Frequent and Daily Communion in the Catholic Church of Spain in the Sixteenth and Seventeenth Centuries." Ph.D. diss., Harvard University, 1952.

Martz, Linda. *Poverty and Welfare in Habsburg Spain: The Example of Toledo*. Cambridge: Cambridge University Press, 1983.

Merino Alvarez, Abelardo. *La sociedad abulense durante el siglo XVI: La nobleza*. Madrid: Impr. del Patronato de Huérfanos, 1926.

Miscelánea conmemorativa del Concilio de Trento (1563–1963): Estudios y documentos. Madrid: CSIC, 1965.

Montalva (de la Madre de Dios), Efrén, and Otger Steggink. *Santa*

Selected Bibliography

Teresa y su tiempo. 2 vols. (Salamanca: Universidad Pontificia, 1982–84.

Nannei, Carlos María. *La "Doctrina Cristiana" de San Juan de Avila.* Pamplona: Universidad de Navarra, 1977.

Peers, E. Allison. *Handbook to the Life and Times of St. Teresa and St. John of the Cross.* London: Burns Oates, 1954.

———. *Studies in the Spanish Mystics.* 2 vols. London: Sheldon Press, 1927.

Pérez, Joseph. *La Révolution des "Comunidades" de Castille (1520–1521).* Bordeaux: Institut d'études ibériques et ibero-américaines de l'Université de Bordeaux, 1970.

Perry, Mary Elizabeth. *Crime and Society in Early Modern Seville.* Hanover, N.H.: University Press of New England, 1980.

Phillips, Carla Rahn. *Ciudad Real, 1500–1750: Growth, Crisis, and Readjustment in the Spanish Economy.* Cambridge: Harvard University Press, 1979.

Pike, Ruth. *Aristocrats and Traders: Sevillian Society in the Sixteenth Century.* Ithaca: Cornell University Press, 1972.

Quadrado, José María. *Salamanca, Avila, y Segovia.* Barcelona: D. Cortezo, 1884.

Rossi, Rosa. *Teresa de Avila: Biografía de una escritora.* Barcelona: Icaria, 1984.

Saínz Rodríguez, Pedro. *La siembra mística del Cardenal Cisneros y las reformas en la Iglesia.* Madrid: FUE, 1979.

Sánchez Bella, Florencio. *La reforma del clero en San Juan de Avila.* Madrid: Rialp, 1981.

Santa Teresa en el IV centenario de la reforma carmelitana, ed. José María Castro Calvo et al. Barcelona: Universidad de Barcelona, 1963.

Sicroff, Albert A. *Los estatutos de limpieza de sangre: Controversias entre los siglos XV y XVII.* Madrid: Taurus, 1985.

Silverio de Santa Teresa. *Historia del Carmen Descalzo en España, Portugal, y América.* 15 vols. Burgos: El Monte Carmelo, 1935–49.

Sobrino Chomón, Tomás. *Episcopado abulense: Siglos XVI–XVIII.* Avila: Institución "Gran Duque de Alba," 1983.

Southern, R. W. *Western Society and the Church in the Middle Ages.* Harmondsworth: Penguin, 1970.

Selected Bibliography

Steggink, Otger. *Experiencia y realismo en Santa Teresa y San Juan de la Cruz.* Madrid: Editorial de Espiritualidad, 1974.

——. *La reforma del Carmelo español: La visita canónica del general Rubeo y su encuentro con Santa Teresa (1566–1567).* Rome: Institutum Carmelitarum, 1965.

Vergara y Martín, Gabriel María. *Estudio histórico de Avila y su territorio.* Madrid: Hernández, 1896.

Weinstein, Donald, and Rudolph M. Bell. *Saints and Society: The Two Worlds of Western Christendom, 1000–1700.* Chicago: University of Chicago Press, 1982.

Wright, A. D. *The Counter-Reformation: Catholic Europe and the Non-Christian World.* New York: St. Martin's Press, 1982.

Secondary Sources: Articles and Contributions to Books

Alonso Cortés, Narciso. "Pleitos de los Cepedas." *Boletín de la Real Academia Española* 25 (1946): 85–110.

Bataillon, Marcel. "Jean d'Avila rétrouvé." *Bulletin Hispanique* 57 (1955): 5–44.

Beltrán de Heredia, Vicente. "Directrices de la espiritualidad dominicana en Castilla durante las primeras décadas del siglo XVI." In *Corrientes espirituales en la España del siglo XVI: Trabajos.* Barcelona: Juan Flors, 1963, pp. 177–202.

——. "Un grupo de visionarios y pseudoprofetas que actúa durante los últimos años de Felipe II: Repercusiones de ello sobre la memoria de Santa Teresa." *Revista Española de Teología* 7 (1947): 373–534.

Bennassar, Bartolomé. "Medina del Campo: Un exemple des structures urbaines de l'Espagne au XVIe siècle." *Revue d'Histoire Economique et Sociale* 4 (1961): 474–495.

Bilinkoff, Jodi. "The Holy Woman and the Urban Community in Sixteenth Century Avila." In *Women and the Structure of Society: Selected Research from the Fifth Berkshire Conference on the History of Women,* ed. Barbara J. Harris and JoAnn K. McNamara. Durham, N.C.: Duke University Press, 1984, pp. 74–80.

Bossy, John. "The Counter-Reformation and the People of Catholic Europe." *Past and Present.* 47 (1970): 51–70.

Selected Bibliography

Brown, Peter. "The Rise and Function of the Holy Man in Late Antiquity." *Journal of Roman Studies* 61 (1971): 80–101.

Bynum, Caroline Walker. "Fast, Feast, and Flesh: The Religious Significance of Food to Medieval Women." *Representations* 11 (1985): 1–25.

Comas, Antonio. "Espirituales, letrados, y confesores en Santa Teresa de Jesús." In *Homenaje a Jaime Vicens Vives*, ed. J. Maluquer de Motes. Vol. 2. Barcelona: Universidad de Barcelona, 1967, pp. 85–99.

Dedieu, Jean-Pierre. " 'Christianisation' en Nouvelle Castille: Catechisme, communion, messe, et confirmation dans l'Archevêché de Tolède, 1540–1650." *Mélanges de la Casa de Velázquez* 15 (1979): 261–293.

Egido, Teófanes. "The Economic Concerns of Madre Teresa." *Carmelite Studies* 4 (1987): 151–172.

———. "The Historical Setting of St. Teresa's Life." *Carmelite Studies* 1 (1980): 122–182.

———. "Santa Teresa y su condición de mujer." *Surge* 40 (1982): 258–275.

———. "El tratamiento historiográfico de Santa Teresa." In *Perfil histórico de Santa Teresa*. Madrid: Editorial de Espiritualidad, 1981, pp. 13–31.

Elliott, J. H. "The Decline of Spain." *Past and Present* 20 (1961): 52–75.

———. "Self-Perception and Decline in Early Seventeenth Century Spain." *Past and Present* 74 (1977): 41–61.

Fita, Fidel. "D. Alonso Sánchez de Cepeda, padre de Santa Teresa: Nuevos datos biográficos." BAH 65 (1914): 138–150.

———. "El gran pleito de Santa Teresa contra el ayuntamiento de Avila." BAH 66 (1915): 266–281.

———. "La verdad sobre el martirio del Santo Niño de la Guardia." BAH 11 (1887): 7–134.

Flynn, Maureen. "Charitable Ritual in Late Medieval and Early Modern Spain." *Sixteenth Century Journal* 16 (1985): 335–348.

Foronda, Manuel de. "Mosén Rubín—su capilla en Avila y su escritura de fundación." BAH 63 (1913): 332–350.

———. "Las ordenanzas de Avila de 1485." BAH 71 (1917): 381–425, 463–520; 72 (1918): 25–47.

Selected Bibliography

Gerardo de San Juan de la Cruz. "María Díaz, llamada la Esposa del Santísimo Sacramento." *El Monte Carmelo* 16 (1915): 174–177, 380–382, 414–418; 17 (1915): 102–105, 166–170, 224–229, 300–304, 410–416; 18 (1916): 56–59.

Gutiérrez Nieto, Juan Ignacio. "Los conversos y el movimiento comunero." *Hispania* 94 (1964): 237–261.

——. "La discriminación de los conversos y la tibetización de Castilla por Felipe II." *Revista de la Universidad Complutense* 22 (1975): 99–129.

——. "La estructura castizo-estamental de la sociedad castellana del siglo XVI." *Hispania* 125 (1973): 519–563.

Haliczer, Stephen H. "The Castilian Urban Patriciate and the Jewish Expulsions of 1480–92." *American Historical Review* 78 (1973): 35–61.

Hernández Hernández, Ferreol. "El convento cisterciense de Santa Ana en Avila." *Cistercium* 11 (1959): 136–144.

Jiménez Duque, Baldomero. "Espiritualidad de María Díaz." *Manresa* 46 (1974): 29–42.

Le Flem, Jean-Paul. "Vraies et fausses splendeurs de l'industrie textile ségoviènne (vers 1460–vers 1650)." In *Produzione, commercio, e consumo dei panni di Lana (nei secoli XII–XVIII)*, ed. Marco Spallanzani. Florence: Olschki, 1976, pp. 525–536.

Lourie, Elena. "A Society Organized for War: Medieval Spain." *Past and Present* 35 (1966): 54–76.

Lunenfeld, Marvin. "Governing the Cities of Isabella the Catholic: The *Corregidores*, Governors, and Assistants of Castile (1476–1504)." *Journal of Urban History* 9 (1982): 31–55.

Márquez Villanueva, Francisco. "Conversos y cargos concejiles en el siglo XV." *Revista de Archivos, Bibliotecas, y Museos* 53 (1957): 503–540.

——. "Santa Teresa y el linaje." In his *Espiritualidad y literatura en el siglo XVI*. Madrid: Alfaguarra, 1968, pp. 141–205.

Molinero, Jesús. "Actas municipales de Avila sobre la fundación del monasterio de San José por Santa Teresa." BAH 66 (1915): 155–185.

——. "La alhóndiga de Avila en 1528 y D. Alonso Sánchez de Cepeda, padre de Santa Teresa." BAH 65 (1914): 258–268, 344–350.

Molinié-Bertrand, Annie. "Les 'Hidalgos' dans le royaume de Castille à la fin du XVIe siècle: Approche cartographique." *Revue d'Histoire Economique et Sociale* 52 (1974): 51–82.

Montalva (de la Madre de Dios), Efrén. "El ideal de Santa Teresa en la fundación de San José." *Carmelus* 10 (1963): 219–230.

Risco, Alberto. "Una opinión sobre los tres primeros confesores Jesuitas de Santa Teresa de Jesús." BAH 80 (1922): 462–469; 81 (1922): 41–52.

Rodríguez, José Vicente. "Cinco cartas inéditas de San Juan de Avila." *Revista de Espiritualidad* 34 (1975): 366–371.

Ruiz Martín, Felipe. "La población española al comienzo de los tiempos modernos." *Cuadernos de Historia* 1 (1967): 189–202.

Serís, Homero. "Nueva genealogía de Santa Teresa." *Nueva Revista de Filología Hispánica* 10 (1956): 365–384.

Sobrino Chomón, Tomás. "Avila." *Diccionario de la Historia Eclesiástica de España*, ed. Quintín Aldea Vaquero et al. Vol. 1. Madrid: CSIC, 1972.

Steggink, Otger. "Teresa de Jesús, mujer y mística ante la teología y los teólogos." *Carmelus* 29 (1982): 111–129.

Tapia, Serafín de. "Avila después de Villalar." *El Diario de Avila.* May 8, 1984, pp. 2–3.

———. "Estructura ocupacional de Avila en el siglo XVI." In *El pasado histórico de Castilla y León*. Vol. 2. *Edad Moderna*, ed. Jesús Crespo Redondo. Burgos: Junta de Castilla y León, 1983, pp. 201–223.

———. "Las fuentes demográficas y el potencial humano de Avila en el siglo XVI." *Cuadernos Abulenses* 2 (1984): 31–88.

———. "La opresión fiscal de la minoría morisca en las ciudades castellanas: El caso de la ciudad de Avila." *Studia Historica* 4 (1986): 17–49.

Vilar, Pierre. "El tiempo del Quijote." In his *Crecimiento y desarrollo: Economía e historia, reflexiones sobre el caso español.* Barcelona: Ariel, 1964, pp. 332–346.

Weisser, Michael. "The Decline of Castile Revisted: The Case of Toledo." *Journal of European Economic History* 2 (1973): 614–640.

Index

Index

Index

Convents. *See* Monastic houses
Conversos, 14, 21–22, 62–68, 83, 85, 89, 94–95, 109–110, 128–130, 142, 146–147, 165, 174, 200–202
Corpus Christi processions. *See* Processions
Council of Trent, 28 n.28, 90, 105–106, 132, 141, 148–150, 164 n.24, 166–172, 177–180, 184
Cristo de la Luz, church, 39
Cruz, Magdalena de la, 118
Cuenca, 87 n.18, 177 n.53
Cuevas, Pedro de las, 86, 95

Dávila, María, 39–49, 56, 59 n.15
Dávila, Pedro, 16–19
Daza, Gaspar, 80 n.4, 84–87, 94–95, 105–108, 118–120, 125, 137, 145–148, 168–172
Deans. *See* Avila: cathedral chapter
Devil, 118–119, 121, 125, 134, 143, 189, 198
Devotio moderna, 36, 79–80, 116–119
Díaz, Mari, 6, 80 n.4, 92, 96–107, 120, 126, 136, 168, 180–183, 187, 190
Discalced Carmelites. *See* Carmelite order: reform
Domestic servants, 54, 59, 99, 113, 126, 137, 157 n.9
Dominican order, 142–143, 192
Dowries, monastic, 88–89, 114, 127, 137, 139, 164–165

la Encarnación, convent, 33 n.40, 39–52, 56, 91, 94, 112–132, 137–139, 190
Enclosure, 112, 115–116, 132, 136, 140, 146, 150, 167, 194
Entail. *See* Mayorazgo
Episcopacy. *See* Avila: bishops
Erasmus of Rotterdam, 79–81, 84, 142
Escudos. *See* Heraldry
Espirituales, 142–144, 192
Eucharist, 13, 23, 83, 90, 100, 105 n.50, 108, 135, 175, 181–183, 188–189, 192 n.81
Experimentados. *See* Espirituales

Fernández Temiño, Pedro, 168–172, 178
Fixed incomes. *See* Rentas
Flanders. *See* Low Countries
Fonseca, Alonso, de, 29, 31 n.32
Franciscan order, 122–125, 160–161

Gallego family, 63–64, 68–69, 72
Gamarra, Francisco de, 174 n.47, 181–183, 194–196
González Dávila, Gil, 6, 101–102
González de Medina, Elvira, 39–49
González Vaquero, Miguel, 193–198
La muger fuerte, 196–198
las Gordillas, convent, 34, 39–49, 56, 123 n.40
Granada, 86, 157, 168
Granada, Luis de, 80 n.3, 144 n.89
Guiera, Catalina, 39–49
Guiera family, 20, 39–40, 139
Guzmán, Diego de, 49, 162–163
Guzmán, Francisco de, 80 n.4, 86, 94 n.30

Heraldry, 47–49, 52, 89–90, 163
Heresy, 140–143, 150–151, 185, 191–192
Herrera, María de, 39–49
Heterodoxy. *See* Heresy
Holy Child of la Guardia, 13
Holy Women. *See* Beatas
Honor, concept of, 15, 18–24, 62–63, 66–67, 80–83, 110–118, 126–132, 136
Hospitals. *See* Poor relief and charity
Host. *See* Eucharist
Huguenots, 122–124, 134–136, 143
Humanism, 79–81, 84, 90

Ibáñez, Pedro, 128
Illuminati. *See* Heresy
Index of Prohibited Books, 142
Inquisition, 13, 34, 82–83, 109, 140–144, 191–193, 200
Isabella I of Castile, 4, 16, 25, 36–37, 198 n.93

Jesuits. *See* Society of Jesus

Index

Jews, 11–14, 20–22, 85, 109, 200–202
  Old Jewish Quarter, 13–14, 17, 33, 64
  See also Conversos
Jiménez de Cisneros, Cardinal. See Cisneros, Cardinal
Joseph, Saint, 114 n.15, 122

Letrados, 142–144
Limpieza de sangre, 20–22, 89, 146–147, 165
Lineage, 18–24, 44–52, 64–68, 82–83, 88–91, 95, 106–107, 112–116, 127–130, 159–166, 196
López, Mencía, 39–49
Low Countries, 134–135, 155
Loyola, Ignatius, 84, 87–93, 111, 119
  Spiritual Exercises, 92–93
  See also Society of Jesus
"Lutherans." See Huguenots

Madrid, 145, 156–157, 158 n.13, 159 n.15, 160–161, 171–172, 201
Madrigal de las Altas Torres, 4, 12, 29 n.29, 31 n.32
la Magdalena, church and hospital, 10, 57 n.12, 60
Manrique de Lara, Jerónimo, 171–179, 181
Mayorazgo, 18, 21–22
Medina, Cristóbal de, 30 n.30, 31, 68
Medina, Luis de, 90, 95
Medina del Campo, 60, 70, 74, 147, 165 n.26
Mendoza, Alvaro de, 85, 100, 105–106, 125, 147–150, 168, 170–171
Mendoza, María de, 105, 148
Mercado Chico, 10, 24, 57, 64
Mercado Grande, 10, 13, 57, 62, 64
Monasteries. See Monastic houses
Monastic houses, 29 n.29, 35–52, 56–59, 88–89, 111–151, 159–167, 184–199; see also entries for individual monastic houses
Moriscos, 11, 157–158
Mosén Rubín, chapel, 39–49
Mújica family, 34–35

Municipal granary. See Avila: al-hóndiga
Mysticism, 96, 106–107, 116–125, 140–145, 151, 184–194, 200

de las Navas family, 63–64, 68–69, 72
New Christians. See Conversos
Niños de la Doctrina Cristiana, 86–87, 94–95, 103, 105, 107, 159–160
Nobles. See Avila: aristocrats
Nuestra Señora de Gracia, convent, 39–49, 57, 111–112, 118
Nuestra Señora de la Anunciación, chapel, See Mosén Rubín, chapel
Nuestra Señora de la Cabeza, church, 11
Nuestra Señora de las Vacas, church and neighborhood, 6, 39, 55, 86, 98–99, 103
Nuestra Señora del Carmen, monastery, 39
Nuestra Señora de Sonsoles, image and shrine, 41, 58, 59 n.15, 158
Núñez Arnalte, Hernando, 41, 47
Núñez Dávila, Juan, 39

Obedience, vow of, 133–136, 150, 188–194, 200
Ocampo, María de, 122
Ordinances, municipal. See Avila: municipal ordinances
Osuna, Francisco de, 116–117, 150
  Third Spiritual Alphabet, 116
Otaduy, Lorenzo, 30 n.30, 179–181, 195

Pajares, Francisco de, 65–67, 72, 75, 76 n.61, 95
Palencia, 148, 165 n.26, 168
Pecheros. See Avila: taxpayers
Pérez, Antonio, 60–61, 69–70
Peso family, 27–28, 49–50, 67, 72
Philip II, 134 n.69, 141–142, 150, 156, 172, 175
Philip III, 174 n.47, 180–181
Philip IV, 196
Plague. See Avila: epidemic disease in
Pleitos de hidalguía, 64–68, 110
Pliego, Alonso de, 72, 75

Index

Index

Library of Congress Cataloging-in-Publication Data

Bilinkoff. Jodi, 1955–
    The Avila of Saint Teresa : religious reform in a sixteenth-century
city/Jodi Bilinkoff.
        p. cm.
    Bibliography: p.
    Includes index.
    ISBN 0–8014–2203–5 (alk. paper)
    1. Teresa, of Avila, Saint, 1515–1582. 2. Avila (Spain)—
Biography. 3. Christian saints—Spain—Avila—Biography. I. Title.
BX4700.T4B53 1989
282'.46359—dc20   89–42886